Cross-Language Relations in Composition

CROSS-LANGUAGE RELATIONS IN COMPOSITION

Edited by
Bruce Horner,
Min-Zhan Lu,
and
Paul Kei Matsuda

Southern Illinois University Press
Carbondale and Edwardsville

13 12 11 10   4 3 2 1

Library of Congress Cataloging-in-Publication Data
Cross-language relations in composition / edited by
Bruce Horner, Min-Zhan Lu, and Paul Kei Matsuda.
    p. cm.
Includes bibliographical references and index.
ISBN-13: 978-0-8093-2982-3 (alk. paper)
ISBN-10: 0-8093-2982-4 (alk. paper)
ISBN-13: 978-0-8093-8575-1 (ebook)
ISBN-10: 0-8093-8575-9 (ebook)
1. English language—Composition and exercises—
Study and teaching. 2. English language—Rheto-
ric—Study and teaching. 3. Report writing—Study
and teaching. 4. Language and languages—Study
and teaching. 5. Rhetoric—Social aspects. 6. Lan-
guage and culture. I. Horner, Bruce, date. II. Lu,
Min-Zhan, date. III. Matsuda, Paul Kei.
PE1404.C753 2010
808'.04207—dc22   2009035613

Printed on recycled paper.♻
The paper used in this publication meets the mini-
mum requirements of American National Standard
for Information Sciences—Permanence of Paper for
Printed Library Materials, ANSI Z39.48–1992.♾

To all unauthorized speakers of English, in our families, our classrooms, and worldwide.

Contents

Acknowledgments

We are grateful to the National Council of Teachers of English for granting us permission to reprint the following essays: Min-Zhan Lu, "Living-English Work," *College English* 68.6, July 2006, copyright 2006 by the National Council of Teachers of English; Paul Kei Matsuda, "The Myth of Linguistic Homogeneity in U.S. College Composition," *College English* 68.6, July 2006, copyright 2006 by the National Council of Teachers of English. We are grateful to the National Council of Teachers of English for also granting us permission to reprint material from the following essays: Anis Bawarshi, "Taking Up Language Differences in Composition," *College English* 68.6, July 2006, copyright 2006 by the National Council of Teachers of English; A. Suresh Canagarajah, "Toward a Writing Pedagogy of Shuttling between Languages: Learning from Multilingual Writers," *College English* 68.6, July 2006, copyright 2006 by the National Council of Teachers of English; Bruce Horner, "Introduction: Cross-Language Relations in Composition," *College English* 68.6, July 2006, copyright 2006 by the National Council of Teachers of English; Gail E. Hawisher and Cynthia L. Selfe, "Globalization and Agency: Designing and Redesigning the Literacies of Cyberspace," *College English* 68.6, July 2006, copyright 2006 by the National Council of Teachers of English; John Trimbur, "Linguistic Memory and the Politics of U.S. English," *College English* 68.6, July 2006, copyright 2006 by the National Council of Teachers of English. We are grateful to Reuters News for granting permission to reprint the image of tongue surgery from the article by Kim Kyoung-wha, "Accent Axed with a Snip," 13 October 2003. We are grateful to Cambridge University Press for granting permission to reprint John Swales', "A CARS model for article introductions" from John Swales', *Genre Analysis: English in Academic and Research Settings*, copyright 1990 by Cambridge University Press.

We thank the University of Louisville's Committee on Academic Publication for providing funding in support of this project, and the University of Louisville English Department chair, Susan Griffin, and colleagues at the University of Louisville for their support and encouragement. Thanks to Jeanne Gunner for her early support of this project in its initial stages and Karl Kageff at Southern Illinois University Press for his encouragement and guidance. Aya Matsuda and our reviewers Mark Hurlbert and Peter Mortensen provided valuable suggestions on earlier versions of the collection, and Samantha NeCamp provided helpful research assistance. For their insights, their patience, and all they've taught us about cross-language relations in composition, we thank our contributors and our students.

Introduction: From "English Only" to Cross-Language Relations in Composition

Bruce Horner

This collection participates in an emerging movement within composition studies representing, and responding to, changes in and changing perceptions of language(s), English(es), students, and the relations of all these to one another. This movement critiques the tacit policy of "English Only" dominating composition and pursues teaching and research that resist that policy. It draws attention to the fact that within much composition teaching and scholarship, both the context of writing and writing itself are imagined to be monolingual: the "norm" assumed, in other words, is a monolingual, native-English speaking writer writing only in English to an audience of English-only readers (Horner and Trimbur).

This tacit policy of monolingualism manifests itself in other ways as well: the institutional divides separating most composition programs and courses from English as a Second Language (ESL) programs and courses, including courses in "ESL composition," and separating composition courses from courses that involve students in writing in any language other than English; the nearly complete absence in composition textbook "readers" of writings by anyone other than North American and British writers whose first language is English (even translations of texts written in languages other than English are rare); the insistence in composition textbooks on standardizing students' English and their neglect of competing standards and definitions of English; composition historians' neglect of writing in languages other than English; and the neglect in composition scholarship of any non-anglophone scholarship on writing. Such practices define composition as composing in, and only in, an English that has a fixed standard that students are told they must learn to produce in order to participate fully in the civic life of the nation (as full citizens). Language, literacy, and citizenship are viewed as interdependent: to be literate is to know the language, and to know the language is requisite to citizenship. To the history and ongoing project of composition, so understood, and to literacy and citizenship, writing in other languages, or in other forms of English, is entirely irrelevant.

This collection contests this state of affairs. Multilingualism, rather than monolingualism, is taken as both the historical and ideal norm. The context of writing and the writing itself are defined as multilingual: not only is the monolingual writer writing only in English to an audience of speakers of only English viewed as an aberration, but even in the case of such aberrations, the "English" being written and the English of the audience is understood to be plural—Englishes—and hence the situation is at least in a certain sense multilingual. Moreover, even the monolingual writers writing only in English to an audience of speakers of only English are viewed as operating in the context of—both responding to and provoking responses in turn from—other languages, including other Englishes and other tongues, and thus they are themselves engaging in cross-language relations, albeit of a peculiar kind.

This position on multilingualism is aligned with scholarship in applied linguistics demonstrating the multiple and fluctuating character of English as not a single, unchanging world language, or lingua franca, but a constellation of ever changing Englishes (see Kachru, *Alchemy*; Parakrama; Pennycook, "English"; and Rubdy and Saraceni, *English*). This scholarship has revealed that treating one set of conventions as posing a universal definition of "English" is at odds with the fact of a variety of different sets of established practices with English effecting its pluralization into "Englishes" (see Kachru, *Alchemy*). Further, it has shown the necessity of approaching all languages and language varieties as inevitably in flux, their defining borders as at best porous and constructed, with even the stability of the plurality of Englishes in question (Gal and Irvine; Parakrama; Pennycook, "English" and "Performativity"). It highlights the politics of standardizing such varieties and the privileging of so-called native English speakers' language practices over those of speakers of English as a "second" language, the practices of both over those of speakers of English as a "foreign" language, and "native" over "indigenized" and creolized Englishes (see Nayar, Singh).

But while the work of this collection is aligned with such scholarship, it necessarily begins from and responds to a different set of conditions and heads in a different direction. Much of the scholarship on English as a Lingua Franca, for example, is concerned with spoken rather than written language (see Matsuda and Matsuda). Thus, at least some of its findings—for example, regarding the phonological character of English as a Lingua Franca—have little direct correlation to questions of writing of concern to compositionists. Further, the focus of much of this scholarship is on norms in, or for, the use of English among those outside the Anglo-American sphere: those who might conventionally be identified as non-native speakers of English. Questions about the uses of English among those located within the Anglo-American sphere—historically the focus of composition studies—are necessarily pushed to the margins in such scholarship.[1]

This collection takes up such questions by resituating the multilingual norm as one appropriate to the Anglo-American sphere and, more specifically, to written language and the teaching of writing there. Thus, against the conventional view of writing as the codification of language into a fixed set of language standards, the chapters gathered here argue that students need to learn to work in their writing within, on, among, and across a variety of Englishes and languages, not simply to (re)produce and write within the conventions of a particular, standardized variety of English. As Gail E. Hawisher and Cynthia Selfe with Yi-Huey Guo and Lu Liu observe in their chapter, ideologies, technologies, languages, and literacies form a complex, interdependent, cultural ecology of literacy both shaping and shaped by writers' literacy practices at the macro-, medial, and micro-levels. Rather than assuming the composition classroom as a site of simple, homogeneous language use among linguistically homogeneous students, these chapters call on us to recognize the fact of this complex ecology operating in the composition classroom as the actual and cultural norm.[2]

This collection thus calls for a radical shift from composition's tacit policy of monolingualism to an explicit policy that embraces multilingual, cross-language writing as the norm for our teaching and research. Some, of course, may understandably be tempted to dismiss calls for such a radical revision of composition as an impractical, futile dream for reversing accidents of the past and to accept the monolingualism of composition as a real, if regrettable, fait accompli. But as the chapters in this collection make clear, such a response in fact evades ongoing history, and it is, in many ways, less practical than an approach that engages composition's multilingual nature.

In one sense, this movement toward multilingualism and cross-language relations in composition can be understood as, and takes the form of, a response to changes in the language backgrounds of the students in our classes, or at least changes in our perceptions of our students' languages. Perhaps most obviously, there are increasing numbers of students taking composition courses for whom English is not their first language (Harklau, Siegal, and Losey, "Linguistically Diverse"). This is a consequence of not only changes in patterns of immigration to the United States but also changes in who among U.S.-born students apply and are admitted to colleges and universities, the increasing tendency of instructors to recognize differences in the language backgrounds of their students, and the increasing permeability of cultural and institutional boundaries separating "native" speakers of English from others. It has been more and more difficult to sustain what Paul Kei Matsuda, in his chapter, describes as the myth of linguistic homogeneity. Further, the methods that he describes for "containing" linguistic differences—admissions policies, entrance exams, placement procedures, the creation of HBUCs (Historically Black Universities and Colleges), separate tracks for ESL students—have become less and less effective in preventing a "critical mass" of language differences from becoming apparent in composition courses. Schools' strategies for identifying and separating ESL from non-ESL students have proven to be unreliable (Matsuda, "Basic").

Moreover, the permeability of the boundaries separating "native" English speakers from ESL speakers is growing. As Kate Mangelsdorf, Jody Millward, and Michelle Hall Kells observe, there are increasing numbers of bi- and multilingual students raised in the United States for whom traditional ESL programs and courses, often designed for international students (Harklau, Siegal, and Losey, "Linguistically Diverse" 2), are ill-suited (see Matsuda, "Myth"). These and other students may define themselves and their language affiliations in ways that defy ordinary attributions, claiming a language identity, for example, that "exists in their minds but not in their tongues" (Chiang and Schmida 87), or identifying themselves "as *in between* worlds" (85; emphasis mine). For these students, as Yuet-Sim D. Chiang and Mary Schmida observe, standard ESL/native-English categories "force [students] to categorize their identity into an either-or sort of framework, when in fact they may not perceive it in such clear-cut distinctions" (90; see also Harklau, Siegal, and Losey, "Linguistically Diverse" 5; and Frodesen and Starna 62). Thus, it is increasingly inappropriate to make simple identifications of students' language and to categorize and place them in courses of instruction according to such identifications.

While it is, of course, possible for teachers and, more commonly, institutions to ignore students' complex self-identifications in favor of neat categories, scholars and teachers are questioning the validity of doing so, on both practical and theoretical grounds. If it is true, as Matsuda observes in his chapter, that second language issues have remained peripheral to composition studies, there is a demonstrable increase in concern among compositionists with recognizing multilingual students, texts, and histories and with the interdependent relations and interactions among different languages and varieties of language in writing (see, for example, Bruch and Marback; Lu, "Professing" and "Essay"; Lunsford and Ouzgane; and Severino, Guerra, and Butler). Post-Pratt, we might say, in their teaching and scholarship, many compositionists have been heeding the call for a "linguistics of contact" focusing on "modes and zones of contact between dominant and dominated groups, between persons of different and multiple identities, speakers of different languages, . . . on how such speakers constitute each other relationally and in difference, how they enact differences in language" (Pratt 60).

The resituating of composition globally mandates pursuit of such a call. It is now the case, for example, that most users of English are in fact non-native speakers of English (see Kachru, "Introduction" 3–4). Not only is multilingualism statistically more common globally; the "globalization" of communication networks occasions far more contact among far more languages and distributes such contacts more broadly. While the "globalization" of English might seem to be bringing about a more monolingual world, in practice it has meant more of a "dispersal" and fragmentation of English, leading to both more interlanguage contact and the establishment of more varieties of English, as the burgeoning scholarly literature in applied linguistics on "world Englishes" and English as a Lingua Franca testify (Brutt-Griffler; Jenkins, *English*). Under such conditions, attempting to teach students to reproduce a single standardized English in their writing is both futile and inappropriate. As Min-Zhan Lu puts it in her chapter, students faced with a plurality of "target" languages, each of which is subject to change, need to become adept at learning to use these languages (in James Baldwin's sense) rather than attempt to imitate a "target." And, as A. Suresh Canagarajah argues in his chapter, rather than locate students on a trajectory from a home or primary language toward competence in a target language, it is more appropriate to examine the process by which writers shuttle between texts, types of texts, and languages and to work at assisting our students themselves in shuttling creatively between these in their writing, not simply to be sensitive to contexts of their texts but to use their writing to transform those contexts. In doing so, we can look at the practices of established writers, as Canagarajah and Lu do, and at the histories of changes in individuals' literacy practices that incorporate movements between languages and technologies, as Hawisher and Selfe with Guo and Liu illustrate in their chapter.

Pursuing multilingual, cross-language relations in composition will require more than simply recognizing the presence of language difference. As John Trimbur notes in his chapter, compositionists' recognition of the multilingual nature of students, though it combats the "ritualized forgetting" of North America's ongoing multilingual character, often goes hand in hand with a drive toward having students produce finished essays in English. In other words, instead of viewing students' command of languages other than English as a resource to promote biliteracy and multilingualism, instructors frequently examine students' language to see whether it hinders or helps their mastery of academic English. Difference is recognized, but, once again, only as something ultimately to be overcome—even, as Lu observes in her chapter, at the cost of tongue surgery.

Trimbur's chapter reminds us that despite the ongoing history of language diversity, contact, and change, and despite the commitment of our professional organizations to policies opposed to English Only legislation (see resolutions of the National Council of Teachers of English), dominant language ideology encourages a "systematic forgetting" of all these. That forgetting operates not only in laws but also in the institutional structuring of our programs of language instruction, in our textbooks, in our curricula, and in our pedagogies. The chapters in this collection combat such forgetting by resituating composition as material and social engagement in interchanges between, among, and across varieties of language practice. As Lu shows in her chapter, the writing practices of such various authors as Chinua Achebe, Arundhati Roy, and Bill Gates's translators show them to be pursuing a living English, one that rejuvenates the language by contesting standardized, dominant English terms, phrasings, and meanings in light of ongoing, and differing, lives, contexts, and values. And, as Hawisher and Selfe with Guo and Liu observe, attention to the interrelationships between students' engagements in various literacy practices and the local and global "cultural ecologies" in which such engagements take place reveals not only how students' literacy practices are shaped by those "ecologies" but also how they in turn reshape those ecologies, resisting any English Only hegemony in both their choice of languages in which to write and also in how they choose to use those languages in their writing. These writers remind us to ask of any composing how and why it engages languages in the ways it does and to ask of ourselves as teachers of composition how and why we involve students in engaging language(s) in the ways we do and how and why we might involve them, and ourselves, more productively in cross-language relations in writing.

Part One: Struggling with "English Only" in Composition

In part 1 of this collection, we present nine chapters investigating the bases and effects of English Only ideology in composition. The opening three chapters by Trimbur, Lu, and Hawisher and Selfe with Guo and Liu place cross-language relations in composition in the context of the history of diverse and changing geopolitical, linguistic, and technological relations and practices. Trimbur identifies in U.S. history not a laissez-faire language policy but a policy of linguistic expediency that assures neglect of the actual multilingual character of the U.S. population. To combat this, he calls for asking not "how cross-language relations inhibit or facilitate students' mastery of academic literacy in English" but "how the available linguistic resources [of students and teachers] can be tapped to promote biliteracy and multilingualism" to make "U.S. English not the center but the linking language in multilingual writing programs, multilingual universities, and a multilingual polity." Lu extends this contextualizing of the work of composition teaching to encompass the current dominance of global fast capitalism. She reminds us that "we live in a world increasingly ordered by the interests of 'developed' countries such as the United States to globalize their hyper-competitive, technology-driven market economies, what critics have termed 'flexible, information economies' or 'fast capitalism,'" an ordering that calls for fluency in a standardizing global "English Only." And she delineates four lines of inquiry that challenge assumptions about the inevitable benefits of achieving fluency in a standardized English and that pursue the possibilities of putting English to work as "living." In Paul Kei Matsuda's chapter, he outlines a "myth of linguistic homogeneity" that has characterized the responses of U.S. composition teachers and scholars to these pressures, responses that align their work with a tacit English Only policy.

In the five remaining chapters of part 1, Elaine Richardson, Kate Mangelsdorf, Scott Richard Lyons, Shondel J. Nero, and A. Suresh Canagarajah identify practices of resistance by (student and other) writers and (sometimes) by teachers to that policy. These practices are aligned with Lu's call for pursuit of "living-English work" and bring back to recognition what the U.S. policy of linguistic expedience encourages us to forget about the history of language use in the territories of the pre- and postcolonial United States and its territories of influence. In her chapter, Richardson highlights Black contributions to the continual remaking of English, identifying ways that, in fact, "African American Vernacular expression is created, in part, by resistance to oppression." Mangelsdorf documents both the creative use of Spanglish by her students outside the classroom and their hesitance to explore Spanglish in the classroom, even despite her encouragement. Lyons argues not just for "the indigenous language revitalization movement . . . as an attempt by Native peoples to claim rhetorical sovereignty in the face of daunting pressures to assimilate linguistically" but also for the metaknowledge acquired through such efforts, exemplified in what he himself learned from Ojibwemowin. Nero describes the ways in which student speakers and writers of Caribbean Creole English challenge not just standard notions of the "ownership" of English but also "the myth . . . of a homogeneous composition class . . . [and] that of a homogeneous English." As she observes, students' use of English demonstrates that "English is not a fixed code (as traditional schooling would have us believe), and so, as they use their variety of English to engage in academic discourse, they are in so doing changing academic discourse itself." In the final chapter of part 1, Canagarajah uses three versions of a text produced by Sri Lankan senior professor K. Sivatamby that show Sivatamby negotiating different genre expectations, audiences, and his own interests in producing each of the three versions—versions that, as it turns out, in the chronology of their production suggest not the expected pattern of the gradual "development" of an argument but a writer "shuttling" between various genres, languages, contexts, and interests in producing each version. Further, Canagarajah's study shows that texts, contexts, and discourses are not just "changing" but "changeable." As Canagarajah observes, if we are interested in "developing not only competent writers but also critical writers," we need to guide and encourage them to "engage critically in the act of changing the rules and conventions to suit their interests, values, and identities."

Part Two: Responses to Struggling with "English Only" in Composition

Part 2 of this volume presents responses to the arguments presented in part 1 by teachers and scholars of composition from across the United States and from a variety of colleges and universities. These responses highlight both the challenges and possibilities involved in addressing cross-language relations in composition teaching and scholarship, providing further context for the arguments already presented and directions to be pursued. Shirley Wilson Logan points to both the potential and the difficulties she faces countering notions of a "standardized" English when training both "native" and non-native speakers of English coming to her as graduate students to teach composition at the University of Maryland. As she notes, many of the "native" speakers are unaware they speak a "dialect" of English, and many of the international students are unaware of how their own multilingual experience may make them "better equipped to develop [undergraduate] students' ability to navigate the complexities associated with learning those conventions, whether the students are monolingual or multilingual English writers and speakers." LuMing Mao, responding to the arguments in the collection in the context of having read recent news of a truck driver fined in Alabama for "speaking with an accent," calls for us and our students to "study and promote words, concepts, categories, and discourses that can debunk the Standard English ideology and that can reveal relationships of subordination, resistance, and re-presentation" so that "we can begin to view 'speaking with an accent' not as a liability but as an asset, . . . as an accentuating synecdoche for promoting discursive copresences, for practicing interdependence-in-difference."

In his response, Anis Bawarshi notes that even if writing programs institute language policies responsive to language difference, they will "still need to contend with the covert, learned inclinations that manage, execute, and maintain the dominance of unidirectional monolingualism." Likening these learned inclinations to what rhetorical genre theorists identify as "uptakes," Bawarshi calls for pedagogies that "delay and, as much as possible, interrupt the habitual uptakes long enough for students to examine critically their sources and motivations, as well as for students to consider what is permitted and what excluded by these uptakes," to "see uptake both as a site of instantiation and regulation of power and as a site of intervention."

Michelle Hall Kells extends Bawarshi's recommendations, calling for composition that teaches not just "global literacy," defined as "the capacity to read (interpret) and write (respond to) the world," but also a rhetoric "by which . . . [teachers, scholars, and citizens] constitute and protect the presence and participation of the diverse groups within a deliberative democracy." She cautions, "Global literacy in and of itself is not enough—we need a cultural ecology ethic that promotes social justice." Noting that movements for social justice have "operated on the assumption that rhetorical situations not only shape discourse, but are shaped by discourse," she calls on compositionists to "exploit the rhetorical resources within our domain as language and literacy experts" to "fram[e] conversations on language 'diversity' and enact . . . advocacy initiatives." She warns that "if we fail to extend our advocacy efforts across the curriculum, ethnolinguistically diverse students will continue to meet with failure, censure, and discrimination in other courses and writing contexts."

Susan K. Miller-Cochran addresses these calls from the perspective of writing program administrators faced with both the myths about linguistic homogeneity and the facts of students' linguistic heterogeneity. Extending Matsuda's exploration of the "myth of linguistic homogeneity" to identify five myths structuring writing programs, Miller-Cochran goes on to describe the dilemmas WPAs face in combating these structuring myths and to make some specific recommendations for WPAs as they work toward meeting their responsibilities to students whose linguistic heterogeneity is increasingly difficult to deny.

Jody Millward accentuates the importance of such recommendations from the perspective of the work of two-year ("community") colleges, whose open admissions policies guarantee student populations even more linguistically diverse than those enrolling in four-year colleges and universities. In addition to echoing calls for more professional development of instructors to prepare them to respond appropriately to their linguistically diverse students, she offers a number of specific assignments for instructors to develop. These aim at building on, rather than working against, the linguistic strengths students bring with them to our campuses.

Catherine Prendergast reminds us that "only a small portion of language acquisition and use, particularly of any form of English globally, takes place in the classroom at all." Drawing on her own work in the post-communist Slovak Republic, she notes that currently much of the learning of English there takes place outside of classrooms, through venues such as Hiphop and gaming. While this doesn't exempt teachers from attempts at cross-language composition, she suggests that this might best be accomplished through "consideration of intersections," "those moments of accidental and purposeful comprehension—and, more important, incomprehension—that result in some upending of the established linguistic order."

Marilyn M. Cooper's response, "Sustainable Writing," suggests that we think of cross-language writing as a way of "enabl[ing] a compelling answer to the question of why diversity in language matters." Languages, Cooper reminds us, are "immensely complex systems, but adherents to the doctrine of standard language try to treat them as if they were the closed systems of classical physics, systems that are predictable and can be controlled." Drawing on both complexity theory and recent critiques of food production in the United States (and elsewhere), Cooper shows how pursuit of an ostensibly more efficient monolingual approach in language in fact "deprives humans of the resources that enable them to make meanings flexibly in response to ever-changing conditions," just as pursuit of an ostensibly efficient "monoculture" approach to food production has deprived us of the means of feeding ourselves. From this perspective, "diversity in language is as essential to the survival of the human species as sustainably produced crops and flocks of animals," for "writing . . . is how we make the connections among people, technologies, and the natural world that enable us to survive." Adopting a cross-language approach to composition is thus not simply the ethical response to linguistic diversity: it is necessary to our survival, enabling "the sustainability of a complex system" that is language.

Victor Villanueva's chapter brings the volume to a close by identifying a peculiarity in the arguments presented in the volume: it is troubling, he observes, that "institutes of higher education would still need to be convinced of the power of multiple language access." He reminds us that those professing language, language learning, and language instruction are, or ought to be, concerned not with "a solitary language spoken and understood by all" but with the "richness in language multiplicity" and that "we can have a greater community in learning from one another." It is toward the articulation of that aim that this collection and its contributors work.

Principles and Future Directions

While many of the contributors to this volume offer suggestions for combating English Only ideology in composition, they understandably, and rightly, resist offering specific requirements for all to follow. They recognize that strategies and tactics for combating that ideology must necessarily be crafted in ways sensitive to immediate local conditions even as these intersect with global forces. While keeping to this caveat, we can nonetheless identify in the contributors' arguments principles by which different strategies and tactics for combating that ideology might be guided and directions to keep in mind.

First, and perhaps foremost, the chapters in this collection put the question of language front and center in the teaching, learning, and study of composition. While in one sense, language has always been at composition's center, it is a restricted, abstract sense of language that, as the chapters show, is at a significant remove from, and in spite of, language practices on the ground: from the statistical norm of multilingualism, from the pluralization and pliability of Englishes, from the power English users can and do exert in putting their language resources to work—in short, from what Lu calls "living-English work." In response, contributors to this volume call for treating English and all languages as the subject of investigation and revision by both students and teachers, in the classroom and in the study—something whose meanings, forms, and values are subject to change and reworking by students through writing rather than fixed abstractions to which they and their writing must simply conform.

In line with this, this volume argues for treating the language practices of all writers, including student writers, as a resource for, rather than interference in, their writing "in," or rather of, English. At the programmatic level, this means at the very least rethinking the institutional labeling and segregation of some students from others on the basis of their histories with English and, more ambitiously, rethinking the developmentalism shaping the design of composition writing curricula. This radically shifts classroom pedagogy from a transmission model aimed at leading students to mastery of a standardized English—a model in which change is expected to occur primarily in the student—to a seminar model, in which students participate in investigating the possible effects of particular uses of language and experiment in changing language (and languages) through their writing.

Scholarship aligned with this approach would involve rethinking previous studies from the perspective of languages as resources while also building on available scholarship hitherto neglected by compositionists because of either its focus on languages, the linguistic medium in which it appears, the linguistic medium of the writing studied, or the peripheralized status of the language users involved—African Americans, language minorities in the United States, pre-college students, and other unauthorized writers and writing practices of varieties of English worldwide. As several of the chapters demonstrate, there is a wealth of scholarship on language and literacy (and language and literacy education) on whose insights compositionists can build, bringing to that scholarship composition's own characteristic focus on the ways in which languages are mediated through specific writing practices, as well as a long tradition in composition studies of working from, and paying respectful attention to, matters on the ground, as it were, in actual literacy practices and conditions. There is also a wealth of scholarship in, and on, languages other than English on which composition can draw that the dominance of English Only ideology over all levels of U.S. education has rendered invisible to most compositionists. It is now long past time for composition scholars to break the English Only barrier in their writing, reading, and thinking as well as teaching.

Breaking through the barriers of English Only ideology in our teaching and scholarship constitutes a political as well as a conceptual break. For insofar as one's language use is a way of positioning oneself (and being positioned) in the social, the approach taken to languages in composition teaching and scholarship will inevitably entail composition's alignment with particular uses of language and against others: composition teaching and scholarship necessarily both promote and engage in particular language practices. This is manifestly the case in the English Only use of language "standards" to exclude and marginalize some people and legitimate others. It is equally the case in teaching and scholarship that honors the power and right of all language users to draw on all their linguistic resources to reinvent English (and other languages) and that actively pursues multilingualism in the kinds of attitudes to and uses of language(s) it honors and encourages.

As contributors make clear, this multilingualism pursues a politics quite different from the familiar laissez-faire accommodationist multilingualism of neoliberalism that effectively leads to a "separate but equal" politics maintaining linguistic and thereby geopolitical boundaries and asymmetrical relations of power. Rather, it is a multilingualism recognizing and honoring the legitimacy of the meshing of languages—in Raphaël Confiant's terminology, *diversalité* in place of the linguistic silo model of *diversité*, and pursuing what Lachman M. Khubchandani identifies as a "plurilingual ethos" (Confiant, "Créolité"; Khubchandani, "Plurilingual"; see also Pennycook, "English" 37–38; and Agnihotri). Further, it is a politics that rejects a model of writing as simply a means of transmitting preexisting meanings, smoothly or not. Instead, it honors the necessary labor of writers and readers, seen as engaging in the production of and struggle over meaning with language. It thus calls for pedagogies, and research practices, built on the characteristics identified in studies of the pragmatics of micro-processes of users of English as a Lingua Franca: attitudes of tolerance, patience, and humility and strategies of negotiation and cooperation (see Canagarajah, "Ecology"; and Rubdy and Saraceni, Introduction 12).

In pursuing these politics, compositionists can draw and build on composition's long tradition of learning to recognize and honor the "logic" of seemingly opaque writings of students deemed illiterate by adherents of English Only standards and of advancing the interests of those students through their teaching and scholarship.[3] Like the work of those engaged in using English as a Lingua Franca, who rework the defining characteristics of English in their exchanges, this work demands tolerance, patience, and humility, as well as skills in negotiation and cooperation. But as difficult as this work promises to be, it is, as several of the contributors remark, vital not only to the interests of the delegitimated and to social justice but also to the well-being of the language and its users. If English Only threatens humanity's cultural ecology by reducing the complexity that sustains it, pursuing cross-language relations in composition can help to reclaim all language as "a persistent kind of creation and re-creation: a dynamic presence and a constant regenerative process" (Williams 31). This does not simply allow more voices to be heard. It helps writers and readers put all their language resources to work to produce meanings in the interests of all.

Notes

1. For example, in the ongoing debate on whether English as a Lingua Franca (ELF) does or should constitute a competing norm to be taught to non-native English speakers as a variety of English alternative to "native speaker" English (see Jenkins, *English*; Friedrich and Matsuda; Pennycook, "English"; Rubdy and Saraceni, Introduction 10; and Seidlhofer), there is little discussion of whether ELF does or should constitute a competing norm for those users of English identified with the Anglo-American sphere. At best, we have Jenkins's anticipation of a time when "any participating [English] mother tongue speakers will have to follow the agenda set by ELF speakers, rather than vice versa, as has been the case up to now" ("Current" 162).

2. The alternative is to assume, despite all evidence to the contrary, that many of our students are somehow interlopers to the Anglo-American sphere, and thus to be shunted elsewhere, or that they are somehow linguistically immature, again despite all evidence to the contrary (Horner).

3. A highly abbreviated and partial list of work in composition participating in this tradition would include Bartholomae, "Study" and "Inventing"; Bean; Brodkey; Chase; Fox, "Basic" and *Social Uses*; Goleman; Hull; Hull and Rose;

Lam; Lees; Miller; Rose; Seitz; Shaughnessy; Smitherman; Soliday; Sternglass; Stygall; and Trimbur. There is also significant scholarship on student writing outside the United States pursuing these same politics. Restricting myself here to English-medium scholarship, I would recommend, for example, Gentil; Ivanič; Ivanič and Camp; Lea; Lea and Street; and Lillis.

Works Cited

Agnihotri, R. K. "Towards a Pedagogical Paradigm Rooted in Multilinguality." *International Multilingual Research Journal* 1.2 (2007): 79–88.

Bartholomae, David. "Inventing the University." *When a Writer Can't Write: Studies in Writer's Block and Other Composing Process Problems.* Ed. Mike Rose. New York: Guildford, 1985. 134–65.

———. "The Study of Error." *College Composition and Communication* 31 (1980): 253–69.

Bean, Janet. "Manufacturing Emotions: Tactical Resistance in the Narratives of Working-Class Students." *A Way to Move: Rhetorics of Emotion and Composition Studies.* Ed. Dale Jacobs and Laura R. Micciche. Portsmouth, NH: Boynton/Cook, 2003. 101–12.

Brodkey, Linda. "On the Subjects of Class and Gender in the 'Literacy Letters.'" *College English* 51 (1989): 125–41.

Bruch, Patrick, and Richard Marback, eds. *The Hope and the Legacy: The Past, Present, and Future of "Students' Right to Their Own Language."* Cresskill, NJ: Hampton, 2005.

Brutt-Griffler, Janina. *World English: A Study of Its Development.* Clevedon: Multilingual Matters, 2002.

Canagarajah, A. Suresh. "The Ecology of Global English." *International Multilingual Research Journal* 1 (2007): 89–100.

Chase, Geoffrey. "Accommodation, Resistance, and the Politics of Student Writing." *College Composition and Communication* 39 (1988): 13–22.

Chiang, Yuet-Sim D., and Mary Schmida. "Language Identity and Language Ownership: Linguistic Conflicts of First-Year University Writing Students." Harklau, Losey, and Siegal 81–96.

Confiant, Raphaël. "Créolité et francophonie: un éloge de la diversalité." *Potomitan.* 30 Sept. 2007 <http://www.palli.ch/~kapeskreyol/articles/diversalite.htm>.

Fox, Tom. "Basic Writing as Cultural Conflict." *Journal of Education* 172.1 (1990): 65–83.

———. *The Social Uses of Writing.* Norwood, NJ: Ablex, 1990.

Friedrich, Patricia, and Aya Matsuda. "When Five Words Are Not Enough: A Conceptual and Terminological Discussion of English as a Lingua Franca." *International Multilingual Research Journal*, forthcoming.

Frodesen, Jan, and Norinne Starna. "Distinguishing Incipient and Functional Bilingual Writers: Assessment and Instructional Insights Gained through Second-Language Writer Profiles." Harklau, Losey, and Siegal 61–80.

Gal, Susan, and Judith T. Irvine. "The Boundaries of Languages and Disciplines: How Ideologies Construct Difference." *Social Research* 62 (1995): 967–1001.

Gentil, Guillaume. "Commitments to Academic Biliteracy: Case Studies of Francophone University Writers." *Written Communication* 22 (2005): 421–71.

Goleman, Judith. *Working Theory: Critical Composition Studies for Students and Teachers.* Westport, CT: Bergin, 1995.

Harklau, Linda, Kay M. Losey, and Meryl Siegal, eds. *Generation 1.5 Meets College Composition: Issues in the Teaching of Writing to U.S.-Educated Learners of ESL.* Mahwah, NJ: Erlbaum, 1999.

Harklau, Linda, Meryl Siegal, and Kay M. Losey. "Linguistically Diverse Students and College Writing: What Is Equitable and Appropriate?" Harklau, Losey, and Siegal 1–14.

Horner, Bruce. "Mapping Errors and Expectations for Basic Writing: From the 'Frontier Field' to 'Border Country.'" *English Education* 26 (1994): 29–51.

Horner, Bruce, and John Trimbur. "English Only and U.S. College Composition." *College Composition and Communication* 53 (2002): 594–630.

Hull, Glynda. "Acts of Wonderment: Fixing Mistakes and Correcting Errors." *Facts, Artifacts, and Counterfacts: Theory and Method for a Reading and Writing Course.* Ed. David Bartholomae and Anthony Petrosky. Upper Montclair, NJ: Boynton/Cook, 1986. 199–226.

Hull, Glynda, and Mike Rose. "'This Wooden Shack Place': The Logic of an Unconventional Reading." *College Composition and Communication* 41 (1990): 287–98.

Ivanič, Roz. *Writing and Identity: The Discoursal Construction of Identity in Academic Writing.* Amsterdam: John Benjamins, 1998.

Ivanič, Roz, and David Camp. "I Am How I Sound: Voice as Self-Representation in L2 Writing." *Journal of Second Language Writing* 10 (2001): 3–33.

Jenkins, Jennifer. "Current Perspectives on Teaching World Englishes and English as a Lingua Franca." *TESOL Quarterly* 40 (2006): 157–81.

———. *English as a Lingua Franca: Attitude and Identity.* New York: Oxford UP, 2007.

Kachru, Braj B. *The Alchemy of English: The Spread, Functions, and Models of Non-native Englishes.* Urbana: U of Illinois P, 1990.

———. "Introduction: The Other Side of English and the 1990s." *The Other Tongue: English Across Cultures.* 2nd ed. Ed. Braj B. Kachru. Urbana: U of Illinois P, 1992. 1–15.

Khubchandani, Lachman M. "A Plurilingual Ethos: A Peep into the Sociology of Language." *Indian Journal of Applied Linguistics* 24 (1998): 5–37.

Lam, Wan Shun Eva. "L2 Literacy and the Design of the Self: A Case Study of a Teenager Writing on the Internet." *TESOL Quarterly* 34 (2000): 457–82.

Lea, Mary. "'I Thought I Could Write till I Came Here': Student Writing in Higher Education." *Improving Student Learning: Theory and Practice.* Ed. G. Gibbs. Oxford: Oxford Centre for Staff Development, 1994. 216–26.

Lea, Mary, and Brian Street. "Student Writing in Higher Education: An Academic Literacies Approach." *Studies in Higher Education* 23 (1998): 157–72.

Lees, Elaine O. "The Exceptable Way of the Society: Stanley Fish's Theory of Reading and the Task of the Teacher of Editing." *Reclaiming Pedagogy: The Rhetoric of the Classroom*. Ed. Patricia Donahue and Ellen Quandahl. Carbondale: Southern Illinois UP, 1989. 144–63.

Lillis, Theresa. *Student Writing: Access, Regulation, Desire*. London: Routledge, 2001.

Lu, Min-Zhan. "An Essay on the Work of Composition." *College Composition and Communication* 56 (2004): 16–50.

———. "Professing Multiculturalism: The Politics of Style in the Contact Zone." *College Composition and Communication* 45 (1994): 442–58.

Lunsford, Andrea, and Lahoucine Ouzgane, eds. *Crossing Borderlands: Composition and Postcolonial Studies*. Pittsburgh: U of Pittsburgh P, 2004.

Matsuda, Aya, and Paul Kei Matsuda. "World Englishes and the Teaching of Writing." *TESOL Quarterly*, forthcoming.

Matsuda, Paul Kei. "Basic Writing and Second Language Writers: Toward an Inclusive Definition." *Journal of Basic Writing* 22.2 (2003): 67–89.

———. "Myth: International and U.S. Resident ESL Writers Cannot Be Taught in the Same Class." *Writing Myths: Applying Second Language Research to Classroom Teaching*. Ed. Joy M. Reid. Ann Arbor: U of Michigan P, 2008. 159–76.

Miller, Richard. "Fault Lines in the Contact Zone." *College English* 56 (1994): 389–48.

National Council of Teachers of English. "Resolution on Developing and Maintaining Fluency in More Than One Language." 21 June 2009 <http://www.ncte.org/positions/statements/fluencyinlanguages >.

———. "Resolution on English as a Second Language and Bilingual Education." 21 June 2009 <http://www.ncte.org/positions/statements/eslandbilingualeduc>.

Nayar, P. Bhaskaran. "ESL/EFL Dichotomy Today: Language Politics or Pragmatics?" *TESOL Quarterly* 31 (1997): 9–37.

Parakrama, Arjuna. *De-hegemonizing Language Standards: Learning from (Post) Colonial Englishes about "English."* London: Macmillan, 1995.

Pennycook, Alastair. "English as a Language Always in Translation." *European Journal of English Studies* 12.1 (2008): 33–47.

———. "Performativity and Language Studies." *Critical Inquiry in Language Studies: An International Journal* 1.1 (2004): 1–19.

Pratt, Mary Louise. "Linguistic Utopias." *The Linguistics of Writing: Arguments between Language and Literature*. Ed. Nigel Fabb, Derek Attridge, Alan Durant, and Colin MacCabe. New York: Methuen, 1987. 48–66.

Rose, Mike. *Lives on the Boundary*. New York: Penguin, 1989.

Rubdy, Rani, and Mario Saraceni, eds. *English in the World: Global Rules, Global Roles*. London: Continuum, 2006.

———. Introduction. Rubdy and Saraceni 5–16.

Seidlhofer, Barbara. "English as a Lingua Franca in the Expanding Circle: What It Isn't." Rubdy and Saraceni 40–50.

Seitz, David. "Making Work Visible." *College English* 67 (2004): 210–21.

Severino, Carol, Juan C. Guerra, and Johnnella E. Butler, eds. *Writing in Multicultural Settings.* New York: MLA, 1997.

Shaughnessy, Mina P. *Errors and Expectations: A Guide for the Teacher of Basic Writing.* New York: Oxford UP, 1977.

Singh, Rajendra, ed. *The Native Speaker: Multilingual Perspectives.* New Delhi: Sage, 1998.

Smitherman, Geneva. *Talkin That Talk: Language, Culture, and Education in African America.* New York: Routledge, 2000.

Soliday, Mary. *The Politics of Remediation: Institutional and Student Needs in Higher Education.* Pittsburgh: U of Pittsburgh P, 2002.

Sternglass, Marilyn S. *Time to Know Them: A Longitudinal Study of Writing and Learning at the College Level.* Mahwah, NJ: Erlbaum, 1997.

Stygall, Gail. "Resisting Privilege: Basic Writing and Foucault's Author Function." *College Composition and Communication* 45 (1994): 320–41.

Trimbur, John. "Beyond Cognition: The Voices in Inner Speech." *Rhetoric Review* 4 (1987): 211–21.

Williams, Raymond. *Marxism and Literature.* Oxford: Oxford UP, 1977.

One

Struggling with "English Only" in Composition

1. Linguistic Memory and the Uneasy Settlement of U.S. English

John Trimbur

Opponents of English Only legislation often argue that the great wisdom of the Founding Fathers is that they made no national language policy, whether through legislating an official language or establishing a corpus-planning language academy along the lines of the Académie française, which John Adams and others proposed. In such accounts, the Founding Fathers' non-institutional stance—their refusal to give official status to English—is offered as historical precedent that in the United States, a national language policy is neither necessary nor desirable. It is not needed because immigrant-settlers have always learned English and not desirable because of its association with xenophobic intolerance. If anything, the very absence of language policy is the heart of the matter.

The idea that an official language policy violates American tradition has been a powerful argument against English Only, and it is easy to see why the Founding Fathers have been invoked as a measure of national sentiment. To say, however, that the Founding Fathers' approach to language provides historical precedent for linguistic tolerance and a multilingual citizenry, as Shirley Brice Heath and others have suggested, memorializes the Founding Fathers' republican prudence but leaves out something critical about their policy on language in the late colonial and early national periods, roughly 1763 to 1830. I don't think it is possible to understand the politics of language in the early United States without putting the Founding Fathers in their post-colonial circumstances, in an English-speaking settler colony that broke away to form a settler empire.

To understand the Founding Fathers, we must recognize them as the political leadership of the merchant and plantation-owning classes that settled new territories in North America for the maritime trade and the slavery system of European mercantile capitalism. I am indebted to Anne McClintock's characterization of the United States as a "breakaway settler colony" to capture how the American Revolution, as the first successful war of national liberation in the modern era, resulted in the formation of a creole republic that shifted control of colonization from the metropolis to the outpost of empire in the colony. What comes to light is a continuity of identity and social purpose, as the former colonials, in the new republic, assumed independent control of the instruments of empire—the slavery system of plantation settlement, fleets of ships in the transatlantic trade, the sovereignty to deal with indigenous populations, and the destiny to occupy and settle new territories.

Mary Louise Pratt says that a common misperception regarding the American public's view of language is that the United States is hostile to multilingualism. Instead, Pratt holds, Americans are ambivalent about the multiple languages spoken on the street, at work, in the schoolyard, and in the homes where at least 20 percent of the population speaks a language other than English. The politics of language in the United States is a tug-of-war between English monolingualism (which, as Pratt notes, has given the country the "well-earned nickname of *cemeterio de lenguas*, a language cemetery" [111]) and the linguistic reality that the United States is now, as it has always been, a multilingual society. The ambivalence that Pratt so acutely identifies has its own specific histories in lived experience and linguistic memory. My task in this chapter is to look for the roots of this ambivalence in the uneasy settlement of English in the late colonial and early national periods, as claims to the linguistic and political priority of English-speaking settler colonists (the Founding Fathers by their proper name) collided not only with languages other than English but also with the agitations within English caused by the circulation of Africanized English-based pidgins and creoles in the slave trade and plantation system.

The Founding Fathers and the Language Politics of Expediency

When one talks about the settler colonists in North America, the term to emphasize is "settled," for it points toward the useful distinction between exploitation and settler colonies. In the first case, as in British India, the Dutch East Indies, French Indochina, and much of colonized Africa, colonial powers administered, directly or indirectly, outposts of economic exploitation without the extensive settlement of metropolitans or the creation of a proto-nationalist creole population. In contrast, white settler colonies, such as those in North America, Australia, New Zealand, South Africa, and Israel, seized and occupied indigenous territory and subdued native populations through war, disease, relocation, and labor policy in order to establish permanent European settlements.

In settler colonies, the proliferation of a creole population served imperial ends by eliminating the need in exploitation colonies to develop a bilingual native elite to mediate between the colonial administration and the colonized masses of indigenous language-speakers. As Benedict Anderson points out, "In the Americas, there was an almost perfect isomorphism between the stretch of the various empires and that of their vernaculars" (78). The settler colonists were ruled, and ruled, monolingually, in the vernaculars of Madrid and London. At the same time, however, the creoles were typically barred from the ranks of imperial administration in the metropolis and the highest positions in the colonies, their career paths in the work of colonization circumscribed by the territory of nativity. It should not be surprising, then, that the imperial administrative units in which creoles found themselves "could," as Anderson puts it, "over time, come to be conceived as fatherlands" (53).

In *Imagined Communities*, a study of the origins of nationalism, Anderson argues that North and South American creoles in the late eighteenth and early nineteenth centuries (Benjamin Franklin, Thomas Jefferson, Simón Bolívar, José San Martín) were the first nationalist revolutionaries, the first in the modern era to develop a national consciousness based on the recognition of others through print-language. Anderson shows that what was distinctive to the consciousness of the creole nationalists was the solidarity of coincidence and simultaneity produced through print-language, an "imagined community" of others (like me), distributed in the "homogeneous, empty space" of the print page, clock, calendar, map, and census: the language field of print capitalism (24). According to Anderson, the availability of the metropolitan vernacular provided creole nationalists with "unified fields of exchange and communication" located "below" the "universal" script-languages of transcontinental religious communities (Latin, Qur'anic Arabic, Hebrew) and dynastic empires (examination Chinese, court French) and "above" differences in spoken dialects (40–41). This was the original linguistic terrain of nationalism, where creoles in the settler colonies first used the means of print capitalism (newspapers, pamphlets, broadsides, print shops, correspondence committees) to imagine the occupied territories as national republics.

What this means further, as Anderson shows, is that decolonization in the creole republics occurred *within* the colonial language. In the United States, unlike the settler colonies of European Jews in Palestine and the Dutch in South Africa, who developed new national languages (modern Hebrew and Afrikaans), the former colonials held to the language of the English-speaking empire, rejecting proposals to make Greek, Hebrew, or French the national language. Instead, English is figured in linguistic memory as the language the Founding Fathers declined to mandate, making it, in effect, the language that required no official sanction, that was, in fact, already there, at moments of settlement and subsequent nativity. At the postcolonial moment, the deregulatory stance of the Founding Fathers deferred to a cultural authority that went deeper than law in English speakers' claim to linguistic and political priority in the occupation and settlement of new territories in North America.

From one angle, the Founding Fathers' refusal to designate an official language for the new nation appears to be in keeping with the laissez-faire spirit of the age and the aims of merchant capitalism in the early modern period to extend the domains of the market and civil society, so that goods, capital, labor, and print language could circulate freely, without state interference. This, at any rate, is the laissez-faire approach to language that opponents of English Only have seized on to argue against a national language policy. Such ostensible neutrality on the part of the Founding Fathers, however, was more apparent than real. The fact is that the political leaders of the merchant-planter coalition were highly interested in language and willing to use it flexibly and in a variety of forms. In the War of Independence, for example, the Continental Congress quite sensibly published its decrees and political propaganda in German and French, the two main languages of the 25 percent or so of European settlers who were not English speakers. The revolutionary army also used languages other than English to recruit non-English speakers and mobilized entire German-speaking regiments. Furthermore, there can be little question that the leading settler colonists valued languages other than English. Jefferson, among others, recommended the learning of classical and modern languages, advising his nephew to go to Canada to learn French; and he took his own advice, learning Spanish by reading *Don Quixote* with the help of an English-Spanish dictionary. Languages other than English were recognized as important for commerce, diplomacy, and knowledge. Benjamin Rush's proposal for a German-language university in the new republic, despite the fact that it was never realized, acknowledged that English was not alone as the medium of modern knowledge. In fact, it was not long in the new republic before George Ticknor became the first in a line of Americans during the nineteenth century to receive a PhD from a German university.

The point to emphasize about the language policy of the postcolonial United States is that while it did not mandate matters of language, neither did it prohibit government action in the realm of language. Behind the ostensible neutrality of a laissez-faire language policy can be found the expedient management of language by the state to establish and maintain its rule in the newly occupied non-English-speaking territories of the settler empire. To put it another way, a politico-linguistic situation inevitably arose when the metropolitan language of empire extended into annexed territories and encountered the languages of the people who already lived there. Such a situation occurred repeatedly throughout the nineteenth century, with the conquest and annexation of California, the Southwest, Alaska, Hawaii, Puerto Rico, Guam, and the Philippines.

We can see how such a language policy of expediency emerged at an early date in the aftermath of the Louisiana Purchase in 1803, Jefferson's dramatic expansion of the boundaries of the United States, which doubled both its geographical size and its francophone population. In the circumstances, there was no way of avoiding the fact that the American occupation was faced with the problem of managing its language relations with newly acquired subjects. At the time of purchase, Anglo-American English speakers in the Louisiana territories were a distinct minority, outnumbered seven to one by an overwhelmingly French-speaking population. Jefferson's first move was to appoint William C. C. Claiborne, who spoke no French, as territorial governor. Claiborne immediately declared an English Only policy in government matters. In response, the Louisiana Remonstrance of 1804 pointed out the flaws in Claiborne's policy: "That free communication so necessary to give the magistrate a knowledge of the people, and to inspire them with confidence in his administration, is by this means totally cut off" (quoted in Crawford, *Hold Your Tongue* 41).

From his side, Jefferson acknowledged, in something of an understatement, "that most of whatever discontent exists among the French inhabitants arises from the introduction of our language too suddenly" (quoted in Crawford, *Hold Your Tongue* 41). What is so evident here is Jefferson's belief in the inevitability that English would ultimately settle in the new territories as the dominant language in use. The issue, for Jefferson, was how to get there. In other words, language policy in the new territories acquired by the early republic arose from the expediency of occupation, and Jefferson quickly appointed bilingual judges and decreed that laws and public records appear in both English and French. In fact, this accommodation of French was continued during the nineteenth century (except for the Reconstruction era, when Union forces were allied against the French-speaking planters). French was widely and officially used in government, courts, schools, and the translation of public documents. Still, as James Crawford wryly notes, when Louisiana gained statehood in 1812, it was the first and last time a state with a minority of English speakers was admitted to the Union (40–43).

As the case of the Louisiana territories illustrates, a language policy of expediency may well allow, either formally or informally, the use of languages other than English according to the particular circumstances. Nonetheless, it is stretching the meaning of the term to say that Jefferson's language policy amounted to "linguistic tolerance" when its motivating force so clearly grew out of the basic need of the American occupation to establish sovereignty in the annexed territories.[1] The term "expediency" better captures Jefferson's politico-linguistic intervention, for it emphasizes, from the perspective of the conquering power, both the appropriateness of the response to the situation and the fact that the response articulated no general principles of a national language policy. There were surely unavoidable lessons to be learned from the experience of the new republic in Louisiana, as Crawford points out, about the uneasy settlement of English in annexed territories, especially later in the nineteenth century in regard to New Mexico where the American occupation again faced a majority of non-English speakers—and, accordingly, withheld statehood until 1911, when there was a majority of English speakers.

While the language politics of expediency in the settler empire posed no obstacle in the occupied territories to accommodating other languages, it also offered no reason the state should acknowledge an obligation to the language rights of non-English speakers except on the grounds of expediency. One of the most salient features of the Founding Fathers' approach to language was the reluctance to recognize, as part of the basic political liberties in the U.S. Constitution, the right of linguistic minorities to communication in their own languages. In this regard, a defining linguistic moment in the new republic occurred in 1795, after German-speaking Virginians petitioned the U.S. Congress to publish federal laws in German. The proposal was defeated, albeit by a single vote, as were further attempts in the early national period to publish federal laws or agricultural reports in languages other than English (although such publication, along with other forms of language promotion, did take place during the nineteenth century at the state and municipal levels). By refusing the responsibility, not to mention civil courtesy, on the part of the federal government in matters of language, the legendary Muhlenburg vote of 1795 set the pattern of favoring English as the national print-language at the expense of another language, in this case German, by refusing to recognize the language right of linguistic minorities to have federal publications available in their own language.[2] This is the characteristic stance of the Founding Fathers: by recognizing no obligation beyond expediency, it permits and prevents.

The Settlement of English and the Multitude

What I hope to have suggested so far is that the language policy of the Founding Fathers, despite its ostensible neutrality and reluctance to legislate, was just as programmatic as overt forms of official language policy. We need to think of language policy not just in terms of state edicts but also in terms of the way the social organization of merchant capitalism produced language relations through the formation of a labor force and the workings of the market and civil society. To understand the language policy of the new republic, we must identify not only the politics of expediency that guided language relations on the part of the settler empire in newly occupied territories but also the covert passages where language circulated in the transatlantic trade and the plantation slavery system. From this perspective, we can see how a linguistic culture forming around the idea of the inevitability of English as the national print-language—and the underlying claim to linguistic and political priority on the part of English-speaking settlers—encountered, in the revolutionary crisis of the 1760s and 1770s, a polyglot and multiethnic multitude that emerged from the very energies of mercantilism aboard ships and in port cities, in the slave castles of West Africa and on the New World plantations, and in pan-Indian resistance movements.

As early as the 1730s and 1740s, urban insurrections against slavery and press gangs, slave revolts, maroonage, mutinies, piracy, and the growing threat of pan-Indian wars had challenged the authority of the British empire in the circum-Atlantic world. Though put down by British might, the revolts of what Peter Linebaugh and Marcus Rediker call the "motley crew" had threatened the heartbeat of mercantile capitalism: the gangs of slaves who labored on the plantations and the gangs of sailors in the ever-growing fleet of naval and merchant ships. According to Linebaugh and Rediker, the motley crew "describes a socio-political formation of the eighteenth-century port or town," in England and the colonies, a multiethnic and polyglot urban mob that embodied the potentiality for an international anti-colonialism of the dispossessed. In the 1760s and 1770s, "at the height of revolutionary possibility," Linebaugh and Rediker write, the "motley crew appeared as a synchronicity or an actual coordination among the 'risings of the people' of the port cities, the resistance of African American slaves, and Indian struggles on the frontier" (213–14).

Tacky's Rebellion in Jamaica in 1760 not only was the most formidable slave uprising to that time in the West Indies but also unleashed plots and revolts across the Caribbean over the next twenty years, some of which veterans of Tacky's Rebellion took part in. Pontiac's Rebellion in 1763 unsettled the western frontier by forging a pan-tribal alliance against British expansion into Indian territory. The ports exploded periodically in the 1760s and 1770s, when multiracial mobs of revolutionary sailors, slaves, free Blacks, abolitionists, and the multitudes of the docklands took their protests against the press gangs and the king's authority into the streets, beyond the control of the moderate patriot leadership. These popular forces were unreconciled to the respectable classes and antinomian in temperament. They had already gone beyond the rights of Englishmen, which were never forthcoming in any case, to base their claims to revolutionary justice on universal rights, putting the moral conscience of humanity above civil law.

Once the dispossessed of the "motley crew" are present in linguistic history, we can see how language policy in the late colonial and early national periods was embedded in the proletarianization of a free and unfree labor force and in the attempt of the settler colonists to establish the linguistic priority of English against the multilingual realities created by the maritime trade and plantation system. The linguistic relations of the settler colony to the polyglot colonial multitude grew out of mercantilist relations of production, articulated in the domain of language through pidginization and creolization, in the uneasy settlement of English in the circum-Atlantic world of merchant capitalism.

Since the 1960s, pidgin and creole studies have overturned the older linguistic history, which held (on the basis of extremely scant evidence) that African slaves in the United States learned a dialect of English that came from Britain (East Anglia was especially favored as the region of origin). Instead of making the white settler colonists the source of all English in the New World and thereby according linguistic priority to the metropolitan English they spoke, pidgin and creole studies locate in West Africa the origin of the English-based creoles so widely distributed in the circum-Atlantic world. This break with a Eurocentric view of English is of great consequence to our investigation of the politics of language in the settler colony, for it reveals, first, that more than one English was settled in the New World and, second, that the social dynamic of language settlement involved not the faulty transmission of English from whites to Blacks, as older accounts explained the inferiority of Black English, but the workings of the circum-Atlantic slave trade.

Linguists generally agree that a West African pidgin English had emerged by the late sixteenth century in the slave castles on the lower Guinea coast. Pidgins are invented, as a rule, to bridge the linguistic gap between mutually incomprehensible language groups. By definition, no one is a native speaker of pidgin. Pidgins rather are interim languages constructed, typically in situations of unequal power relations, to manage work, trade, social relations, and territory. West African pidgin English could well have drawn its inspiration in part from Portuguese pidgin, which was already present along the Guinea coast by the 1490s, or from the nautical pidgin English that circulated, as we will see in a moment, in the transatlantic maritime trade. Whatever the case may be, there was no question that the political economy of the slave trade produced an interlanguage that enabled communication both between European slavers and Africans and among Africans themselves, who in the maelstrom of the slave trade had been cast together from various language groups. Slave traders learned to separate speakers of the same African languages as a means of social control, and accordingly the formation of pidgin English was as much a response to the need of slaves to communicate with each other as a means to facilitate communication with Europeans. Certainly, the majority of pidgin speakers were Africans, who spoke in pidgin to other Africans, as well as to Europeans.

Pidgins become creoles when they are taken up as the first language of native speakers. The shift is not primarily in the linguistic structure of the language but in its use, as pidgin becomes a creole mother tongue. In the New World, this occurred when African slaves settled West African pidgin English in the form of English-based plantation creoles. These were mutually comprehensible languages that ranged throughout the circum-Atlantic world from North America throughout the Caribbean to Guyana and Surinam on the Atlantic coast of South America. Creoles that are part of this language continuum were settled in West Africa—Sierra Leone Krio, Liberian Pidgin English, WesKos in Nigeria and Cameroon. The similarities among all of these creoles have led a number of linguists to argue that they must have had a single English-based ancestor in West Africa (Baker; Hancock; McWhorter). By this account, it was not a matter of African slaves inventing plantation creole in the New World and then transplanting it on a plantation-by-plantation basis. Instead, a language that had already been developed by Africans in West Africa was taken to the New World, where slaves settled West African pidgin as their native language in the plantation creoles of the circum-Atlantic world.

The view that plantation creole is nothing more than a form of broken English appears repeatedly in the writings of slave owners and European visitors to the New World throughout the late eighteenth and early nineteenth centuries. The truth, however, is more the reverse: namely, that Africans began to *break* English—to tame it for use—in the slave castles on the West African coast at least a century before, seeking some linguistic traction in relations of drastically unequal power. Two telling points enable us to glimpse the hybridic labor that produced the interlanguage of pidgin from the available linguistic resources of English and West African languages. First, although English was the lexifier or language of power, the linguistic motive, nonetheless, was not so much to acquire English wholesale as to pidginize it by eliminating features of English that were unusual or difficult for relevant language groups to learn and by interjecting into English ways of forming words and sentences that came from African languages. Second, and related, is John H. McWhorter's critique of the "limited access" theory that argues that creole develops in circumstances where the majority of speakers do not have sufficient exposure to learn fully the target European language, as supposedly was the case on plantations where slaves significantly outnumbered native European language-speakers and often had little direct contact with them. The issue here, to put it more bluntly than McWhorter might, is not a matter of numbers but the fact that, in their hybridic formation, creoles do not target European languages at all and then fail to approximate them fully. Rather, creoles use European languages, in hybridic linguistic activity, to develop new languages that were not there before in order to deal with asymmetrical relations of power and to pursue social purposes for which no other language is available.

Certainly, slave owners collaborated in the formation of plantation creole by suppressing the use or teaching of African languages, often under threat of such harsh punishment as having an offending slave's tongue cut out. Nonetheless, the linguistic agency in the matter must go to the West Africans who invented pidgin and the African American slaves who developed and maintained it as plantation creole. Moreover, as McWhorter notes, once the "limited access" theory is dismissed, it removes one of the main hypothetical barriers to slaves learning the English of the planter class. There was no intrinsic reason they could not; and in fact, many slaves were bidialectal, using the metropolitan English of the planter class to work as relatively privileged house slaves, to learn artisan trades, and to read the Bible and abolitionist tracts and newspapers. Still, for African American slaves, maintaining plantation creole provided valuable resources of representation, sociality, intimacy, and secrecy.

This uneasy (because unequal) settlement of English through pidgin and creole produced the paradoxical situation, as J. L. Dillard points out, "of a variety of English being taught to some Englishmen by non-Europeans" (147). There is ample historical record that the slave-owning classes learned to speak plantation creole from African Americans, often at an early age through play with slave children, and then used it as a means of managing the slave labor force. But there are other equally revealing examples of how forms of Africanized English were transmitted in the New World. Dillard presents circumstantial evidence that a "time table for the spread of Pidgin English from African slaves to Indians is a workable one" (143). There is no doubt that African slaves and Indians encountered each other in the early part of the seventeenth century, within colonial institutions, as fellow slaves (where Indian servitude preceded the arrival of Africans), or as fellow pupils in missionary schools. Whether pidgin English was transmitted from Africans to Indians, as Dillard suggests, there are persuasive attestations in literary works and travelers' accounts that Indians spoke pidgin at an early date. For bidialectal slaves, who could manage language relations with whites and, in some instances, wrote passes in the name of their masters, flight to the north may have been more thinkable than it was for monodialectal slaves who spoke only plantation creole. For these slaves, running away to receptive Indians could well have been the better or only option, and it is easy to imagine how pidgin English would have been of great use in the circumstances.

Relations between Africans and Indians were various and extensive and have for long been a neglected chapter in American history. In the case of the Seminole, relations between Indians and Africans formed the basis of resistance to the United States in the two Seminole wars of self-defense in 1817–18 and 1835–42. The Seminoles had already split from the Creek confederacy by the late eighteenth century, leaving Georgia and Alabama to settle in Florida, which was not under U.S. jurisdiction until 1813. The name "Seminole" derives from the Spanish word *cimarron* (or runaway) and is related to "maroon" in English. In Florida, the Seminole formed alliances with the largest African American maroon community in North America, perhaps a thousand former slaves, many of whom were Gullah speakers, who had run away from the lowland plantations in South Carolina and Georgia to join the four thousand or so Seminoles. Once in Florida, the maroons developed an Afro-Seminole creole to accommodate their relations with the Indians and to pursue the joint purposes of staying free from the reach of the U.S. state and its persistent efforts to wipe out the maroon community in Florida, reenslave its members, and remove the Seminole to the west.

The nautical pidgin that took shape aboard the merchant ships and in the imperial navies, among the multiethnic crews of sailors waylaid into service by press gangs and the pressures of poverty, offers another instance of how language relations and labor policy were linked in the circulation of English. As partially free labor, sailors made up what Rediker calls the "deep sea proletariat," the workforce of merchant capitalism that imported and exported millions of pounds of commodities annually in the circum-Atlantic trade. As Rediker notes, "The ship was not only the means of communication between continents, it was the first place where working people from the continents communicated" (134). The use of nautical pidgin has deep roots in the European maritime trade, going back to *sabir*, the lingua franca of the Mediterranean, established as a continuous linguistic tradition since at least the time of the Crusades and maintained into the twentieth century. As an available linguistic resource to sailors, *sabir* may have served as an ancestral language to the English, French, and Portuguese pidgins and creoles that spread across the world in the era of European exploration and colonization.

According to Linebaugh and Rediker, the nautical pidgin that took shape in the maritime trade combined "first, nautical English; second, the 'sabir' of the Mediterranean; third, the hermeticlike 'cant' talk of the 'underworld'; and fourth, West African grammatical construction" to produce "the pidgin English that became in the tumultuous years of the slave trade the essential language of the Atlantic" (153). The "vehicular languages" invented in part to facilitate shipboard communication for purposes of command and discipline, Linebaugh and Rediker note, became in turn a "revolutionary vector" by providing the nautical proletariat with a means of self-organization and self-expression in strikes, mutinies, and piracy. Sailors, as Walter Benjamin notes, along with other migratory types, have always been storytellers, bringing news to far-flung peoples. In the maritime trade of mercantile capitalism, sailors' nautical pidgin helped to foster an emerging proletarian sphere that linked the polyglot multitude by transmitting the anticolonial potentialities of abolition, resistance to press gangs, slave revolts, and urban riots from port to port, fueling the revolutionary crisis that shook the circum-Atlantic world in the 1760s and 1770s.

The Anglo-Saxon Surrogate

To establish the linguistic and political priority of English-speaking settler colonists and, in the face of the polyglot multitude, to make English the inevitable language of settlement and nativity, the settler colonists performed what Joseph Roach in *Cities of the Dead: Circum-Atlantic Performance* calls an act of "surrogation." "Newness," Roach says, "enacts a kind of surrogation—in the invention of a new England or new France out of memories of the old" (4). Surrogation, as Roach explains it, involves a substitution for the missing original that results in a systematic (and systematically incomplete) forgetting. When "actual or perceived vacancies occur in the network of relations that constitutes the social fabric"—when, say, someone dies or retires from work or, for our purposes, settles new lands or breaks ties with the old—then the incumbents, according to Roach, "attempt to fit satisfactory alternates." However, since "collective memory works selectively, imaginatively, and often perversely, surrogation rarely if ever succeeds." Whether through deficit or surplus, the "intended substitute" is never an exact fit, a source of ambivalence more than a resolution to the anxiety of displacement. Thus, as Roach notes, "selective memory requires public enactments of forgetting, either to blur the obvious discontinuities, misalliances, and ruptures or, more desperately, to exaggerate them in order to mystify a previous Golden Age, now lapsed" (2–3).

We can find the rhetorical action of surrogation in the moment of settlement by English-speaking colonists in North America. To establish the priority and legitimacy of settlement (and consequently to erase the presence of indigenous people), the colonists made the freeborn Anglo-Saxons of British political tradition the historical ancestors of the land they were occupying. As Allen J. Frantzen writes, "Jefferson and other early American revolutionaries were immersed in myths of Anglo-Saxon democracy, and among the patriots discussing them were George Washington, Patrick Henry, and Benjamin Franklin" (18). In Jefferson's design for the Great Seal of the United States (which was not adopted), on one side appeared the mythical Anglo-Saxon warriors Hengst and Horsa, while the other featured the pillar of fire that guided God's chosen people into the promised land in Exodus 13:21–22. Iconically, the United States, as heir to the primitive democracy of an Anglo-Saxon past, was, for Jefferson, "chosen" to settle a new world by recovering ancient English liberties and institutionalizing the Anglo-Saxon tradition of common law. Expansionist premises and an overriding sense of manifest destiny were the clear prospects of Jefferson's Anglo-Saxonism. For Jefferson, however (and, as we will see, for Franklin and Noah Webster), this was a future verified by looking backward, to the historical primacy of Anglo-Saxon origins and linguistic memories of an older, purer English speech settled and preserved in the New World. This is what Roach calls the "myth of monocultural autochthony" (109) that offsets the illegitimacy of settlement by erasing evidence of dislocation and the seizure of territory.

The "genius of Anglo-Saxonism," as Roach says—and Franklin, Jefferson, and Webster demonstrate—is its capacity "to perpetuate itself by simultaneously expanding its boundaries in the name of freedom and disavowing its consequent affiliations in the name of race" (109). Franklin's infamous tirade against Pennsylvania Germans in his "Observations Concerning the Increase of Mankind," written in 1751, presents a remarkable instance of Anglo-Saxon expansionism and its racialized affiliations and disaffiliations. Here is a key passage from Franklin's "Observations":

> Why should the Palatine Boors be suffered to swarm into our Settlements, and by herding together establish their Language and Manners to the Exclusion of ours? Why should Pennsylvania, founded by the English, become a colony of Aliens, who will shortly be so numerous as to Germanize us instead of our Anglifying them, and will never adopt our Language or Customs, any more than they can acquire our Complexion? (234)

As can be seen, for Franklin, the English claim to Pennsylvania rested on priority of settlement and the purported originality of the English settler colonists. The very notion that Pennsylvania could be "founded" by Europeans depends, in the first instance, on the replacement of aboriginal sovereignty and native patterns of land use by English settlement and the assumed entitlement of freeborn subjects of the British empire to expand the territory of Anglo-Saxon liberty. By installing such an Anglo-Saxon surrogate in the gap between the mother country and the New World, the displaced English settlers in North America seized on a readily available fiction to represent themselves as being at home in the colonies—a means of remembering and forgetting that in turn erased native inhabitants and cast the "swarm" of Pennsylvania Germans as illegitimate invading rivals.

Franklin may well have been drawing on his own experience as an entrepreneurial printer when he called on his fellow English-speaking settlers to recognize the danger posed by Germans, who made up perhaps 40 percent of the population in Pennsylvania. By the time he wrote his "Observations," Franklin had already encountered Germans as "foreign" economic competition, failing in his attempt in 1732 to establish the first German-language newspaper in North America and later being cut out of the publishing business by a rival German printer who cornered the German-language book market in Pennsylvania (Shell 6–7). Franklin's xenophobic fear of a "colony of Aliens" certainly anticipates a larger pattern in the United States, where the language of non-English speakers who are seen to pose a social, economic, or political threat becomes, as Shirley Brice Heath puts it, the "focus of argument" about linguistic status and political legitimacy (10). In a sequence of rhetorical moves that have become standard to the idea of the inevitability of English, Franklin begins by asserting the linguistic priority of English and its authenticity as the language of settlement. Then he constructs an unbridgeable divide between English speakers and German speakers that is warranted not only by linguistic and cultural difference but also, revealingly, by the lack of a shared "Complexion."

Franklin's move from language to complexion leads him to disaffiliate English settlers from Germans on the grounds of racialized identities. In a now familiar gesture, language and race become proxies for each other as Franklin divides the world between the "black or tawny" people of Africa, Asia, and Native America; the "swarthy" people of Europe (which includes not only the predictable Spaniards and Italians but also Swedes and Germans); and the Anglo-Saxons alone who "make the principal Body of White People on the Face of the Earth." Linguistic memory merges with natural history as Franklin maps a racialized taxonomy across the surface of the globe. What is most troubling to Franklin is the recognition that, according to the categories of his own invention, "the number of white People in the World is proportionately very small." In Franklin's articulation of language and race, the installation of an Anglo-Saxon surrogate in the multilingual and racialized world of the circum-Atlantic provokes the realization that English-speaking white people are surrounded and outnumbered. "I could wish their Numbers were increased" (234), Franklin says, in one of those moments of Anglo-Saxon linguistic and racial paranoia, when the settler colony becomes aware of the multitude.

The diaspora of the circum-Atlantic world, as Roach says, put pressure on the myth of monocultural autochthony, "threatening its imputed purity, both antecedent and successive, because it appears to make available a human superabundance for mutual assimilation" (43). In the case of Franklin, the founding myth of the English colonies, with its claims to priority of settlement, takes place in a geohistorical landscape in which the Anglo-Saxon minority is threatened by swarming multitudes and a Babel of languages. The overwhelming number—the "herd"—of racialized others threatens miscegenation and promiscuous liaisons of all sorts. Predictably, Franklin calls for a halt to immigration to Pennsylvania that might "darken its People" (234). As we see, Franklin's desire to bring forward an authorizing, autochthonous Anglo-Saxon origin of language and liberty kept colliding with the linguistic and cultural impurities of the circum-Atlantic world, the "alien double," as Roach puts it, who appears "in memory only to disappear" (6).

In the case of Noah Webster, Franklin's rival German was no longer the source of linguistic, cultural, and racial anxiety but instead was assimilated and refigured in a shared Teutonic linguistic culture that reaches back to biblical times before the separation of Noah's sons Shem, Ham, and Japheth. Vernacular words in Celtic and Teutonic languages—the foundation, for Webster, of an English rooted in antiquity—acquired a primacy and historical pedigree in their affinity with words that were part of a common language before the linguistic dispersion of Babel. According to Webster, while Shem and Ham are the sources of Semitic and Hamitic languages and cultures, Europeans are the descendants of Japheth. From these ancient roots, Webster argues, Teutonic influences shaped not only Greek and Latin but, more tellingly for his purposes, the English spoken in the United States and England.

In a stroke of linguistic nationalism, Webster made American English historically antecedent to British English. As Webster says in his *Dissertations on the English Language*, published in 1789, there is a "surprising similarity between the idioms of the New England people and those of Chaucer, Shakespeare, &c. who wrote in the true English stile" (108). Webster's linguistic nationalism hinges foremost not on postcolonial innovation but on a restoration of the linguistic memory of an English that "seldom use[s] any words except those of Saxon origin," a language free of the Latin contaminants of the Roman conquest and the Norman yoke (not to mention the Africanized English that Webster ignores). "The people of America, in particular the English descendants," Webster says, "speak the most pure English known in the world" (288). For Webster, the English of the British empire was a language in decline, a decadent and impure product of neologism, loss of standards, and intercultural contact. "Let it be observed," Webster says in 1816, "that so far as a difference between the language of Englishmen and of Americans consists in our use of words obsolete in the higher circles of Great Britain, the change is not in our practice but in that of Englishmen. The fault, if any is theirs" (quoted in Baron 58). American English, as Webster saw it, "still adhere[s] to the analogies of the language, where the English have infringed them. So far therefore as the regularity of construction is concerned, we ought to retain our own practice and be our own standards" (129).

According to Webster, American English not only had a purity of origin but also a uniformity of expression that guaranteed its function in binding the nation into a common monolingual speech community. In contrast to the linguistic situation in England, Americans were not divided by local dialects. "The people of distant counties in England," Webster says, "can hardly understand one another, so various are their dialects." In the United States, however, "in the extent of twelve hundred miles in America," he continues, "there are very few, I question whether a hundred words . . . which are not mutually intelligible" (288–89). Perhaps, but only if you "forget" to count the languages of non-English speakers; the plantation creole spoken by slaves, who made up more than one-fifth of the population when Webster was writing; the nautical pidgin of the "deep sea proletariat"; and the various linguistic hybrids spoken along the borders of the United States, where French, Spanish, and Native American languages interacted with English through annexation, trade, and diplomacy. The uniformity of English that Webster had in mind, as has so often been the case in the United States, is the language of the New England settlers, the Anglo-Saxon descendants whose own regional dialect became the surrogate for a missing English of national unity.

For Webster, the incomplete substitution afforded by the Anglo-Saxon surrogate only revealed the limits of systematic forgetting in linguistic memory. Webster notes that the people of New England have been living "in the situation of an island" where they "have not been exposed to any of the causes which effect great changes in language and manners" (quoted in Baron 59). Known by its insularity, American English, for Webster, was protected from the linguistic and political turbulence of the circum-Atlantic world. The troubling exceptions, however, were the "commercial towns," the ports through which the hybridic vernaculars of pidgin and creole circulated. More muted than in Franklin, there is nonetheless in Webster the unsettling recognition of the polyglot multitudes gathered dockside, where the port cities figured as conduits of linguistic contamination and seditious ideas. For Webster, the preservation of Anglo-Saxon linguistic origins imputed an isolated purity to English in the United States and amounted, accordingly, to an incomplete erasure of its wider linguistic relations and the innovations of its pidginized and creolized forms. Looming at the edge of linguistic memory was the uneasy settlement of English in North America—and what Roach calls the necessary "failures of memory to obscure the mixtures, blends, and provisional antitypes necessary for its production" (6).

Toward a National Public Policy on Language

There is no doubt, as Michael P. Kramer puts it, that Webster shaped "American linguistic history into a final, open-ended chapter of the Anglo-Saxon spirit" (62) or that his dictionaries, spellers, and linguistic tracts helped promote U.S. English as the national print-language of the settler empire. Certainly this linguistic memory has been institutionalized in English studies, U.S. college composition, and the modern U.S. university. Since the overturn of the classical curriculum and the establishment of graduate education on the German model in the late nineteenth and early twentieth centuries, the U.S. university has drastically curtailed the educational role of languages other than English—whether Greek and Latin in the old-time American colleges or German for those Americans who went to German universities to get PhDs. Instead, English has become the unquestioned medium of instruction and the vernacular of modernity, identified with science, technology, and the professions. In turn, the other modern languages have been territorialized in departments of French, German, Spanish, and so on, as national literatures, in the tacit language policy of the modern research university that assigns only to English the status of a living language (Horner and Trimbur).

The issue here is not simply Anglo-Saxon hegemony in linguistic memory but the relentless monolingualism of American linguistic culture, the strategies by which English is meant to replace and silence other languages. This unidirectional monolingualism has been codified in the view that African American English is a faulty derivative of U.S. English and in melting-pot ideologies as a "natural" language shift to the use of English only (with consequent loss of mother tongue) that occurs by the third generation in immigrant families, thereby making bilingualism and the maintenance of home languages appear to be aberrant and un-American. U.S. English figures as a loss of memory, a language of forgetting whose very ground of speech is the displacement of other languages. And yet, as Roach suggests, "the most persistent mode of forgetting is memory imperfectly deferred" (4). Linguistic memory—the incomplete forgetting of ancestral languages—virtually guarantees the ambivalence about multilingualism that Pratt describes, as traces of other languages and other Englishes (embedded residually in mundane rituals, music, ethnic and racial identifications, the names and taste of food, the sound of a word, a style of dress, and so on) collide with English mono-lingualism and its Anglo-Saxon heritage.

From a certain angle, it would appear that "memory imperfectly deferred" is compulsively resurfacing in the U.S. university in the form of multicultur-alism, postcolonial theory, and transnational studies. The emergence of this counter-memory has indeed recast the study of history, literature, and culture, with works such as Roach's *Cities of the Dead*, among many others, that take as their unit of analysis not the nation-state and the national character of the old American exceptionalism but instead the circulation of people and cross-language relations across national borders. Still, as Marc Shell and Werner Sollors have pointed out, there is a remarkable silence within this recent and important body of work, as well as across the university curriculum, about the multilingualism that linguistic memory has erased. The primacy of Eng-lish as the medium of instruction retains a powerful hold on teaching and learning, curtailing the development both materially and programmatically of a multilingual curriculum. In contemporary English studies, for example, while English-language writers across the global diaspora are widely read, there is no apparent institutional or critical space for the vast non-anglophone literature written in the United States. To test this point, check the table of contents of Shell and Sollors's groundbreaking *Multilingual Anthology of American Literature*, with its original texts and English translations, to see how many writers you've ever heard of. Another instance of systematic forgetting is the reference volume *Asian-American Literature: An Annotated Bibliography*, which explicitly excludes "works written in Asian languages, unless they have been translated into English" (Sollors 14).

In the field of writing studies, until quite recently there has been very little discussion of writing in languages other than English in composition class-rooms, and the writing that takes place in Spanish, French, German, Chinese, Arabic, and other language courses has remained largely invisible, both con-ceptually and programmatically. The question traditionally asked in writing studies is how cross-language relations inhibit or facilitate students' mastery of academic literacy in English. I think the question needs to be reframed, to ask how the available linguistic resources can be tapped to promote biliteracy and multilingualism. I want to imagine a new configuration of languages in the U.S. university and in U.S. college composition that realigns the relations among languages, with U.S. English not the center but the linking language in multilingual writing programs, multilingual universities, and a multilingual polity. To do this would require a shift from the unidirectional and subtrac-tive monolingualism that has long dominated writing programs to an active and additive multilingualism in which a range of languages are involved as the medium of writing, as the medium of instruction across the university curriculum, and as the medium of deliberation in the public sphere.

To say, as liberal opponents of English Only often do, in line with the presumed wisdom of the Founding Fathers, that the United States does not need a national language policy has the unintended effect of reinforcing the ambivalence that results from the uneasy settlement of English and the "incomplete forgetting" of other languages and other Englishes. Despite such predictable consequences, it is nonetheless arguable to hold that the United States should keep language out of the hands of the state, making it a matter for civil society to determine through custom rather than law. The key point to recognize, however, is that, for better or worse, such a laissez-faire approach does constitute a language policy, and not the absence of one, based on the principle of muddling through the uneasy settlement, past and present, of English in the United States. To my mind, a more promising approach to the politics of language in the United States is Geneva Smitherman's call, in 1987, for academics in speech, language, and writing studies to "take up the unfinished business of the Committee on the Students' Right to Their Own Language" and put forward a national public policy on language that would (1) teach standard edited English as the language of wider communication, (2) recognize the legitimacy of African American English and non-mainstream languages and dialects and promote such mother tongues as the medium of instruction, and (3) promote the learning of one or more additional languages, such as Spanish or other relevant language. The exact configuration of languages to be studied and learned will depend on individual interest and local circumstances. But as Smitherman insists, the "three-prong policy . . . constitutes an inseparable whole" (31) that is meant to change the status of languages in the United States by reconfiguring their relation to each other.

What Smitherman's proposal for a national language policy makes clear is that multilingualism does not mean simply affirming the linguistic rights of minority language groups to use their own language as they see fit. Certainly, a national public policy on language must defend such rights, which, as noted earlier, have never been fully recognized in the United States. As I see it, however, multilingualism signifies more than simply the tolerance of many languages in America. It also entails the status planning of languages and an additive language policy where all students as a matter of course speak, write, and learn in more than one language and all residents of the United States thereby become capable of communicating with each other in a number of languages. The goal of such a national language policy, I believe, goes beyond a discourse of linguistic rights to imagine the abolition of English monolingualism altogether and the creation in its place of a linguistic culture where being multilingual is both normal and desirable, as it is throughout much of the world. If anything, the multilingual language policy I'm advocating would loosen the identification of language with racialized and ethnic groups by putting multiple languages and multiple Englishes into circulation as means of participating in public life and as linguistic resources of reciprocal exchange.

Notes

1. In "Anatomy of the English-Only Movement," James Crawford sees Jefferson's language policy in Louisiana as a betrayal: "For the United States, the Louisiana Purchase of 1803 posed an early test of the nation's commitment to its founding principles. Would democracy be extended without reservation to cultural and linguistic minorities? Would President Jefferson honor his own rhetoric about 'unalienable rights'? Apparently not. His policy toward the Louisiana Territory illustrates a classic choice of expediency over principle." As should be evident, my view, rather, is that expediency is the principle.

2. The narrow defeat of the proposal was made possible when Speaker of the House F. A. Muhlenburg, one of the original sponsors, vacated his post in order not to prejudice the vote. During the nineteenth century, this incident, curiously, turned into the legend that Congress had come within one vote of abolishing English as the national language and replacing it with German (Kloss 29–30; Schiffman 219). See Kloss on nineteenth-century language promotion at municipal and state levels.

Works Cited

Anderson, Benedict. *Imagined Communities: Reflections on the Origin and Spread of Nationalism*. London: Verso, 1991.

Baker, Philip. "Investigating the Origin and Diffusion of Shared Features among Atlantic English Creoles." *St. Kitts and the Atlantic Creoles*. Ed. Philip Baker and Adrienne Bruyn. London: U of Westminster P, 1998. 315–64.

Baron, Dennis. *Grammar and Good Taste: Reforming the American Language*. New Haven: Yale UP, 1982.

Benjamin, Walter. *Illuminations*. Ed. Hannah Arendt. Trans. Harry Zohn. New York: Schocken, 1969.

Crawford, James. "Anatomy of the English-Only Movement." *James Crawford's Language Policy Web Site and Emporium*, 2000. 10 Nov. 2007. <http://ourworld. compuserve.com/homepages/JWCRAWFORD/anatomy.htm>.

———. *Hold Your Tongue: Bilingualism and the Politics of "English Only."* Reading, MA: Addison-Wesley, 1992.

Dillard, J. L. *Black English: Its History and Usage in the United States*. New York: Random House, 1972.

Franklin, Benjamin. *The Papers of Benjamin Franklin*. Vol. 4. Ed. Leonard W. Labaree et al. New Haven: Yale UP, 1959.

Frantzen, Allen J. *Desire for Origins: New Language, Old English, and Teaching the Tradition.* New Brunswick, NJ: Rutgers UP, 1990.

Hancock, Ian. "The Domestic Hypothesis, Diffusion, and Componentiality: An Account of Atlantic Anglophone Creole Origins." *Substrata Versus Universals in Creole Genesis.* Ed. Pieter Muysken and Norval V. Smith. Amsterdam: John Benjamins, 1986. 71–102.

Heath, Shirley Brice. "English in Our Language Heritage." *Language in the USA.* Ed. Charles A. Ferguson and Shirley Brice Heath. New York: Cambridge UP, 1981. 6–20.

Horner, Bruce, and John Trimbur. "English Only and U.S. College Composition." *College Composition and Communication* 53 (2002): 594–630.

Kloss, Heinz. *American Bilingual Tradition.* McHenry, IL: CAL and Delta Systems, 1998.

Kramer, Michael P. *Imagining Language in America: From the Revolution to the Civil War.* Princeton: Princeton UP, 1992.

Linebaugh, Peter, and Marcus Rediker. *The Many-Headed Hydra: Sailors, Slaves, Commoners, and the Hidden History of the Revolutionary Atlantic.* Boston: Beacon, 2000.

McClintock, Anne. "The Angel of Progress: Pitfalls of the Term 'Postcolonialism.'" *Colonial Discourse and Post-Colonial Theory.* Ed. Patrick Williams and Laura Chrisman. New York: Columbia UP, 1994. 291–304.

McWhorter, John H. *The Missing Spanish Creoles: Recovering the Birth of Plantation Contact Languages.* Berkeley: U of California P, 2000.

Pratt, Mary Louise. "Building a New Public Idea about Language." *Profession* 2003: 110–19.

Rediker, Marcus. *Between the Devil and the Deep Blue Sea: Merchant Seamen, Pirates, and the Anglo-American Maritime World, 1700–1750.* New York: Cambridge UP, 1987.

Roach, Joseph. *Cities of the Dead: Circum-Atlantic Performance.* New York: Columbia UP, 1996.

Schiffman, Harold F. *Linguistic Culture and Language Policy.* London: Routledge, 1996.

Shell, Marc. "Babel in America." *American Babel: Literatures of the United States from Abnaki to Zuni.* Ed. Marc Shell. Cambridge, MA: Harvard UP, 2002. 3–33.

Shell, Marc, and Werner Sollors. *The Multilingual Anthology of American Literature: A Reader of Original Texts with English Translations.* New York: New York UP, 2000.

Smitherman, Geneva. "Toward a National Public Policy on Language." *College English* 49 (1987): 29–36.

Sollors, Werner. "For a Multilingual Turn in American Studies." *ASA Newsletter* 20.2 (1997): 13–15.

Webster, Noah. *Dissertations on the English Language.* Boston: Isaiah Thomas, 1789.

2. Living-English Work

Min-Zhan Lu

In "American English: Quest for a Model," Shirley Brice Heath reminds us that efforts to standardize English have been around since the beginning of our nationhood. John Adams, in a series of letters to the Continental Congress and in the midst of his mission to gain money for continuing the American Revolution, proposed that an institution be formed and charged with two responsibilities: to prescribe a language standard and to consider political and economic forces critical to the international spread of American English (Heath 220, 221). I see Adams's proposition as a classic example of "English Only" projections. It illustrates that English Only efforts involve geopolitical, economic, and cultural transactions. These efforts aim to control not merely which language can be used, where, and when but also and always how that language is to be used by its actual, possible, or imagined users. And they discipline users to be preoccupied with two and only two questions: What counts as correct usage in the eyes of those in positions to withhold educational and job opportunities? How might I best learn to work English strictly according to these rulings? Both questions render ambivalence toward standardized uses of English a barrier to personal and social development.

We get a glimpse of the global spread of U.S. English Only projections since Adams's time from two media reports on the popularity of tongue surgery (a snip of tissue, the frenulum, linking the tongue to the floor of the mouth using local anesthetic) in two "developing" countries: the People's Republic of China and South Korea—an archenemy and an ally, respectively, of the United States during the Korean and the Cold War. One report, titled "Accent Axed with a Snip," states that one mother's "hope" of turning her son into "a fluent English speaker" recently "drove [her] to take her six-year-old son for surgery aimed at ridding him of his Korean accent when speaking the language of choice in global business" (Kim). Another report, titled "Chinese Find Learning English a Snip," claims that "with China's growing internationalisation," people are "begging for" tongue surgery because "they're taking interpreters [*sic*] exams or wanting to go abroad or get a job [in China] with a foreign company" and because they want to be freed "from that tongue-tied feeling" when using English (Markus). When shown photographs attached to such reports (see figure 2.1), the first reaction of most readers, myself included, is, "Yuck! Gross!" While such images still invoke an involuntary shudder in me, I am increasingly convinced of my need to see the "popularity" of tongue surgery in "developing" countries as intricately informed by what we in "developed" countries do and do not do when addressing our own and our students' ambivalence toward English Only rulings.

The reports on tongue surgery also illustrate the domination of English Only assumptions in popular representations, what Braj B. Kachru has called fallacies of English users and uses ("Alchemy"). Although both news reports question the surgery's effectiveness in ensuring "clear" English, they imply a consensus among all users of English that only one way of using English

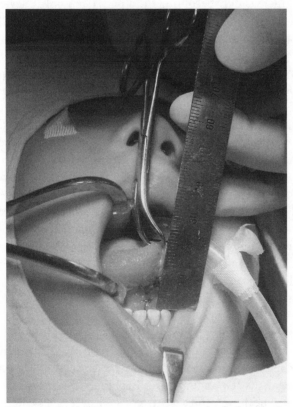

Fig. 2.1. A South Korean oral surgeon checks the length of a four-year-old patient's frenulum after tongue surgery, during which 1 to 1.5 centimeters are sliced off the frenulum to help give the tongue more flexibility for fluent English speaking (Seoul, 16 October 2003). Copyright © Ho/Reuters.

counts as accent-free and, thus, proper or good. Furthermore, the only motivation for learning English is to improve one's career prospects in the capitalist global market. The reports can also serve as reminders that we live in a world increasingly ordered by the interests of "developed" countries such as the United States to globalize their hyper-competitive, technology-driven market economies, what critics have termed "flexible, information economies" or "fast capitalism" (Castells; Harvey). People from all strata of the world are living under exponential pressure to use English and use it only with the kind of "demeanors"—accent, lexicon, grammar, rhythm, pitch, and so on—that appeal to the few with the cultural, political, and economic capital to dispense "job and educational opportunities" (Lu, "Essay"). By the same token, how to make learners feel tongue-loose in the "English of global business" is increasingly becoming the a priori and only relevant question for language education. For example, according to a CBS News report, the College Board's National Commission on Writing turns to the hiring and promotion personnel of corporations affiliated with the Business Roundtable to identify the English "skills" college students need to "acquire" ("Too Many"). The spokesperson of the College Board asserts that instructional "responsibility" for these sought-after skills lies in three sites: grade schools, universities, and training programs. Given the currency of such commissions in the current day United States, all of us in English studies need to wrestle with our charge to produce only bodies (with a particular length of frenulum) and affects (such as tongue-tied or tongue-loose feelings) that are useful for a "biopolitical structuring of the world" according to the "business" logic of "developed" countries (Hardt and Negri 32). We need to raise and pursue two related questions: What gross actions and inactions on our part might have directly and indirectly pressured users of English to see symbolic and surgical fixes as the only viable resolution to their own and their children's tongue-tied feelings? How might we best go about problematizing English Only rulings on the uses and users of English?

English as a *Yuyan*: Living-English Work

The Chinese character-combination for the term "language" is *yuyan*. Used alone or in combination with other characters, both *yu* and *yan* can mean "a language"; elements of a language (words, phrases, or expressions); the act of "speaking" or "meaning"; and a written or spoken text (a saying or proverb). So images of a living language, in actual use by actual users, are never absent in any reference to language as a system or *yufa* (the laws of language—its grammar). My lived difficulty in not seeing English as a *yuyan* has triggered an interest in representations of living-English. Let me invoke a few examples of such representations to delineate four lines of inquiry consistently blocked by the focal point of English Only projections.

My first example dates back to about fifty years after John Adams made his American English Only propositions to the Continental Congress. Francis Lieber, a political philosopher and the first editor of the *Encyclopædia Americana*, had this to say about English: "A *living language* does not only mean a language spoken by a *living people*, but also a living thing itself with all the capacities, rights, and necessities of life, that is, of *change*, expansion, and elimination" (quoted in Heath 231; emphasis mine). The second example comes from a 1975 essay by Chinua Achebe titled "The African Writer and the English Language." Achebe writes: "The price a world language must be prepared to pay is submission to many different kinds of use" (432). In the same essay, Achebe quotes James Baldwin as saying that "perhaps [English] was not my own because I had never attempted to use it, had only learned to imitate it. If this were so, then it might be made to bear the burden of my experience if I could find the stamina to challenge it, and me, to such a test" (433). My last example comes from Toni Morrison's 1993 Nobel Prize lecture. Morrison states, "The vitality of language lies in its ability to *limn* the actual, imagined and possible lives of its speakers, readers, writers" (20; emphasis mine). "We die. That may be the meaning of life. But we *do* language. That may be the measure of our lives" (22).

The ideal user of English posed in these examples is someone who is not only acutely aware of the pressure to function as an English Only user but also attentive to the capacities, rights, and necessities of change in all living things: people, their lives, society, culture, the world, and the language itself. These examples depict English as kept alive by many and having many different ways of using it, each of which is itself a living process in-the-forming: informing and informed by the specific different and dynamic historical and social contexts of individual acts. We can use such depictions of living-English to pose four lines of inquiry against the grain of English Only instructions.

Line one: English Only instruction parades the (seldom delivered) promise of ensuring access to wider communication and better educational and job opportunities. But living-English users carefully weigh dominant stories of what English Only instruction can do for them against what such training has historically done to them and to peoples, cultures, societies, and continents whose language practices do not match standardized English usages. For instance, Achebe depicts English as having become a "world language" and a "national language" in countries like Nigeria as part of a "package deal" that includes the "atrocity of racial arrogance and prejudice which may yet set the world on fire" (430). He thus reminds us to ask what specific historical atrocities have made English the "language of choice for global business" in China, South Korea, and the United States. Living-English users of English situate their relations to diverse languages and diverse uses of English in the context of a reading of history and of the world that treats intra- and international transactions on all levels (military, geopolitical, economic, cultural, technological, linguistic) and in all areas (school, home, paid work, civic, life worlds) as co-constitutive.

Line two: Living-English users also weigh the promise of better educational and job opportunities against what English Only instruction cannot do: it cannot address their needs to use English to articulate—work out meaningful connections across—experiences and circumstances of life consistently discredited by standardized English usages. If we approach "experience" in terms of socially constructed relations between individual selves, others, and the world, then the act of trying to "limn" or make a language "bear" or "carry" the burden of a particular lived experience would necessarily involve efforts to use language to interpret and represent such relations and their interrelations: not only to make sense of such relations while describing and legitimizing them but also to shape how one lives such relations in light of one's interpretation and representation (Lu and Horner). Achebe advises the African writer to "aim at fashioning out an English which is at once universal and able to carry his peculiar experience" (432). I take his emphasis on the "peculiar," and Baldwin's warning of the need to make the language his "own," to refer to those lived relations that are "particular," that is, socially and historically specific to the individual user and his or her people, culture, and region but rendered "odd" and thus "non-representative" and "irrelevant" by English Only projections. Living-English users keep deliberate track of the "peculiar" experiences they are having difficulty limning in a specific standardized usage. They thus comprehend English Only usages as resulting from voluntary or involuntary efforts to fix the contexts and purposes of using English, efforts not always in the interests of all its users and certainly not on all occasions. To Achebe, the "value of English as a medium of international exchange" or a "universal language"—that is, its communicative power— depends on its ability to "carry the peculiar experience" of its diverse users rather than on its ability to universalize the language practices of all its users according to the logic of global business (Achebe 432). When employing a standardized usage on a particular occasion, living-English users refuse to treat the tongue-tied or the tongue-loose feelings they and others experience as a sign of their failure or ability to access "communicative power." Instead, they approach such different experiences when using the same usage from the perspectives of the particular but different social, historical experiences each of us is interested in limning.

Line three: Living-English users are also always conducting research on how diverse users have grasped their "problems" with English-only instruction. Achebe, for instance, turns to Baldwin to map alternative ways of presenting the challenges facing living-English users. By posing the word "use" as an antonym to the word "imitate," Baldwin foregrounds individual users' rights to transform rather than mechanically reproduce standardized usages. The image of a user actively fashioning a different way of using English, making it do things it has not been historically geared to do, puts the formation of English in the hands of all its users. By identifying his "[having] only learned to imitate" as the source of his problem with English, Baldwin suggests further that whether people see a language as their own depends on whether they have "learned to imitate" or to "use" it. Baldwin thus marks all sites of learning as potentially "benign or coercive sponsors" of English-only dispositions (Brandt). Baldwin's use of the word "own" suggests that those of us committed to Students' Right to Their Own Language(s) would need to fight not only for the students' rights to use their "home" or "first" languages but, more important, for their right to own the "language of wider communication": to learn to use—actively fashion and transform—rather than merely imitate its standardized rules. That is, we need to fight for students' right to fashion an English that bears the burden of experiences de-legitimized by English Only usages. Moreover, we need to "challenge" ourselves to unlearn a "learned" disposition: our fear that attention to the need and rights to transform standardized usages will interfere with rather than enhance the ability of individuals to learn English.

Line four: Living-English users focus energy on how to tinker with the very standardized usages they are pressured by dominant notions of educational and job opportunities to "imitate." For instance, Achebe uses standardized pronouncements such as, "The price non-native English speakers (or non-standard English speakers) must be prepared to pay for better education and job opportunities is to learn the English of wider communication." Achebe opts for the familiar sentence pattern: "The price such-and-such must be prepared to pay is to do such-and-such." Yet, he names standardized English rather than its so-called non-native, non-standard users as the party paying the price: "The price a world language must be prepared to pay is submission to many different kinds of use" (432). By replacing the verb "to learn" with the word "submission," Achebe also reminds us that subjugation is the end objective of any instruction underwritten by the fantasy of a world using one language, English, and using English strictly according to a fixed set of usages. Furthermore, he highlights the agency of users worldwide by depicting them as submitting English to many, and many different, uses.

Achebe, Baldwin, and Morrison remind us in both the content and style of their writing that it is "neither necessary nor desirable" for users of English to "imitate" a standardized usage simply because it has been marketed as native, proper, accent-free, most sought-after, and thus correct (Achebe 432). Instead of seeking symbolic or physical surgical procedures to "free" one another from our tongue-tied feelings or to treat our tongue-loose feeling with standardized usages as a life insurance policy to be clung to and gloated over, we need to use them as critical resources—motivations—for pursuing the goals of "critical affirmation" (Lu, "Redefining" 173). We need to probe the ways our sense of ease with a particular usage might inadvertently sponsor systems and relations of injustice, even and especially when that usage seems to make normal and standard a particular experience that appears common, natural, and beneficial to us. We need to affirm our yearning for a better world for all by critically engaging with all words and deeds that present symbolic or physical tongue surgery as the only alternative for the subjects of domination. English can be a link language for users committed to social justice if, and only if, we combat English Only projects by pursuing living-English work.

Notes on Living-English Composition

The four lines of living-English inquiry are in keeping with work in U.S. composition that marks as assets—critical resources—two aspects of individual users' lives: (1) their actual, often complex, and sometimes conflicting relations with diverse languages and diverse ways of using English and (2) their interests in using English to articulate aspirations for life that are consistently de-legitimized by the logic of global business but critical to the well-being of peoples bearing the cost of existing structures and relations of injustice. To further explore how U.S. composition might actively pursue the four lines of living-English, I turn to some of my notes to delineate two potential points of departure.

One cluster of my notes centers on scholarship across the disciplines that takes a relational and historical approach to the world we share with other users of English, such as *The Other Tongue: English across Cultures* (Kachru), *The Cultures of Globalization* (Jameson and Miyoshi), and *Beyond Dichotomies: Histories, Identities, Cultures, and the Challenge of Globalization* (Mudimbe-Boyi). I am particularly interested in scholarship that approaches the transrelations of nations, cultures, peoples, and language(s) in terms of transactions that transform, transfuse, translate, transport, transverse, transubstantiate, transvalue, transpose, and transplant established ways of doing things and in terms of multidirectional transactions—not merely top-down but also bottom-up and sideways. What follows are two sets of questions I see this body of scholarship posing for my work in U.S. composition.

How can I stay vigilant toward my professional training and thus often inadvertent sponsorship of the various English Only fallacies? As Kachru cogently illustrates, the "fallacy" that "English is essentially learned to interact with native speakers of the language" crumples as soon as we learn to study (instead of ignore) the diverse ways English is used outside the so-called native-speaking countries, in regions where English is used as a "second language" (for example, India, Kenya, Zambia) or a "foreign language" (for example, China, Korea, the former Soviet Union, Saudi Arabia, Zimbabwe) (Kachru 357–58). For instance, English is being used in multilingual countries such as South Africa as a "link language" for collective struggle against long and complex histories of intra- and international injustices along lines of race, ethnicity, gender, class, and so on (see Trimbur; Desharzer). The Cojti Cuxil in Guatemala are interested in learning English because they see it as a potential force for counteracting the residual hegemony of Spanish Only instruction on the national scene (Mignolo and Schiwy 266). Speakers of Tlingit on Prince of Wales Island in the Gulf of Alaska are fighting the threat of the extinction of Tlingit by translating into that language anything they can get their hands on, including Christmas carols like "Jingle Bells" and nursery rhymes such as "Hickory Dickory Dock" (Cronin 142). Subaltern groups across the world are using English and transnational information networks to initiate what critics have termed "globalization from below"—building national and international alliances, including the "internationalization of indigenous organizations" in Latin America, to affect national language and education policies, human rights struggles, and the fight for women's rights, workers' rights, and environmental well-being (Mignolo 43–44). How might U.S. composition tap into the knowledge and theory emerging from such a wealth of living-English work by users of English as a "second" and "foreign" *yuyan* so that accounts of the planetary scope of the hegemony of English are complicated by accounts of the ways in which English has been continually and consistently broken and invaded and thus kept alive by users using it in and in the interest of "developing," "under-developed," or "undeveloped" areas of the United States, the Americas, and the world (Mignolo; Mudimbe-Boyi; Pratt; Harvey; Trouillot; Dirlik)?

How might I put my work in the context of escalating U.S. political and economic interests in harnessing information technology to maintain its global hegemony (Harvey)? What is the viability of approaching our word-work in

English or across languages not only in terms of fixed territorial spaces (the United States, China, Zimbabwe) but also in terms of the technologically constructed "time zones"—relations defined "chronologically" by access to the kind of telecommunication and information networks providing the infrastructure underwritten by and underwriting post-Fordist economic logic (Cronin 82–83, 112)? How might I best attend to issues of class, gender, place, and history as well as race and ethnicity when approaching the agency of peripheralized users and avoid the danger of "unmooring" concepts such as "hybridity," "in-between-ness," and "global flow" from the actual, specific, physical-social-historical contexts of particular language use—the different realities facing the small number of winners and the majority of losers in the global restructuring of capitalism (Dirlik 102, 104–7; Hardt and Negri 150)? How might U.S. composition articulate a global perspective that attends to rather than blurs the actual, specific, physical-social-historical contexts of individual students' life and work?

In the second cluster of my notes, I read texts to glean materials conducive to living-English inquiry when teaching courses labeled business and technical writing, basic writing, ESL, EFL, or first-year composition and under rubrics such as cultural, genre, and literacy studies or rhetorical or discourse analysis. I am interested in materials that call into question our English-only fixation on "fluency" in the "skills" sought after by the hiring and promotion practices of members of the Business Roundtable. For instance, in a section in Achebe's essay "African Writers and English," Achebe starts with a passage from his novel *Arrow of God* where the chief priest is telling one of his sons why it is necessary for the chief to send the son to church:

> I want one of my sons to join these people and be my eyes there. If there is nothing in it you will come back. But if there is something there you will bring home my share. The world is like a Mask, dancing. If you want to see it well you do not stand in one place. My spirit tells me that those who do not befriend the white man today will be saying had we known tomorrow. (Achebe 432)

He then poses a standardized version of the passage from *Arrow of God* to make a case that it is neither necessary nor desirable for all users of English to mechanically abide by English Only rulings:

> I am sending you as my representative among these people—just to be on the safe side in case the new religion develops. One has to move with the times or else one is left behind. I have a hunch that those who fail to come to terms with the white man may well regret their lack of foresight. (Achebe 432–33)

Using the two passages, we might engage students in identifying the words, expressions, and sentence structures in the standardized version that fall within our sense of colloquial English and those in the passage from *Arrow of God* that appear "thick"—not immediately "intelligible" and "dense" or even "dumb" to our native-trained ears. Then we might re-read *Arrow of God* to consider the ways in which the original, less idiomatic sounding version carries the burden of the specific circumstances, experiences, thoughts, feelings, actions, and relations the novel is trying to limn, plus the ways in which these conditions and relations are being dismissed or trivialized in the second version. We might use the passages to consider the value of reading methods that pay "thicker"—closer and more "intimate"—attention to the historical, social, geopolitical, economic, cultural, linguistic reasons for a particular user of English (in this case, a self-identified African writer, Chinua Achebe) to act (to produce a text, oral or written) in a particular way on a specific occasion (Appiah; Spivak). We might use the two versions to call into question our learned distaste for non-idiomatic English lexicons and grammar—our learned inclination to view them as either exotic or downright stupid, nonsensical, incorrect. And we might use such passages to consider the ways in which various usages in the English Only, standardized version might also directly and indirectly undercut conditions and relations critical to the day-to-day well-being of individual students.

War Talk is a collection of articles and print versions of speeches by Arundhati Roy, some initially published in India and others in the United States. We can use the collection to engage students in exploring ways of reading that treat glossaries or annotations as integral rather than as appendages to be glossed over. Take, for example, two sentences from the book. The first sentence comes from "Democracy: Who Is She When She Is at Home," which the footnote tells us was "first published in the May 6, 2002, issue of *Outlook* magazine (India)":

> Once the Muslims have been "shown their place," will milk and coca-cola flow across the land? . . . Or will there be someone else to hate [next year]? Alphabetically: Adivasis, Buddhists, Christians, Dalits, Parsis, Sikhs? Those who wear jeans or speak English or those who have thick lips or curly hair? (22–23)

In "Ahimsa," which the footnote indicates is "based on the version published in the *Christian Science Monitor* on July 5, 2002," but "first published in the *Hindustan Times* (India), June 12, 2002," we encounter this sentence: "It [the government] says quite openly if it were to give in to the demands of the Maan 'oustees' (that is, if it implemented its own policy), it would set a precedent for the hundreds of thousands of people, most of them *Dalits* (un-

touchables) and *Adivasis . . .*" (Roy 11; emphasis mine). The glossary to the book provides a "thick" translation for the term "Dalit": "Those who are oppressed or literally 'ground down.' The preferred term for those people who used to be called 'untouchables' in India" (113). The *Webster's New World Dictionary* (third college edition) defines "untouchables" as: "In India, any member of the lowest castes, whose touch was regarded as defiling to higher-caste Hindus; discrimination against these people (now called Scheduled Castes) was officially abolished in 1955." Using the passages from the two essays, the entry from the "college edition" of the "new world" dictionary, the glossary to *War Talk*, and the footnotes to the essays, we might ask students to consider the loss of meaning if we ignore the glossary when making sense of the sentences. For instance, in what ways does the Dalits' preference for a term of self-naming that bears the literal meaning of "ground down" (over the standardized label "untouchable") and Roy's use of that term in her writing make English better bear the burden of the Dalits' lived experiences both before and after the 1955 "official" abolishment of discrimination against the "untouchables"? Using the footnotes on the publishing history of a piece such as "Ahimsa," we might also consider how and why a standardized English translation-reduction would be attached to the term "Dalits" when the article appeared in a publication such as the *Christian Science Monitor*. And we can ask what we can do as readers of popular magazines to intervene with such standardized practices.

In *Translation and Globalization*, Michael Cronin tells of the efforts of translators in recent decades to use e-mail, bulletin boards, newsgroups, and mailing lists to get instant help globally when encountering problems in translating something (45). For instance, in her description of the Russian translation of Bill Gates's *Business @ the Speed of Thought*, Natalie Shahova talks about a query she and her colleagues posted on Lantra (an international forum for translators and interpreters) concerning the "contemporary meaning" of the term "knowledge worker" (quoted in Cronin 45). Instead of a definitive answer, they found that "even natives have different opinions." Using such stories as points of departure, we might ask students to compose a series of replies to the query, including one that offers a definition of "knowledge worker" from the perspective of Microsoft headquarters, another defining "knowledge worker" from the perspective of a life world critical to their sense of self and life but peripheralized by dominant notions of "educational" or "career" prospects, and a third that tinkers with the Microsoft headquarters' definition of the term from the peripheralized perspective.

This type of assignment is in keeping with the goal of a whole range of classrooms housed in English studies: requiring students to perform close analyses of the content and style of a written text—for instance, Bill Gates's book; conducting research by gathering policy statements, commercials, and the like from Microsoft and related Web sites while performing discourse analyses to get a sense of dominant goals and values of global business; and composing auto-ethnographic accounts of the language practices of users of English in life worlds critical to one's sense of self and life but peripheralized by English Only rulings. This assignment can also initiate "thick" descriptions of the peculiar circumstances and relations endorsed by the kind of vocabulary and lexicon standardized by U.S. corporations such as Microsoft and generate deliberations over the need and right of diverse users within and outside the United States to "use" rather than "imitate" such hegemonic usages.

Both clusters of my notes, as in my other work, speak to the peculiar circumstances of my life and thus are best used to call attention to rather than to obscure the actual but different circumstances facing each of us in spite of the general encroachment of the fast-capitalist logic of "space-time compression," "time-to-market," and the "trinity of quality, price, deadline" on the visions and operations of all U.S. colleges and universities (Cronin; Readings). To animate exchange of the different turns those of us interested in living-English uses and users of English must continue to improvise in our day-to-day lives, let me close by pointing to one aspect of my own work I am having the most difficulty with and therefore am most concerned to interrogate. Composition courses are traditionally housed in English departments and are often taught by people with training in areas of study titled "literature," "linguistics," "comparative literature," and the like. However, there has been a long-standing tradition in these departments and areas of study to treat "thick" inquiry into the politics of reading-writing-translation as bearing primarily or solely on the study of "literary" texts while assigning "non-literary" work—so-called scientific, technical, commercial, legal, and administrative writing—to "the realm of no-nonsense, commonsensical instrumentalism" (Cronin 1–2). For instance, most of the works informing my own reading of the politics of language use, including a majority of the texts I discuss in this chapter, focus on the reception and production of "literary" texts across historical and national borders. In fact, my own difficulty in coming up with examples of living-English work other than the writing of established figures in "literary" studies—Achebe, Baldwin, Morrison, Roy—speaks to my own inscription in that tradition. (For "non-literary" examples by unpublished writers, see my "Professing Multiculturalism" and "Essay.")

However, so long as U.S. composition continues to identify as its central objective writing in or across the disciplines or professions, teachers and researchers like myself must continue to challenge ourselves to construct a global perspective on the politics of "non-literary" uses of English. In their aspiration to join the professions or gain access to career prospects, students across the disciplines along with professionals (research scientists, engineers, systems analysts, investment bankers, authors, editors, and so on) are increasingly pressured to perceive and market their competence in terms of their ability to process and manipulate information—deliver products and services in the form of data, words, and images and to do so in the English most sought-after by the hiring and promotion practices of corporations surveyed by the College Board's National Commission on Writing. A global perspective on the work of U.S. composition in a world driven by the logic of fast capitalism must address the politics of language practices in scientific, technical, commercial, legal, and administrative writing. I call attention to my own difficulty in moving in that direction to mark it as an imperative for all of us interested in using English to build a more just world for all.

Coda

While working on this chapter, I read a front-page report in the *New York Times* titled "For Mongolians, E Is for English, F Is for Future" (Brooke). The report covers a national drive in Mongolia to make English its official foreign language (and eventually, its official second language). It begins by citing Mongolia's prime minister as stating, in an "American English honed in graduate school at Harvard," "We see English . . . as a way of opening windows on the wider world." The report then cites Mongolia's foreign minister ("speaking American English, also honed at Harvard") as saying, "If there is a shortcut to development, it is English." The report ends by citing Mongolia's minister of education, culture, and science, "a graduate of a Soviet University" who "laboriously explained in English," "If we can combine our academic knowledge with the English language, we can do outsourcing here, just like Bangalore" (A9). The report also claims that what's taking place in Mongolia is "a reflection of the steady march of English as a world language," a phenomenon "fueled by the growing dominance of American culture and the financial realities of globalization." Other evidence of English "taking hold" across the world includes the establishment of six private "English villages" in South Korea where "paying students can have their passports stamped for intensive weeks of English-language immersion, taught by native speakers from all over the English-speaking world." In addition, "in Iraq, where Arabic and Kurdish are to be the official languages, a movement is growing to add English, a neutral link for a nation split along ethnic lines" (A1).

Given the continued currency of "native-speakers" from the "English-speaking world" in the English language industry, how U.S. composition represents English and its uses and users will have intense and lingering effects on the future of the world. If we continue to sponsor English Only assumptions in our day-to-day practice, chances are that English will be used as a supposedly "neutral" tool for perpetuating the logic of a "free market economy" rather than as a link language for Arabic and Kurdish speakers to exchange among themselves and peoples of the world their experiences combating ethnic divisions on the local, regional, and global levels. If we continue to sponsor English Only assumptions in our day-to-day practice, chances are that the paying students in South Korea seeking "immersion" in "English villages," once they get their "passports stamped" by the "native speaking" villagers, will continue to see physical and symbolic tongue surgery as the only viable resolution to their trouble with the usages standardized by the English of global business. All of us interested in the future of a world sustainable for not only the few of us benefiting from the logic of fast capitalism but also the majority grossly impoverished by it need to get involved in living-English work.

Works Cited

Achebe, Chinua. "The African Writer and the English Language." Burke, Crowley, and Girvin 427–33.

Appiah, Kwame Anthony. "Thick Translation." Venuti 417–29.

Brandt, Deborah. *Literacy in American Lives*. Cambridge: Cambridge UP, 2001.

Brooke, James. "For Mongolians, E Is for English, F Is for Future." *New York Times* 15 Feb. 2005, national ed.: A1, A9.

Burke, Lucy, Tony Crowley, and Alan Girvin, eds. *The Routledge Language and Cultural Theory Reader*. New York: Routledge, 2000.

Castells, Manuel. *The Information Age: Economy, Society and Culture, II: Rise of the Network Society*. 2nd ed. Oxford: Blackwell, 2000.

Cronin, Michael. *Translation and Globalization*. London: Routledge, 2003.

Desharzer, Mary K. "Postapartheid Literacies: South African Women's Poetry of Orality, Franchise, and Reconciliation." *Women and Literacy*. Ed. Beth Daniell and Peter Mortensen. Urbana, IL: NCTE, 2007.

Dirlik, Arif. "Bringing History Back In: Of Diasporas, Hybridities, Places, and Histories." Mudimbe-Boyi 93–128.

Hardt, Michael, and Antonio Negri. *Empire*. Cambridge, MA: Harvard UP, 2000.

Harvey, David. *The New Imperialism*. Oxford: Oxford UP, 2003.

Heath, Shirley Brice. "American English: Quest for a Model." Kachru, *Other Tongue* 220–32.

Jameson, Fredric, and Masao Miyoshi, eds. *The Cultures of Globalization*. Durham, NC: Duke UP, 1998.

Kachru, Braj B. "The Alchemy of English." Burke, Crowley, and Girvin 307–29.

———, ed. *The Other Tongue: English Across Cultures*. 2nd ed. Urbana: U of Illinois P, 1992.

Kim, Kyoung-wha. "Accent Axed with a Snip." *Aljazeera.net* 19 Oct. 2003. 17 Nov. 2003 <http://english.aljazeera.net/NR/exeres/4794AA93-CDAE-4E8C-BAEB-977E2DA59BOE>.

Lu, Min-Zhan. "An Essay on the Work of Composition." *College Composition and Communication* 56 (2004): 16–50.

———. "Professing Multiculturalism: The Politics of Style in the Contact Zone." *College Composition and Communication* 45 (1994): 442–58.

———. "Redefining the Literate Self: The Politics of Critical Affirmation." *College Composition and Communication* 51 (1999): 172–94.

Lu, Min-Zhan, and Bruce Horner. "The Problematic of Experience: Redefining Critical Work in Ethnography and Pedagogy." *College English* 60 (1998): 257–77.

Markus, Francis. "Chinese Find Learning English a Snip." *BBC News World Edition* 31 July 2002. 17 Nov. 2003 <http://news.bbc.co.uk/2/hi/world/asia-pacific/2161780.stm>.

Mignolo, Walter. "Globalization, Civilization Processes, and the Relocation of Languages and Cultures." Jameson and Miyoshi 32–53.

Mignolo, Walter, and Freya Schiwy. "Beyond Dichotomies: Translation/Transculturation." Mudimbe-Boyi 251–86.

Morrison, Toni. *Lecture and Speech of Acceptance, upon the Award of the Nobel Prize for Literature, Delivered in Stockholm on the Seventh of December, Nineteen Hundred and Ninety-Three.* New York: Knopf, 1994.

Mudimbe-Boyi, Elisabeth, ed. *Beyond Dichotomies: Histories, Identities, Cultures, and the Challenge of Globalization.* Albany: State U of New York P, 2002.

Pratt, Mary Louise. "Modernity and Periphery: Toward a Global and Relational Analysis." Mudimbe-Boyi 21–48.

Readings, Bill. *The University in Ruins.* Cambridge, MA: Harvard UP, 1996.

Roy, Arundhati. *War Talk.* Boston: South End, 2003.

Spivak, Gayatri Chakravorty. "The Politics of Translation." Venuti 397–416.

"Too Many Workers Are Bad Writers." *CBSNEWS.com* 14 Sept. 2004. 21 June 2009 <http://www.cbsnews.com/stories/2004/09/14/national/main643250.shtml?tag=contentMain;contentBody>.

Trimbur, John. "Language Policy and Normalization in South Africa: Some Other Lessons." *JAC* 22 (2002): 646–57.

Trouillot, Michel-Rolph. "The Perspective of the World: Globalization Then and Now." Mudimbe-Boyi 3–20.

Venuti, Lawrence, ed. *The Translation Studies Reader.* London: Routledge, 2000.

3. Globalization, *Guanxi*, and Agency: Designing and Redesigning the Literacies of Cyberspace

Gail E. Hawisher and Cynthia L. Selfe
with Yi-Huey Guo and Lu Liu

"*Guanxi*" (kuan-hsi) literally means "relation" or "relationship," as a noun, and "relate to" as a verb, though as commonly used in contemporary Chinese societies, it refers more narrowly to "particularistic ties." . . . These ties are based on ascribed or primordial traits such as kinship, native place, and ethnicity, and also on achieved characteristics such as attending the same school (even if not at the same time), serving together in the same military unit, having shared experiences, such as the Long March, and doing business together. . . . While the bases for *guanxi* may be naturally occurring or created, the important point is that *guanxi* must be consciously produced, cultivated, and maintained over time.
　　　　　—Thomas Gold, Doug Guthrie, and David Wank,
　　　　　　"An Introduction to the Study of *Guanxi*"

During the past twenty-five years, we have come to recognize with others (for example, Norris; Castells) that computer networks increasingly serve as sites within which people from around the world design and redesign their lives through literate practices. In both global and local contexts, the relationships among digital technologies, language, literacy, and an array of opportunities are complexly structured and articulated within a constellation of existing social, cultural, economic, historical, and ideological factors that constitute a cultural ecology of literacy. These ecological systems continually shape and are shaped by people (Giddens)—at a variety of levels and in a range of ways—as they live out their daily lives in technological and cultural settings (Selfe and Hawisher). In this chapter, we attempt to explore these interdependent relationships between learning English(es) and learning digital literacies in such contexts by focusing on the crucial role that both traditional and changing practices of *guanxi* have played in advancing the digital literacies of two women: Lu Liu and Yi-Huey Guo.

The literal meaning of *guanxi* refers to "social relationships or social connections" (Yang, "Gift Economy" 35). The art of *guanxi*, which stresses the "importance of the length and quality of personal relationships" (48), involves the tactical deployment of "minute [social] mechanisms" that serve the symbolic and pragmatic function of "breaking down . . . boundaries between people" (41) and can involve the exchange of "symbolic capital" as well as the exchange of gifts, positions, and political capital (46). For many scholars, *guanxi* describes a set of practices based on kinship relations, family ties, connections, and experiences (for example, the Long March of the Cultural Revolution) that have developed during the long history of China. In this chapter, we focus on the dynamic nature of *guanxi* practices and *guanxi* networks, *guanxiwang* (Yang, *Gifts, Favors* 3), especially as these are shaping—and being shaped by—people's literate practices in and around globalized digital environments.

In our exploration of the term *guanxi*, we recognize the connection between *guanxi* and Pierre Bourdieu's notion of social and cultural capital, that is, as something akin to a complex set of social networks operating through personal connections. The connections forged through *guanxi*, we believe, operate at many levels within global and local environments—at the macro-, medial, and micro-levels of culture and development—and their effects may be amplified within and complicated by and through the use of literate exchanges within the globalized web of computer networks (Castells, *Rise*; *Power*; *End*). The connections established through *guanxi*, and the changing practices of *guanxi* in digital environments, may allow some individuals to begin the work of addressing "barriers to knowledge and participation" and to increase their "access to information and communication" both within and across cultures (*Human Development* 32).

We begin with the literacy narratives of our two coauthors: Lu Liu, a recent graduate student at Purdue University from the People's Republic of China, and Yi-Huey Guo, a recent graduate student at the University of Illinois at Urbana-Champaign from Taiwan. We interviewed both in 2003, when they were thirty-one years old, and both continue to correspond with us on-line, whether here or abroad.[1] Our goal—which is part of a larger project in which we have been engaged for several years—is to tell the stories of these two women who have acquired English and digital literacies over the course of their thirty-some years and who have used these literacies to communicate within and between cultures as they advance their educations. As we worked with Lu and Yi-Huey, we came to realize the intimate relationship between their learning of English and their acquisition of digital literacies. English enabled them initially to work with the U.S. computer interfaces while, at the same time, their growing digital proficiency gave them more opportunities for learning English. Especially in their first years of learning software programs, English was implicated in all aspects of the pains they took with computing. In undertaking these efforts, both women have in addition depended on localized and globalized forms, and traditional and changing practices, of *guanxi*—the Chinese concept originally introduced to us by Lu. Their stories, we believe, provide a valuable snapshot for literacy and language educators in the twenty-first century.

Lu Liu

On 23 March 1972, in Chengdu, the capital city of Sichuan province, Lu Liu was born into the modern People's Republic of China (PRC). Two years after Lu's birth, Zhou Enlai outlined his program of modernization that eventually led to China's entry into the world of cyberspace. The hope at the time was that computerization could help "transform a primarily agrarian society into a global economic power for the 21st century."[2] In beginning its move into cyberspace, however, China first had to modernize its infrastructure and educate its populace while addressing, among other challenges, widespread poverty and political repression, both legacies of Maoist communism. Lu's family, for instance, while part of the dominant Han ethnic group, was far from wealthy, as she explains:

> The "house" I lived in was actually part of a mansion situated in a big yard. The mansion belonged to a big landlord in Chengdu, capital of Sichuan province before P.R. China was founded. The two rooms my family lived in were part of the kitchen of that big house. Actually we had only one room but my father extended the roof himself and added another small room (altogether the two rooms took up about twenty square meters). Our "house" was two steps away from the public toilet. It looked very simple and shabby, but my father did create a very small garden for me in front of the house.

Like many Chinese families, Lu's family valued literacy and provided Lu with Chinese picture books along with children's versions of fiction and poetry that she memorized even before she attended school. In her early literacy efforts, Lu was encouraged in a range of ways, often by members of her immediate family who served as role models. Lu's father, who left college in his sophomore year to support his family as a skilled electrician, bought her and her brother *lianhuanhua*, illustrated storybooks that were "simplified versions" of "Chinese classical novels." In addition, he subscribed to magazines that were "relevant" to her studies when Lu was in primary school and high school.

Using somewhat different strategies, Lu's mother, who held a high school diploma and was a skilled factory worker, also supported her daughter's early literacy practices:

> My mother encouraged us to read and write. She herself likes to keep to-do lists. She used to use chalk to write down to-do lists on the concrete floor of our house. She says writing helps her to remember things. Both of my parents valued education. They told me that I was born in a poor family and education is the only way for me to help myself to get a better life. I cannot remember what kind of writing/reading except my mother's to-do lists that my parents did when I was little. They were always busy with housework at home.

Lu's grandparents also served as literacy role models. Although her grandfather, her mother's father, never spoke of his work as a secretary to the Chinese Nationalist Party, the Goumindan, after the PRC was formed in 1949, his life and household were informed by traditional intellectual values. As Lu remembers:

> He taught me to recite Chinese poems and rhymed short stories when I was about three years old. He read from books while I listened and learned the lines by heart. After I went to school, I still went to live with my grandpa and grandma during the school breaks. Every day my grandpa would ask me: "Did you read and write what you are supposed to?" He was always there reminding me that reading and writing are very important things I need to do on a daily basis.

Her grandmother, too, played an active role in Lu's early literacy development. She was, as Lu remembers it, keenly appreciative of the English language and sensed the importance this language would assume both in the world and in Lu's life. She also introduced Lu to her first encounter with *guanxi*:

> I learned my first English word when I was very young, about three years old. My grandma was going to send me to a kindergarten. Because I was not a registered resident in the district where the kindergarten was, my grandma had to ask the lady in charge to bend the rules. I was an adorable kid, so my grandma thought I had a chance. To impress the lady more, my mom taught me to say "How are you?" and "Good morning." So when my grandma brought me to that lady, saying the English phrases was part of my "talent show." I was admitted.

Given her home training and her ability to depend on familial *guanxi* networks, Lu's success in school was, at least in part, predictable—first at Chengdu Kuixinglou ("tower of the talented") Primary School and later at

Chengdu Shude ("morality cultivation") Middle School. Lu's secondary education was profoundly influenced by the dramatic political reforms taking place
in China. In 1981, the same year that the IBM personal computer appeared on
the market, Deng Xiaopeng introduced large-scale programs to modernize
the country. Rapidly, these efforts began to pay dividends. By 1987, the PRC
had applied to join Bitnet, a network developed by U.S. universities, and Qian
Tianbai, a professor in Beijing, had sent out the first e-mail in China through
the Chinese Academic Network (*China Internet*).

When she entered the foreign language university at the age of seventeen,
Lu felt as though she was not only fulfilling her mother's dream but also following through with her own "love affair with English." It was at this time
too that Lu had her first experiences with digital literacy:

> My first encounter with computers dates back to my freshman year in
> college. It was 1989 when I took my first computer class and learned
> BASIC (a computer language, if I remember correctly). I believe I sat
> in front of a personal computer and learned to type words of a simple
> language so that the computer can show me all the files, I can set up a
> folder, or I can delete and copy documents to floppy disks. It was that
> simple. . . . We would talk about how to use that language in class and
> then have access to computers for forty-five minutes every two weeks.
> The computers were located in a special room where we all had to wear
> slippers. . . . Computers at that time were not a big deal for my parents
> and other relatives. I actually told them little about my computer literacy
> because the computer class was a bit boring to me.

Lu recalls being taught classes in Chinese although she needed English to
read the computer programs and viewed her growing proficiency in English
as contributing substantively to her gradual accumulation of digital literacies.
Interestingly, in this first experience with computers, she needed English in
order to learn yet another language, BASIC, which she used to program the
computer. By 1999, after she completed a master's degree in American studies at Beijing Foreign Studies University, Lu enrolled in the London School
of Economics and Political Science at the University of London. There, she
used a borrowed computer until she purchased a secondhand 486 UNISYS
laptop for £150.

As is the case for increasing numbers of young Chinese, Lu's English literacy practices and values continued to be connected to, and supported by,
her uses of technology. This linkage—overdetermined and formulated around
interactions at school, in the workplace, and in social networks—indicates
just how inextricably literacy practices became tied to digital technologies

in the closing years of the twentieth century and the opening years of the twenty-first: hence our use of the term "digital literacy" here and in other work we have done (Selfe and Hawisher).[3] Other scholars have helped describe the robust nature of this linkage. Mark Warschauer, for instance, notes that networked digital environments like the Internet have helped hasten the globalization of English literacy practices when individuals in China and elsewhere use digital networks "on a daily basis" for reading and writing as they engage in "finding information and communicating with peers and colleagues" (par. 8). Sei Hwa Jung focuses on this important linkage between English literacy practices and Information Communication Technologies (ICTs), noting that "English and ICT . . . , especially to non-native speakers of English, have become the essential literacy skills of our time" (16). Perhaps the most pointed description of this fundamental connection between literacy and digital environments, however, comes from a nineteen-year-old Chinese woman, Lin Yan, who was reported as explaining to President Bill Clinton on a visit to China in 1998, "If you don't know English, you can't use computers. And if you can't use computers these days, you can't get ahead" (quoted in McCarthy 33).

The combination of her English literacy practices and her imaginative and tactical deployment of computer networks allowed Lu to develop and expand her professional and social networks, her *guanxiwang*, on a global scale. As she pursued her graduate studies and continued to form relationships through face-to-face interactions at the London School of Economics, Lu also exploited the increasing accessibility of global computer networks in a tactical way to initiate e-mail exchanges with other scholars within the profession, thus extending her *guanxi* networks beyond national and cultural borders. For example, Lu e-mailed a speech communication scholar in the United States and told him about her research on U.S. images in Chinese best-sellers from the 1980s and 1990s. Although he was retired, he invited Lu to send him her work for a possible book he was doing on rhetoric and communication. Also via e-mail, he invited Lu to join a panel on Chinese communication studies at the National Communication Association Conference in Chicago. With his help, she presented her first conference paper in 1999 and, later in 2000, published her first book chapter. In this way, Lu's own increasing skill in writing, reading, and speaking English was amplified by the globalized communication environment of the Internet, making it possible for her to expand her *guanxi* networks in ways she could not have done under other circumstances.

As Andrew B. Kipnis observes, it is true that "because practices of *guanxi* production involve more than one person, they necessitate communication"

(24). We are making a slightly different statement here, however, claiming that, in a globalized world increasingly dependent on on-line communication, the ability to undertake literate exchanges within computer networks serves to amplify and magnify the power of communication in establishing, sustaining, and extending *guanxi*. These cross-cultural *guanxi* represent, we believe, a potent form of accumulating and deploying social capital in an increasingly globalized world. That is not to say that people do not extend their *guanxi* networks using other technologies and networks, such as writing and posting letters, albeit with different results. It is only to stress the amplified role that the globalized communication environment of the Internet can serve in expanding *guanxiwang*.

By 2001, Lu had moved to Purdue and had purchased a desktop computer. At Purdue, enrolled in a PhD program first in communication and then in rhetoric and composition, Lu found technology to be plentiful. When we interviewed her in 2003, Lu was reading and writing e-mail and making e-cards for family, friends, colleagues, and professors; conducting much of her academic research on the Web; contributing to electronic mailing lists connected with her profession; designing PowerPoint and conference presentations for the Purdue Writing Lab; designing Web sites; downloading free antivirus software from the Web; participating in chat rooms; and taking and manipulating digital photographs. As she noted, despite her reservations about some young people who developed a "morbid" obsession with on-line life,

> I think computers are now playing a very important role in our daily life. E-mail accounts and surfing the net for all kinds of information have become an indispensable part of many people's daily activities. The Internet has . . . helped people to transcend space and keep in touch. Virtual communities on the Web have grown dramatically. I know of several virtual communities for overseas Chinese.

Today, Lu reads and writes on-line in Chinese and is able to use a Chinese interface to connect with people and to access Chinese Web sites. She also finds, however, that her Chinese can prove inadequate for the technological terms she wants to convey:

> Learning computers confirmed my interest in learning English because English seemed to enable me to have access to the latest computer technologies. My learning of English enabled me to continue to use the computer via an interface in English. Sometimes when I talk to my brother about some computer technology issues, I do not even know the terms in Chinese.

In some respects, then, English has contended with Chinese as Lu's academic language and has become—at the moment—her language of preference insofar as digital literacies are concerned. At the same time, however, her growing proficiency with English has distanced her from her brother: Lu can speak about computer technology in English but not in her family language. She has, nevertheless, invested a great many years in learning how to make both English and computers work for her professionally as she moves culturally, linguistically, and geographically through diverse academic settings. Today, computers and English are essential to Lu's daily literate activities in the profession.

In this respect, Lu is like many young urban Chinese who increasingly find their specialized professional lives unsuited to a sole reliance on familial *guanxi* because the "areas of specialization" they have pursued "do not overlap" (Hanser 153) with their families' networks. Instead, growing numbers of young professionals, like Lu, are developing *guanxi* that extend beyond family contexts, often using computer networks to support the formulation of relationships across cultures and conventional geopolitical borders, making a "global practice" of *guanxi* (Jirik 20). In such contexts, young professionals like Lu are inventing their own identities through their interactions with others on-line, thus making of themselves, as Sherry Turkle observes, "multiple, distributed" identities (par. 1).

Yi-Huey Guo

Yi-Huey Guo, a Taiwanese citizen who completed a doctoral program at the University of Illinois at Urbana-Champaign and who is author of our second literacy narrative, was born on 23 November 1972, the same year as Lu. In talking about the education and languages of her grandparents, parents, and own generation, she encapsulates Taiwan's eventful and difficult history. Depending upon the political rule of the time, different languages—and different people—have predominated in her country, which has been known throughout the years as Nationalist China, the Republic of China, Taiwan, and Formosa, the name of the island given by the Portuguese as far back as the 1500s. Here is how she contextualizes her country's language history in terms of her own family:

> My grandparents only attended elementary school. Due to the history of Taiwan, my grandparents learned some Japanese in school (since Taiwan was the colony of Japan at that time). During their whole life, they couldn't speak any Mandarin Chinese. They only spoke Taiwanese.
>
> Before World War II, Taiwan was the colony of Japan. People spoke Japanese and Taiwanese. After World War II, many non-communist

Chinese came to Taiwan. . . . They also became the ruling class of Taiwan; they forbid us to speak Taiwanese. We then started to learn Mandarin Chinese from then on.

Therefore, there was some transitional change of our language use. In my grandparents' generation, they could only speak Taiwanese (or if they attended school, they could speak Japanese). My parents' generation used both Taiwanese and Mandarin Chinese. But many people of this generation are not good at speaking Mandarin Chinese, particularly if they don't receive higher education. They code-switch a lot. In my generation, we can speak fluent Chinese.

Like Lu, who as a child learned the Chengdu dialect, Yi-Huey's first language was not Mandarin Chinese. Yi-Huey grew up speaking Taiwanese, essentially a dialect of Minnan spoken in southern China's Fujian province and from which many Taiwanese originally emigrated. Thus, both women first needed to learn Mandarin Chinese—in addition to the English they eventually acquired—if they were to become fully educated in their home countries.

As Yi-Huey continued to tell us more of the history of Taiwan, we learned that although the Chinese annexed Taiwan as a province, Taiwan became a part of Japan when Japan defeated China in 1895. It was during the next fifty years that the Japanese language became prominent among the Taiwanese, a situation that persisted until Japan's defeat in World War II. These events had many historical repercussions in the daily language use of people in Taiwan.

In 1943 at the Cairo Conference, an agreement was made regarding the future of Taiwan. The Allied forces, without the benefit of Taiwanese input, agreed to give China over to Chiang Kai-shek and his Nationalist Republic of China. In 1949, though, as Chiang Kai-shek and 2 million refugees fled mainland China and its rising communist government, the Republic of China essentially moved to Taiwan. Although many Taiwanese see these years as difficult and fraught with problems, they concede that economically—because of the hard work of the Taiwanese people and the social infrastructure established by the Japanese—this period yielded some major improvements in their country, and literacy rates rose dramatically. Since 1949, Mandarin Chinese has been the official language of Taiwan, although, as Yi-Huey points out, several other languages, especially Taiwanese and Hakka, are spoken in the more rural areas, and English has become a prized language among the educated.

Yi-Huey Guo and her family benefited from the good economic times that marked the 1970s and 1980s in Taiwan. She herself was born in Taichung, the third largest city in Taiwan, into an educated, middle-class Taiwanese family. She was raised in a four-story house in which she and her brothers all had their own bedrooms. From the very first, Yi-Huey realized that education would be central to her life and to that of her two younger brothers. Her mother, an English teacher of twenty-five years, constantly stressed the importance of English and the value of being educated. Her father—a university professor—was, for his children, the epitome of an educated man, and he continues today to teach and write books about law. Although, in comparison to Lu, Yi-Huey seems to come from an affluent background, she insists that her family is middle class. If they are mistaken for a family from the upper-middle or upper class, Yi-Huey notes, it is only because of the high value her parents have placed on education and literacy, especially that which is valued in schools and leads to academic advancement:

> Although my parents are teachers and we three children all hold master's degrees or above, we don't consider ourselves as upper- or upper-middle class. I would only consider ourselves as middle class since we are not wealthy. Since I was a child, my parents have told us that "our family is as average as those of others, so if you want to buy anything luxurious, you should work hard to get them by yourselves. But if you want to study for the higher degrees, we'll always support you. So, you don't need to worry about tuition [for schools here or for graduate school abroad]."

Given this background and her familial *guanxi*, Yi-Huey and her brothers attended one of the best schools available in Taichung. As noted, however, their first language was Taiwanese, and they did not learn Mandarin Chinese until they went to school. All of the children continued to speak Taiwanese at home. Although they attended public elementary school in their neighborhood, Yi-Huey and her siblings transferred to a private school when Yi-Huey was in the sixth grade. This school, Tong-Hai University Elementary School, was connected to the university where her father worked and was especially well known for its excellent instruction in English.

Yi-Huey excelled in English throughout her school years but often had trouble with science and math, which she earnestly disliked. During these years, Mandarin Chinese became her primary language and was constantly reinforced in school and through the flood of television programs she watched in Chinese. According to Yi-Huey's mother, Yi-Huey's Chinese became more and more fluent even as her proficiency in Taiwanese declined. Although the English language became increasingly important as well, it was Chinese that gradually replaced her home language of Taiwanese.

When Yi-Huey was in junior high school, Taiwan experienced a great deal of prosperity—in part due to its early research and development in technology, its successful foreign trade, and its digital connections with high-tech firms around the globe. In the late 1980s, the explosion of innovation in the computer sector was picking up speed both at home and abroad, and the Internet was gaining momentum in multiple countries around the world. At this time, Yi-Huey graduated from the Taichung Second High School and entered Providence University, where she received her BA in English language and literature in 1995. It was here that she first encountered computers:

> In my undergraduate years, I had computer classes in school. I needed to learn WordPerfect and Lotus. But I never used computer before. I had difficulty to get used to computers at that time. I thus turned to a private institute for help, where it offered computer lessons. However, the computer lessons I learned in both private institute and school did not help me a lot. I was very slow in learning anything technical. I was confused and afraid of using computer at that time.

From the start, however, Yi-Huey used both Chinese and English when she worked with computers. The keyboards she typed on in Taiwan contained the English alphabet at the center of the keys and Chinese on the upper-right side of the keys. Her instructions either through manuals or through her teachers were similarly in English and Chinese, as were the interfaces on WordPerfect and Lotus, the first programs she learned.

It was while Yi-Huey was still in junior high school that her family began to show an interest in computers, especially her two younger brothers, who became avid gamers. Although never as expert as her brothers, Yi-Huey eventually became somewhat comfortable with computers and even more proficient with English when attending graduate school at Ohio State University. After earning an MA in 1996 in language arts, reading, and literature education, she returned to Taiwan as a teacher who relied increasingly on computers for her schoolwork and e-mailed her friends at Ohio State on a daily basis. In her doctoral program at the University of Illinois, Yi-Huey continued to hone her computer skills, which she still sees as insufficient for today's world: "I have low computer skills and this sometimes made me feel it difficult to survive. Computer use is not just a fashion but another form of literacy. Possessing low computer skills is just like possessing low literacy." Recently, Yi-Huey has returned to Taiwan as a college English instructor at Chang-Jung University, and despite feeling that her digital literacy abilities could still improve, she nevertheless surrounds herself with the computer tools that enable her work.

Increasingly, she has come to recognize the intimate relationship of English and Chinese in her teaching and use of computers. Although the Internet today is populated by great numbers of Chinese Web sites unavailable before the World Wide Web took off in Taiwan during the first decade of the twenty-first century, it also remains a ubiquitous resource for the learning of English. The English Web sites help Yi-Huey immerse her students in English-only worlds replete with words, images, and sounds, despite her students' preference for the Chinese sites.

Within this context, Yi-Huey's English literacy practices (like Lu's)—her skill in writing, reading, and speaking English, as well as Chinese—have been amplified within the globalized communication environment of the Internet, allowing her to take advantage of geographically distributed, cross-cultural *guanxi* as well as familial relationships and resources. Recognizing the power of deploying English literacy practices within computer networks—and the relationship of computer networks in formulating increasingly global *guanxi*—Yi-Huey encourages students to follow her lead.

Discussion

What sorts of themes can we draw from Lu and Yi-Huey's narratives of literacy and English learning as they intersect with the cultural ecology in which these two women live out their lives? In many respects, their stories serve to underscore and extend at least four themes that have emerged in current scholarship on digital literacies, but they also demonstrate the challenges facing people from around the world as they design and redesign their literacies in cyberspace.

1. *Digital literacies, indeed all literacies, exist and develop within the context of complex and interrelated local and global ecologies.* Our study of digital literacies in the United States, for example, and the work of scholars like Brian V. Street, James Paul Gee, Harvey J. Graff, and Deborah Brandt (*Literacy*) remind us that we cannot hope to understand any literacy or language use—print or digital—until we understand the complex social and cultural ecology, both local and global, within which literacy practices and values are situated. As these two narratives indicate, the ways in which people from various nations acquire and develop digital literacy—or are prevented from doing so—depend on a constellation of factors: among just a few of them, income, education, access and the specific conditions of access, geographical location, proficiency in English, and support systems, sometimes in the form of *guanxi* and sometimes practiced over the Internet.

The literacy narratives of Lu and Yi-Huey also demonstrate the multiple dimensions in which technology helps to shape the lived experiences of people within a cultural ecology. Related macro-level trends such as the globalization of markets and monetary systems, the growth of information networks, the rapid pace of technological innovation, China's efforts to modernize an agrarian society, and Taiwan's experiment with democracy clearly shaped the lives of these two women, their language resources, and the digital literacy practices they have acquired and valued. These women came of age and attended school in the early 1980s just as the PRC began to realize the dividends of massive economic and technological reforms and Taiwan began a period of increasing economic prosperity. Both women's literacy practices and values were influenced by their countries' emphasis on building technological infrastructures, assembling a critical mass of skilled engineers and scientists, investing in education and educational technology, establishing political stability, and formulating technology policies that made a difference in the lived experiences of its citizens.

Linked to these macro-level trends, of course, have been factors that manifested themselves at the medial level of their environments. The high schools that Lu and Yi-Huey attended were beginning to offer courses that incorporated the use of computers—although, as in the United States, these first passes at integrating technology into teaching met with varied success and failure. Each school Lu and Yi-Huey attended, moreover, had achieved an excellent reputation for the teaching of English, a language that proved essential in advancing their educations and digital literacies. Similarly, at the micro-level, the high value that both Lu's and Yi-Huey's parents placed on literacy and their determination to ensure that their offspring attended the best schools available have given their daughters opportunities to accumulate the requisite cultural capital (Bourdieu) to acquire English and the literacies of technology.

As in the United States, however, physical access to computers has, at times, been sporadic, and even when access has been available, the specific conditions have sometimes proven less than conducive to learning and practicing digital literacies. Lu, for example, found that learning BASIC was pretty boring, and as Yi-Huey notes:

> I started to learn computers when I was a freshman in my college life. I had not much motivation to learn computer at all at that time. The courses did not help me at all. Rather, after taking the course, I felt that the computer was a very inconvenient invention. I did not have access to the computer at that time except the class time. Although the school had a computer lab, it was always full. And that somehow made me lose patience in learning to use computer.

Yi-Huey did, however, excel in English in school—the only subject, she tells us, in which she really succeeded. Her expertise in English and her subsequent schooling in the United States eventually provided her with a kind of access that allowed her to develop digital literacies, although never to the extent she thought was necessary. Each time she began to master a particular technology, the technology shifted and more mastery of a greater number of computer applications seemed to be demanded. While today she enjoys e-mailing, instant messaging, texting, and social networking Web sites, she has greater problems with Web authoring, which she learned early on but had less impetus to pursue as she moved back and forth between the United States and Taiwan.

2. *The ecology of literacy is seldom monocultural and never static; it is always a site of contestation between emerging, competing, changing, accumulating, and fading languages and literate exchanges.* The cultural ecology of literacy consists of a dynamic mosaic of patches, mini self-organizing systems characterized variously by different languages and histories and locations, different literacy practices and digital environments, different belief systems and hegemonic relationships, different "organisms, artifacts, landscapes, dialects, communities, cultures, and social individuals" (Lemke 94). Within this dynamic environment, both hegemonic and counter-hegemonic forces contend at many levels, and different literacies and languages emerge, compete, change, accumulate, and fade.

In this context, scholars have continued to express concerns about the overlapping processes of informatization and globalization, especially when considering U.S. technological expansionism, but increasing numbers have also identified counter-hegemonic tendencies developing in various patches around the world. As Randy Kluver has argued, "If informatization and globalization have the capacity to transform culture (the yang), then they also strengthen them (the yin)." And, as Kewen Zhang and Xiaoming Hao add, the recent proliferation of ethnic media in cyberspace may serve to fortify and strengthen the cultures of ethnic immigrants rather than weaken them.

Certainly, the literacy narratives of Lu Liu and Yi-Huey Guo bear out this latter understanding. In 1995, when these women were twenty-three, for example, Netscape began supporting both Chinese and Japanese sites. Soon thereafter, as Joe Lockard notes, "Asian nets started expanding exponentially," and by the time that Yi-Huey and Lu were using computers in graduate school, they were able to access Web sites not only in English but also in Chinese. As Lu and Yi-Huey were working on their doctoral degrees in the United States, Stefan Jarvis was writing in 2001 that Asian governments probably have little to fear from the preponderance of English on the Internet. Those in many countries, such as Japan, primarily access local sites written in their own language despite much of the Internet's content featuring English. In other words, as Anthony D. Smith argues, it is a mistake to think that the global landscape of the Internet necessarily leads to a monologic global culture or language like English. Statistical studies also support Smith's argument. In 2002, Daniel Pimienta—an author associated with Funredes, a non-governmental organization active in defending cultural and linguistic diversity on the Web—reported:

- The relative presence of English on the Web has declined from 75% in 1998 to 50% today (in terms of the web pages in English).
- The presence of each language on the Web appears to be proportional to the number of web users who speak that language (at least for the 7 languages . . . studied).
- The growth of English-speaking users has slowed and is close to saturation, whereas numbers in other linguistic areas are often growing very strong (with Chinese in the lead).

We should also note that—given the literacy practices of individuals like Lu and Yi-Huey in a number of different parts of the world, including Africa, Egypt, India, Greece, and Korea—cyber-English itself is changing and being redesigned, some think, as "cyberneopolitan" (Lockard). Consider, for example, this post cited by Lockard in 1996:

> I am sorry with purists but cultural domination of a language has always determined in non-native or culturally dominated a development, maybe unconsciosly of riot, towards a strong contamination. In USA this is clear in blacks' slung and latinos like it happens for maya indigenous in Mexico, irish in Ireland, Catalanouse in Spain and others. I personally don't love English like don't love italian, prefering usually talk in neapolitan.

As Lockard continues, this kind of language recalls "Brathwaite's description of nation language: 'It may be in English: but often it is in an English which is like a howl, or a shout or a machine gun or the wind or a wave. . . . Sometimes it is English and African at the same time.'"

In discussing similar variations of language in the Caribbean, Emily Williams suggests that such efforts, while they might at first glance seem simplistic, often represent an effective form of linguistic resistance, a "sophisticated code of communication" that, while "largely unintelligible to the colonizers," can serve as a "distancing mechanism from the European power structure while simultaneously providing an enclave of survival for the slave" (22). Min-Zhan Lu notes that such literate responses represent "diverse visions of what life and success have meant and could and should mean" (34) and "senses of self, visions of life, and notions of one's relations with others and the world" (28) that are resistant to dominant hegemonies.

These resistant Englishes—cyberneopolitan, pidgin, or sometimes creole—grow out of specific ecological patches in Italy, India, Egypt, or China, among many other locations. On the Internet, and in the far-flung *guanxi* networks of individuals like Lu and Yi-Huey, these variations compete with each other, change over time, and also accumulate and fade. As they do so, they also change the larger ecological system for Englishes and digital literacies. These efforts do not mean, of course, that the hegemony associated with the potent overlapping formations of globalization, informatization, and U.S. culture has been obviated (see Bollag; Dor; Chang). Rather, they indicate that a complex set of factors within patches of an ecological system—and the play of difference among patches—may support ongoing efforts of resistance and change.

Lu's and Yi-Huey's use of resistant Englishes, or not, in their on-line conversations with family and friends remains essentially hidden to us in our roles as their U.S. teachers and colleagues. At the same time, however, we have watched firsthand as Yi-Huey has at times struggled with the language and arrangement of the World Wide Web. In one instance, she tried to secure U.S. airline tickets to travel to Taiwan but felt she was misled by the English on-line advertising at a discount commercial Web site and was charged for an added service that she had not ordered. She was angry enough to write of this "consumer threat" in a formal academic paper that she presented at the 2003 Conference on Computers and Writing. In her paper, she wraps her concerns in an academic discourse that in its own way is every bit as resistant and critical of the status quo as Lockard's example. She writes, for example, that "even though the multiplayered and nonlinear information system of the hypertext liberates a reader from reading linear texts, it has generated violence in the network community, where the readers are forced to struggle against the writer's hegemony. This phenomenon is particularly serious when the readers engage in the process of hypertext reading for the purpose of commerce." Here she argues that far from setting a reader free, the Web's hypertext format is at best confusing and at worst a venue that enables English-writing Webmasters to deceive consumers. Her paper began as an outraged complaint in a graduate class that eventually made its way into a written response that she reworked into a conference proposal and presentation.

3. *People exert powerful agency, both individually and collectively, in, around, and through digital literacies.* As Min-Zhan Lu (this volume) also points out, people continually design and redesign the local ecological patches they inhabit through literacy practices and values. The stories of Lu Liu and Yi-Huey Guo and the work of scholars such as Anthony Giddens remind us that, even

as people's language acquisition and digital literacies are being shaped by macro-, medial, and micro-level factors in the literacy ecology they inhabit, they also shape these environments through their language practices and values. Although Yi-Huey struggled within her early educational environments, for example, her desire to please her parents and her determination to acquire English were factors that helped make it possible for her to succeed in school and to pursue an advanced education. Similarly, although Lu's early experiences with computers were limited and less than applicable to her interests in language studies, her personal commitment to education—and the shaping influence of her family's literacy values—encouraged her to persevere in school.

This same theme of personal agency also played itself out in terms of gender expectations and computer use. Yi-Huey, for instance, persisted in developing computer expertise despite the fact that women in her country tend to pursue studies in the humanities:

> In Taiwan, females prefer humanities or social science majors; meanwhile, males prefer science or engineering majors. Not knowing why, people tend to believe that women are gifted for memorization and men for analytical skills. In addition, people also tend to think that it's better for the women to choose humanities-related majors since engineering majors are more related to blue-collar jobs. This leads to more female students in humanities/social science majors and more male students in engineering/science majors. And I do think this affects our acquisition of computer literacy, because humanities major students didn't have many computer courses compared with other engineering/science majors. Take me, for example; I only learned some word processing skills in my undergraduate days in Taiwan.

It is especially important in light of our previous discussions of *guanxi* to note that the social agency practiced by both Lu and Yi-Huey has extended far beyond the micro- and medial levels. People like Lu and Yi-Huey have contributed to our understanding that *guanxi* in the age of the Internet involves "networks of trust" that "form and dissolve, collapsing space according to need," networks that flourish "across cultures" as a "global practice" that entail literate exchanges (Jirik 20).

The changing nature of *guanxi*, a cultural practice historically focused on personal networks formulated primarily through face-to-face interactions and relationships, seems congruent, in our opinion, with Giddens's structuration theory (1979) in which neither cultural formations nor "the experience of the individual actor" wholly constitute social practices but, rather, exert a recursive, mutually shaping influence on social practices (119–20). *Guanxi*, as Thomas Gold, Doug Guthrie, and David Wank have pointed out, involves a dynamic set of social practices and understandings that "recursively constitutes the conditions of its production and reproduction" and is, moreover, continually changed through the "situated activities of human agency" (Jirik 20).

Within the digital environment of the Internet, Lu and Yi-Huey are only two individuals among millions continually designing and redesigning landscapes of cyberspace through their literacy practices on bulletin boards and in chat rooms, in e-mail and on nonprofit Web sites, and through their efforts to teach and to learn. Although both women's lives have clearly been shaped by the overlapping, macro-level trends of globalization and informatization and by the U.S. efforts of technological expansion—their acquisition of digital literacies, their interest in English, their study in the United States—these trends have also been clearly influenced by their literacy and language practices, values, and *guanxi* of parents and family, peers and teachers. And just as clearly, they have made their own code-switching language and literacy practices work for them. Yi-Huey notes, for instance:

> The language [I] use depends on whom I write to or what I want to search or research about. In terms of English, I often do three things: (1) e-mail contact with my international friends, (2) searching for shopping information on-line, and (3) academic writing. In terms of using Chinese, I usually do the following things: (1) workplace writing, (2) read the news thru the Internet.

Lu and Yi-Huey seem to know, as John Tomlinson has argued, that the articulated formations of globalization, informatization, and technology have resulted in a cyber landscape that "no one—not the West, America, nor multinational capitalism—can fully control" (189). *Guanxi*, too, as John Jirik notes, encompasses an exceedingly complex set of cultural practices and values that continuously changes: the "multiple systems that are constituted through the different practices of *guanxi* in different cultural contexts" are shaped by multiple agents and social forces that are mutually influential and far from "closed to one another" (20).

4. Schools, homes, and increasingly the Internet itself are primary gateways through which people gain access to digital literacies. Finally, we find it useful to pay some attention to the gateways—supported again by the practices of *guanxi*—that provided Lu and Yi-Huey access to the acquisition and development of digital literacies. Individuals who gain access to technology through the standard gateways of school, home, and increasingly the Internet also frequently network with those who may serve as literacy sponsors. Brandt uses this term "sponsor" to denote "agents, local or distant, concrete or abstract, who enable, support, teach, model, as well as recruit, regulate, suppress or withhold literacy—and gain advantage by it in some way" ("Sponsors" 166). As we mentioned, a related notion of *guanxi* emerges from the stories of Lu and Yi-Huey. Lu tells us that *guanxi* is widely used when people talk about doing business in China and that the term refers to networks constituted by relatives, acquaintances, teachers, or organizations that can help people achieve something they might not be able to achieve alone. The *guanxi* in Lu's and Yi-Huey's lives, for example, often took the form of academic connections of parents and friends that facilitated their studies abroad, supported their developing sophistication in the use of information technologies, and finally became crucial to their literacy development. These more conventional *guanxiwang*, personal networks, expanded as Lu traveled from the PRC to London and then to the United States for her conference paper and subsequently her graduate school education. These conventional networks of relationships—in combination with the digital *guanxiwang* that both women established—laid the foundation for additional extended networks and digital literacy practices, as well. At Ohio State University and the University of Illinois, for example, Yi-Huey was able to develop subsequent digital literacy expertise and to connect with other graduates of those institutions who would form her expanded *guanxiwang*. The Chinese term *guanxi*, then, serves to extend Brandt's explanation of literacy sponsorship—providing a more complex, concrete, and global perspective on how such relationships function, and dynamically change, in an increasingly networked world (*Literacy*).

By Way of Ending, but Only for the Moment

Lu and Yi-Huey have taught us a great deal about the complex local and global ecologies within which they have worked to develop digital literacies. These literacies and the computer environments within which the two women enacted many of their literate practices helped them extend and expand their cross-cultural *guanxiwang*. Using the Web as a communicative environment, they have shown us how their own language and literacy practices both reflect and resist the linguistic formation of Standard English and the dominance of English in digital spaces. They have also demonstrated how their interests, values, and practices have shaped the cultural exchanges of information in which they have participated and how their literacies have functioned to redesign the world they inhabit as well as the *guanxi* networks they have formed. Their narratives, we believe, also emphasize the complex relationships between learning English(es), learning digital literacies, and acquiring the means of success in an increasingly technological world. As mentioned,

Lu's and Yi-Huey's stories highlight the connections between *guanxi* and Bourdieu's concept of social and cultural capital: personal connections that form social networks and help individuals acquire the means of succeeding in both personal and economic arenas. In this context, we understand the family, friends, and spouses of the two women—their shared knowledge, education, and beliefs—as valuable sets of personal resources. The academic background of Yi-Huey's family, for instance, provided her a context—and a set of resources—that helped to encourage and enable her to pursue her own education and to learn English and develop the digital literacies that were critical to her educational success. Similarly, the academic connections that Lu forged with scholars in the United States, China, and London over the Internet helped her to present her first conference paper and publish her first book chapter. By contrast, learning any digital practices in the absence of learning English or without the opportunities provided through personal connections might well have resulted in different life trajectories for Lu and Yi-Huey.

In short, we have come to understand *guanxi* as a useful term not only for describing the richly textured constellations of connections and resources that structure the lives of individuals but also for suggesting how these connections and resources are linked—at various levels in a range of ways—to the related social, cultural, ideological, technological, and economic formations that structure the "information age" (Castells, *Rise*). The term also gives us a sense of how complexly rendered are the challenges that confront contemporary students who must learn to operate effectively within dynamic and rapidly changing economic contexts shaped by the logic of flexible accumulation at the local, regional, and global levels. In an increasingly technological world, personal connections and language resources can be amplified in reach and scope—but also complicated in their formation and deployment—within the expanding complex of computer networks and through the practice of digital literacies. Lu Liu and Yi-Huey Guo have discovered their own ways to cope successfully with these challenges and, along the way, have taught us about *guanxi*—and about the influence of digital literacies—in their personal and professional lives.

Notes

1. For the past eight years, we (Gail Hawisher and Cynthia Selfe) have collected literacy autobiographies from more than 350 individuals. When publishing these narratives, we have asked contributors to work with us in a collaborative relationship to tell their stories accurately and to set them within robust historical, social, economic, and educational contexts. In these published accounts, we

have generally identified contributors as "coauthors," in an attempt to honor their generosity in responding to our questions and, in doing so, telling us the stories of their lives. The term "coauthor" is also meant to signal the hours contributors have spent reading our accounts of their lives, contributing additional information that made them come alive, answering follow-up e-mail inquiries, combing over drafts for inaccuracies, and suggesting revisions.

Over time, however, and after conferring with a number of contributors, we have come to understand that "coauthor" may not be serving as an accurate or adequate descriptor. These individuals have reminded us that we have assumed both slightly different roles and slightly different responsibilities than have the contributors of life history narratives: we identified the original questions for this series of interviews, we selected the historical and social frameworks within which to recount the narratives, we chose the publication venues in which to place the narrative accounts, we served as editors and principal researchers.

Thus, although we remain convinced that the life history narratives that these individuals have shared represent the heart of every piece we have collectively published in this series and we understand that these accounts could not have been written without contributors' voices and help, we also recognize the importance of identifying our own responsibility as the primary authors of these reports. Any shortcoming that characterizes these published works, we consider our own.

2. Information regarding Lu Liu and Yi-Huey Guo was gathered from autobiographical accounts written in 2003, as well as from a series of conversations and on-line correspondence collected between 2003 and 2006.

3. It is for this reason that we use the term "digital literacy" (or digital literacies) to signal the practices involved in reading, writing, and exchanging information in on-line environments, as well as the values associated with such practices—cultural, social, political, and educational. For us, the term differs from computer literacy in that it focuses primarily on the word "literacy"—and thus on communication skills and values—rather than on the skills required to use a computer. When we talk about digital literacies, we reference, as well, a complex set of social practices that shape and are shaped by people's literate exchanges in digital environments, which, we recognize, are embedded in a larger cultural ecology of literacy (Selfe and Hawisher; Hawisher, Selfe, Coffield, and El-Wakil). All these terms are synonymous with our use of technological literacy, and we use them in this chapter interchangeably. In all cases, they focus on literacy practices and values in on-line environments rather than on the skills required to use computers themselves.

Works Cited

Bollag, Burton. "The New Latin: English Dominates in Academe." *Chronicle of Higher Education* 8 Sept. 2000, international section. 10 Oct. 2005 <http://chronicle.com/free/v47/i02a07301.htm>.

Bourdieu, Pierre. *Language and Symbolic Power.* Ed. John B. Thompson. Trans. Gino Raymond and Matthew Adamson. Cambridge, MA: Harvard UP, 1991.

Brandt, Deborah. *Literacy in American Lives.* Cambridge, MA: Cambridge UP, 2001.

———. "Sponsors of Literacy." *College Composition and Communication* 49 (1998): 165–85.

Brathwaite, Edward Kamau. *Contradictory Omens: Cultural Diversity and Integration in the Caribbean.* Mona, Jamaica: Savacou Publications, 1974.

Castells, Manuel. *End of the Millennium.* Malden, MA: Blackwell, 1998.

———. *The Power of Identity.* Malden, MA: Blackwell, 1997.

———. *The Rise of the Network Society.* Malden, MA: Blackwell, 1996.

Chang, Chi-Yu. "How American Culture Correlates the Process of Globalization." *Asian EFL Journal* 6.4 (Sept. 2004). 10 Oct. 2005 <http://www.asian-efl-journal.com/site_map_2004.html>.

China Internet Network Information Center Web site. 2003. Retrieved 7 Oct. 2007 <http://www.cnnic.net.cn/html/Dir/2003/12/12/2003.htm>.

Dor, Daniel. "From Englishization to Imposed Multilingualism: Globalization, the Internet, and the Political Economy of the Linguistic Code." *Public Culture* 1.16 (2004): 97–116.

Gee, James Paul. *Social Linguistics and Literacies: Ideology in Discourses.* 2nd ed. London: Taylor, 1996.

Giddens, Anthony. *Central Problems in Social Theory: Action, Structure and Contradiction in Social Analysis.* Berkeley: U of California P, 1979.

Gold, Thomas, Doug Guthrie, and David Wank. "An Introduction to the Study of *Guanxi.*" Gold, Guthrie, and Wank 3–20.

———, eds. *Social Connections in China: Institutions, Culture, and the Changing Nature of Guanxi.* Cambridge: Cambridge UP, 2002.

Graff, Harvey J. *The Legacies of Literacy: Continuities and Contradictions in Western Culture and Society.* Bloomington: Indiana UP, 1987.

Guo, Yi-Huey. "Between the Lawful and the Fraudulent: The Myth of Internet Shopping." Paper presented at 2003 Computers and Writing Conference. Purdue University, West Lafayette, Indiana. 22–25 May 2003.

Hanser, Amy. "Youth Job Searches in Urban China: The Use of Social Connections in a Changing Labor Market." Gold, Guthrie, and Wank 137–62.

Hawisher, Gail E., and Cynthia L. Selfe with Kate Coffield and Safia El-Wakil. "Women and the Global Ecology of Digital Literacies." *Women and Literacy: Local and Global Inquiries for a New Century.* Ed. Beth Daniell and Peter Mortensen. New York: LEA, 2007. 207–28.

Human Development Report 2001: Making New Technologies Work for Human Development. United Nations Development Programme. New York: Oxford UP, 2001.

Jarvis, Stefan. "Asia's Internet Experience." *Asian/Pacific Book Development (ABD)* 32 (2001): 3–5. UNESCO's Asia-Pacific Cooperative Programme in Reading

Promotion and Book Development. 10 Oct. 2005 <http://www.accu.or.jp/appreb/report/abd/32–2/abd3221.html>.

Jirik, John. "The AOL Time Warner CCTV (China) Television Exchange: *Guanxi* in Globalization Theory." (Tracking Number ICA-19–10805). Paper presented at the annual meeting of the International Communication Association. Marriott Hotel, San Diego. 27 May 2003. 12 Oct. 2007 <http://www.allacademic.com/meta/p111969_index.html>.

Jung, Sei-Hwa. *The Use of ICT in Learning English as an International Language*. Diss. U Maryland, 2006. College Park, MD: Digital Repository of the University of Maryland, 2004. 16 Oct. 2007 <https://drum.umd.edu/dspace/bitstream/1903/3885/1/umi-umd-3733.pdf>.

Kipnis, Andrew B. *Producing Guanxi: Sentiment, Self, and Subculture in a North China Village*. Durham, NC: Duke UP, 1997.

Kluver, Randy. "Globalization, Informatization, and Intercultural Communication." United Nations Online Network in Public Administration and Finance 2004. *United Nations Public Administration Network*. 10 Oct. 2005 <http://www.unpan.org/>.

Lemke, Jay L. *Textual Politics: Discourse and Social Dynamics*. London: Taylor and Francis, 1995.

Lockard, Joe. "Resisting Cyber-English." *Papyrus News*, 1996. 10 Feb. 2005 <http://eserver.org/bs/24/lockard.html>.

Lu, Min-Zhan. "An Essay on the Work of Composition: Composing English against the Order of Fast Capitalism." *College Composition and Communication* 56 (2004): 16–50.

McCarthy, Terry. "The Pulse of China." *Time Magazine* 29 June 1998, 31–36. 25 Oct. 2007 <http://www.time.com/time/magazine/article/0,9171,988617,00.html>.

Norris, Pippa. *Digital Divide: Civic Engagement, Information Poverty, and the Internet Worldwide*. Cambridge: Cambridge UP, 2001.

Pimienta, Daniel. "Put Out Your Tongue and Say, 'Aaaa': Is the Internet Suffering from Acute 'Englishitis'?" Communication and Information in the Knowledge Society: An International Gateway. *UNESCO*, 2002. 10 Oct. 2005 <http://www.unesco.org/webworld/points_of_views/300102_pimienta.shtml>.

Selfe, Cynthia L., and Gail E. Hawisher. *Literate Lives in the Information Age: Narratives of Literacy from the United States*. Mahwah, NJ: Erlbaum, 2004.

Smith, Anthony D. "Towards a Global Culture". *Global Culture: Nationalism, Globalization and Modernity*. Ed. Mike Featherstone. London: Sage, 1990. 171–91.

Spoken and Written Languages. Web site of the Central People's Government of the People's Republic of China. 2006. 7 Oct. 2007 <http://english.gov.cn/2006–02/08/content_182616.htm>.

Street, Brian V. *Social Literacies: Critical Approaches to Literacy in Development, Ethnography, and Education*. London: Longman, 1995.

Tomlinson, John. "Cultural Globalization and Cultural Imperialism." *International Communication and Globalization: A Critical Introduction*. Ed. Ali Mohammadi. London: Sage. 170–90.

Turkle, Sherry. "Who Am We?" *Wired* 4.1 (Jan. 1996). 14 Oct. 2007 <http://www.wired.com/wired/archive/4.01/turkle_pr.html>.

Warschauer, Mark. "Millennialism and Media: Language, Literacy, and Technology in the 21st Century." Paper presented at the World Congress of Applied Linguistics (AILA). Tokyo. Aug. 1999. *Papyrus News*. 25 Oct. 2007 <http://members.tripod.com/vstevens/papyrus/16sep99a.htm>.

Weber, Ian. "Shanghai Baby: Negotiating Your Self Identity in Urban China." *Social Identities* 8.2 (2002): 347–68.

Williams, Emily Allen. *Poetic Negotiation of Identity in the Works of Brathwaite*. Lewiston, NY: Edwin Mellen Press, 1999.

Wu, J. "Overseas Chinese Capitalism and the Marginalization of the Rule of Law: A Reassessment of the Relationship between Law and Economic Development." *Berkeley NcNair Journal* (on-line), Sept. 1996. 12 Oct. 2007 <http://www-mcnair.berkeley.edu/96journal/wu.html>.

Yan, Yunxiang. *The Flow of Gifts: Reciprocity and Social Networks in a Chinese Village*. Stanford, CA: Stanford UP, 1996.

Yang, Mayfair Mei-Hui. "The Gift Economy and State Power in China." *Comparative Studies in Society and History* 31.1 (1989): 25–54.

———. *Gifts, Favors, and Banquets: The Art of Social Relationships in China*. Ithaca: Cornell UP, 1994.

Zhang, Kewen, and Xiaoming Hao. "The Internet and Ethnic Press: A Study of Electronic Chinese Publications." *Information Society* 15 (1999): 21–30.

4. The Myth of Linguistic Homogeneity in U.S. College Composition

Paul Kei Matsuda

In "English Only and U.S. College Composition," Bruce Horner and John Trimbur identify the tacit policy of unidirectional English monolingualism, which makes moving students toward the dominant variety of English the only conceivable way of dealing with language issues in composition instruction. This policy of unidirectional monolingualism is an important concept to critique because it accounts for the relative lack of attention to multilingualism in the composition scholarship. Yet it does not seem to explain why second language issues have not become a central concern in composition studies. After all, if U.S. composition had accepted the policy of unidirectional monolingualism, all composition teachers would have been expected to learn how to teach the dominant variety of English to students who come from different language backgrounds. This has not been the case. While Geneva Smitherman and Victor Villanueva argue that coursework on language issues should be part of every English teachers' professional preparation (4), relatively few graduate programs in composition studies offer courses on those issues, and even fewer require such courses. As a result, the vast majority of U.S. college composition programs remain unprepared for second language writers who enroll in the mainstream composition courses. To account for this situation, I want to take Horner and Trimbur's argument a step further and suggest that the dominant discourse of U.S. college composition not only has accepted "English Only" as an ideal but already assumes the state of English Only, in which students are native English speakers by default.

That second language writing has not yet become a central concern in composition studies seems paradoxical given the historical origin of U.S. college composition as a way of "containing" language differences from the rest of U.S. higher education. Robert J. Connors has suggested that U.S. composition arose in response to perceived language differences—texts written by ostensibly some of the brightest native English speakers that included numerous errors in "punctuation, capitalization, spelling, [and] syntax" (*Composition* 128). Susan Miller also points out that college composition "has provided a continuing way to separate the unpredestined from those who belong . . . by encouraging them to leave school, or more vaguely, by convincing large numbers of *native speakers* and otherwise accomplished *citizens* that they are 'not good at English'" (Miller 74; emphasis added). To a large extent, however, issues that prompted the rise of the composition requirement are weak forms of language differences that affect native speakers of English—matters of convention and style as well as performance errors that arise from factors such as unfamiliar tasks, topics, audiences, or genres. While U.S. composition has maintained its ambivalent relationship with those weak forms of language differences, it has been responding to the presence of stronger forms of language differences—differences that affect students who did not grow up speaking privileged varieties of English—not by adjusting its pedagogical practices systematically at the level of the entire field but by relegating the responsibility of working with those differences to second language specialists (Matsuda, "Composition"; Shuck).

I am not trying to imply that there has not been *any* effort to address second language issues in composition studies. I recognize that a growing number of writing teachers who face those issues in their classes on a daily basis have developed, often on their own initiative, additional expertise in issues related to language differences. What I want to call into question is why the issue of language difference has not become a central concern for *everyone* who is involved in composition instruction, research, assessment, and administration. I argue that the lack of "a professionwide response" (Valdés 128) to the presence of strong forms of language differences in U.S. composition stems from what I call the myth of linguistic homogeneity—the tacit and widespread acceptance of the dominant image of composition students as native speakers of a privileged variety of English. To show how the myth of linguistic homogeneity came into being, I examine here the early history of various attempts at linguistic containment, which created a condition that makes it seem acceptable to dismiss language differences. My intention is not to argue against all forms of linguistic containment. Rather, I want to problematize its long-term implication—the perpetuation of the myth of linguistic homogeneity—that has in turn kept U.S. composition from fully recognizing the presence of second language writers who do not fit the dominant image of college students.

The Image of College Students and the Myth of Linguistic Homogeneity

Behind any pedagogy is an image of prototypical students—the teacher's imagined audience. This image embodies a set of assumptions about who the students are, where they come from, where they are going, what they already know, what they need to know, and how best to teach them. It is not necessarily the concrete image of any individual student but an abstraction that comes from continual encounters with the dominant student population in local institutional settings as well as from the dominant disciplinary discourses. Images of students are not monolithic; just as teachers incorporate pedagogical practices from various and even conflicting perspectives, student images are multiple and complex, reflecting local institutional arrangements as well as teaching philosophies and worldviews of individual teachers. Although there is no such thing as a generalized college composition student, overlaps in various teachers' images of students constitute a dominant image—a set of socially shared generalizations. Those generalizations in turn warrant the link between abstract disciplinary practices and concrete classroom practices.

Having a certain image of students is not problematic in itself; images of students are inevitable and even necessary. Without those images, discussing pedagogical issues across institutions would be impossible. An image of students becomes problematic when it inaccurately represents the actual student population in the classroom to the extent that it inhibits the teacher's ability to recognize and address the presence of differences. Just as the assumption of whiteness as the colorless norm has rendered some students of color invisible in the discourse of composition studies (Prendergast 51), theoretical practices that do not recognize and challenge inaccurate images reinforce the marginal status of those students by rendering them invisible in the professional discourse. By the same token, pedagogical practices based on an inaccurate image of students continue to alienate students who do not fit the image.

One of the persisting elements of the dominant image of students in English studies is the assumption that students are by default native speakers of a privileged variety of English from the United States. Although the image of students as native speakers of privileged varieties of English is seldom articulated or defended—an indication that English Only is already taken for granted—it does surface from time to time in the work of those who are otherwise knowledgeable about issues of language and difference. A prime example is Patrick Hartwell's "Grammar, Grammars, and the Teaching of Grammar," a widely known critique of grammar instruction in the composition classroom. In his analysis of a grammar exercise, he writes that "the rule, however valuable it may be for non-native speakers, is, for the most part, simply unusable for native speakers of the language" (116). While this is a reasonable claim, to argue against certain pedagogical strategies based on their relevance to native speakers seems to imply the assumption of the native-English-speaker norm. Hartwell also claims that "native speakers of English, regardless of dialect, show tacit mastery of the conventions of Standard English" (123), which seems to trivialize important structural differences between privileged varieties of U.S. English and many other domestic and international varieties of English.

Language issues are also inextricably tied to the goal of college composition, which is to help students become "better writers." Although definitions of what constitutes a better writer may vary, implicit in most teachers' definitions of "writing well" is the ability to produce English that is unmarked in the eyes of teachers who are custodians of privileged varieties of English or, in more socially situated pedagogies, of an audience of native English speakers who would judge the writer's credibility or even intelligence on the basis of grammaticality. (As a practicing writing teacher, I do not claim myself to be immune to this charge.) Since any form of writing assessment—holistic, multiple-trait, or portfolio assessment—explicitly or implicitly includes language as part of the criteria, writing teachers regularly and inevitably engage in what Bonny Norton and Sue Starfield have termed "the covert language assessment" (292). As they point out, this practice is not problematic in itself, especially if language issues are deliberately and explicitly included in the assessment criteria and if students are receiving adequate instruction on language issues. In many composition classrooms, however, language issues beyond simple "grammar" correction are not addressed extensively, even when the assessment of student texts is based at least partly on students' proficiency in the privileged variety of English. As Connors has pointed out, "the sentence . . . as an element of composition pedagogy is hardly mentioned today outside of textbooks" and has become a "half-hidden and seldom-discussed classroom practice on the level of, say, vocabulary quizzes" ("Erasure" 97, 120). It is not unusual for teachers who are overwhelmed by the presence of language differences to tell students simply to "proofread more carefully" or to "go to the writing center"; in the same classrooms, non-native speakers of dominant varieties of English are being held accountable for what is not being taught.

The current practice might be appropriate if all students can reasonably be expected to come to the composition classroom having already internalized a privileged variety of English—its grammar and rhetorical practices associated with it. Such an expectation, however, does not accurately reflect the student population in today's college composition classrooms. In the 2003/2004 academic year, there were 572,509 international students in the United States (Institute of International Education, *Open Doors 2004*), most of whom came from countries where English is not the dominant language. Although the number has declined slightly in recent years, international students are not likely to disappear from U.S. higher education any time soon. In fact, many institutions continue to recruit international students—because they bring foreign capital (at an out-of-state rate), increase visible ethnic diversity (which, unlike linguistic diversity, is highly valued), and enhance the international reputation of the institutions—even as they reduce or eliminate instructional support programs designed to help those students succeed (Dadak; Kubota and Abels).

In addition, there is a growing number of resident second language writers who are permanent residents or citizens of the United States. Linda Harklau, Meryl Siegal, and Kay M. Losey estimate that there are at least 150,000–225,000 active learners of English graduating from U.S. high schools each year (2–3). These figures do not include an overwhelmingly large number of functional bilinguals—students who have a high level of proficiency in both English and another language spoken at home (Valdés)—or native speakers of traditionally underprivileged varieties of English, including what has come to be known as world Englishes. The myth of linguistic homogeneity—the assumption that college students are by default native speakers of a privileged variety of English—is seriously out of sync with the sociolinguistic reality of today's U.S. higher education as well as the U.S. society at large. This discrepancy is especially problematic considering the status of first-year composition as the only course that is required of virtually all college students in a country where, according to a 2000 U.S. census, "more than one in six people five years of age and older reported speaking a language other than English at home" (Bayley 269).

The Policy of Linguistic Containment in U.S. College Composition

The perpetuation of the myth of linguistic homogeneity in U.S. college com-position has been facilitated by the concomitant policy of linguistic contain-ment that has kept language differences invisible in the required composition course and in the discourse of composition studies. Since its beginning in the late nineteenth century at Harvard and elsewhere, the first-year composition course has been a site of linguistic containment, quarantining from the rest of higher education students who have not yet been socialized into the dominant linguistic practices (Miller 74). While using the composition course as a site of linguistic containment for native speakers of privileged varieties of English, institutions have found ways to exclude more substantive forms of language differences even from the composition course by enacting several strategies for linguistic containment. The first and most obvious strategy is to exclude language differences from entering higher education altogether by filtering them out in the admission process. Another common strategy, especially when the number of students from unprivileged language backgrounds is relatively small, is to ignore language issues, attributing any difficulties to individual students' inadequate academic preparation. Even when language differences are recognized by the teacher, those differences are often contained by sending students to the writing center, where students encounter peer tutors who are even less likely to be prepared to work with language differences than composition teachers (Trimbur 27–28).

The policy of containment is enacted most strongly through the placement procedure, which is unique to composition programs in the sense that students do not normally have the option of choosing a second language section—perhaps with the exception of speech communication courses. The all-too-common practice of using language proficiency tests for composition placement (Crusan 20) is a clear indication that the policy of linguistic containment is at work. Even when direct assessment of writing is used for placement, the use of holistic scoring may lead raters to give disproportionate weight to language differences because "a text is so internally complex (e.g., highly developed but fraught with grammatical errors) that it requires more than a single number to capture its strengths and weaknesses" (Hamp-Lyons 760). Based on the placement test results, many students are placed in non-credit "remedial" courses where they are expected to erase the traces of their language differences before they are allowed to enroll in the required composition course. In other cases, students are placed—sometimes after their initial placement in mainstream composition courses—in a separate track of composition courses for non-native English speakers that can satisfy the composition requirement. These courses, though sometimes costly to students, provide useful language support for students and are necessary for many who will be entering the composition course as well as courses in other disciplines where the myth of linguistic homogeneity prevails. At the same time, these placement practices also reify the myth by making it seem as if language differences can be effectively removed from mainstream composition courses.

In the remainder of this chapter, I examine the emergence of the myth of linguistic homogeneity and the concomitant policy of linguistic containment in the late nineteenth and early twentieth centuries—the formative years of U.S. college composition. U.S. higher education during this period is marked by several influxes of international students, many of whom came from countries where English was not the dominant language. Each of these influxes was met not by attempts to reform composition pedagogy but by efforts to contain language differences—efforts that continue even today. I focus on developments before the 1960s because it was the period when a number of significant changes took place. Although English had long been part of U.S. higher education, the English language began to take center stage in the late nineteenth century through the use of English composition as part of the college entrance exam (Brereton 9) and through the creation of the English composition course that tacitly endorsed the policy of unidirectional monolingualism (Horner and Trimbur 596–97). It was also during this period that language differences in the composition classroom became an issue because of the presence of a growing number of international students, and many of the placement options for second language writers were created (Matsuda and Silva; Silva). My focus is on international students because, until the latter half of the twentieth century, resident students from underprivileged language backgrounds were systematically excluded from higher education altogether (Matsuda, "Basic" 69–72).

Waves of International Students and the Policy of Containment

The image of U.S. college students as native speakers of more or less similar, privileged varieties of English had already been firmly established by the mid-nineteenth century. Although the larger U.S. society had always been multilingual (Bayley 269), language differences were generally excluded from English-dominated higher education of the nineteenth century. The assumption of the native-English-speaker norm was, at least on the surface, more or less accurate in the mid-nineteenth century, when access to college education was restricted to students from certain ethnic, gender, religious, socioeconomic, and linguistic backgrounds. As David Russell notes, U.S. colleges before the end of the Civil War were "by modern standards extraordinarily homogeneous, guaranteeing a linguistic common ground" (35). While U.S. higher education began to shift from exclusive, elitist establishment to a more inclusive vehicle for mass education during the latter half of the nineteenth century, the traditional image of college students remained unchallenged for the most part. Although the creation of what have come to be known as Historically Black Universities and Colleges provided African American students access to higher education since the early nineteenth century, they did not affect the dominant image because they were physically segregated from the rest of the college student population. In fact, those colleges served as sites of containment—ethnic as well as linguistic. The Morrill Act, first passed in 1862 and then extended in 1890, gave rise to land-grant institutions across the nation that made college education open to women as well as students from a wider variety of socioeconomic groups. Yet, non-native speakers of privileged varieties of English did not enter higher education in large numbers because the ability to speak privileged varieties of English was often equated with the speaker's race and intelligence.

One of the major institutional initiatives that contributed to the exclusion of language differences was the creation of the entrance exam—first instituted at Harvard in 1874 and then quickly and widely adopted by other institutions. The entrance exam at Harvard was motivated in part by "a growing awareness of the importance of linguistic class distinctions in the United States" (Connors, *Composition* 128). Harvard course catalogs during this period indicate that the entrance exam included "reading English aloud" or writing with "correct spelling, punctuation, grammar, and expression" (quoted in Brereton 34). Miller also points out that "forms of this examination became the most powerful instrument for discriminating among students in higher education" (63), effectively excluding students who did not fit the dominant linguistic profile. Even in the nineteenth century, however, the assumption of linguistic homogeneity in higher education was not entirely accurate, and it moved farther and farther away from the sociolinguistic reality of U.S. higher education. One group of students who brought significant language differences was made up of international students who entered U.S. higher education through different admission processes; they therefore were not subject to linguistic filtering (Matsuda, "Basic" 71–72).

The history of international ESL students in U.S. higher education goes at least as far back as 1784, when Yale hosted a student from Latin America; in the mid-1800s, students from China and Japan also attended Yale and Amherst College (King 11). The first influx of international students came in the latter half of the nineteenth century, when U.S. higher education began to attract an increasing number of students from other countries as it developed research universities modeled after German institutions. Most of these international students were from Asian countries that were "undergoing modernization with the help of knowledge acquired from Western countries" (Bennett, Passin, and McKnight 26). During the late nineteenth century, European students also came to U.S. higher education "not so much seeking an education that was not available to them at home, as out of a desire to see America, the 'country of the future'" (Institute of International Education, *Handbook* [1955] 6).

In the late nineteenth century, when many of the international students were sponsored by their governments, language preparation was generally considered to be the responsibility of individual students or their sponsoring governments, and U.S. colleges and universities usually provided little or no institutional support for international students' cultural and linguistic adjustments. For instance, students from China and Japan, most of whom were sponsored by their respective governments, usually received language instruction before coming to the United States. In many cases, however, their language preparation was less than adequate by the standard of U.S. institutions, and they were sent to preparatory schools, where they were "placed in classes with the youngest children" (Schwantes 194). The Japanese government continued to send students to U.S. colleges; however, they were selected by a rigid examination, and their progress was monitored by a supervisor sent by the Japanese government (Institute of International Education, *Handbook* [1955] 4). By the 1880s, the practice of holding the sponsoring government responsible for providing language preparation became difficult to sustain as the number of government-sponsored students declined, giving way to an increasing number of privately funded students (Bennett, Passin, and McKnight 32).

The second influx came in the early part of the twentieth century, when internationally known research institutions began to attract a growing number of international students, most from countries where English was not the dominant language. Although there were only 3,645 international students in U.S. higher education in 1911, the number began to grow rapidly after the conclusion of World War I (1914–18). This change was due partly to European students' dissatisfaction "with their own traditions of education" as well as Asian students' need for "new foundations for modern systems of education" (Kandel 39). Another factor that contributed to the growth was the national interest of the United States. The U.S. government's growing concern with post–World War I international relations—especially with European nations—prompted the establishment in 1919 of the Institute of International Education (IIE) with support from the Carnegie Endowment for International Peace. The IIE was successful in "stimulat[ing] interest in student exchange, encouraging public and private groups to sponsor international students" (Institute of International Education, *Handbook* [1955] 7). By 1920, the number of international students had reached 6,163 and was continuing to increase (Institute of International Education, *Handbook* [1961] 230). In 1930, U.S. colleges and universities reported the presence of 9,961 international students (Darian 105).

The growing presence of international students from non-English-dominant countries became an issue among hosting institutions. Some educators recognized the problem of the traditional pedagogy based on the dominant image of students. Isaac Leon Kandel, for example, wrote that international students did not benefit as much from the instruction, not because of their lack of ability but because "courses were organized primarily with the American student, familiar with American ideals, aims, history, and social and political background, in mind" (50). The solution, however, was not to challenge the dominant image but to contain issues of linguistic and cultural differences by providing additional instruction—an approach that might have seemed reasonable when the number of international students was relatively small. To provide linguistic support for those who did not fit the traditional image of college students, institutions began to develop special English language courses. According to a 1923 survey of four hundred institutions, all but two stated that they had "provision for special language help by official courses or by voluntary conversation classes" (Parson 155). Although it continued to be "a common rule to refuse admission to students who are unable to speak and read English," about 50 percent of institutions offered "special courses for backward students" (155).

In 1911, Joseph Raleigh Nelson in the Engineering College at the University of Michigan created the first English courses specifically designed for international students (Klinger 1845–47), followed by Teachers College of Columbia University, which created special courses for matriculated international students in 1923 (Kandel 54). Harvard University created its first English courses for international students in 1927, and George Washington University and Cornell University followed suit in 1931 (Allen 307; Darian 77). While there were some exceptions—such as the program at Michigan, which continued for several decades—many of these early programs were ad hoc in nature. The initial innovation at Harvard ceased to exist after a while, and by the 1940s, second language writers at Harvard had come to be mainstreamed into "regular" sections of composition courses with additional help from individual tutoring services (Gibian 157). At George Washington, the separate section of composition used "the same materials as the sections for Americans and . . . was conducted by the same teacher"; however, "none of the English instructors really desired to teach that group," and this program was later found to be unsuccessful (Rogers 394). The courses at Columbia, which allowed students to enroll simultaneously in college-level courses, were also found to be ineffective in containing language differences (Kandel 54). Other institutions, especially where the number of international students was relatively small, dealt with language differences "by a process of scattering foreigners through different courses, so that they must mingle freely with others, rather than segregating them for group study in classes where they may persist in using their own language" (Parson 155).

Following the announcement of the Good Neighbor Policy in 1933, the State Department began to bring international students from Latin America to provide scientific and technical training. This development led to the creation, in 1941, of the English Language Institute (ELI) at the University of Michigan. As an intensive program, it separated students from the college-level courses for a period of several months while students focused on developing their English language proficiency. Although the program was initially intended for Spanish-speaking graduate students from Latin America, it later broadened its scope to include undergraduate students and students from other language backgrounds. The Michigan ELI provided a model for intensive English programs throughout the United States and in many other countries, paving the way for the next wave of ESL courses that were created in response to the post–World War II influx of international students (Matsuda, "Composition" 701–6).

Although the number of international students declined somewhat during the Depression and World War II, the conclusion of the war brought another influx of international students. The international student population surged from less than 8,000 in 1945 to 10,341 in 1946 (Darian 105), when the United States replaced Germany as the most popular destination for international students. The number doubled in the next two years, and by 1949, there were 26,759 international students (Institute of International Education, *Open Doors* 7, 14). To contain the language differences these students brought with them, an increasing number of institutions—including those that had relatively small but steady enrollments of international students—began to create separate English courses and programs on a permanent basis (Schueler 309). In 1949, Harvard once again created a special non-credit course for small groups of students from Europe, providing a preparation for the required composition course (Gibian 157). At about the same time, Queens College developed a multilevel intensive English language program with its own teaching and testing materials (Schueler 312–14). Tulane University also created a non-credit English course for second language writers. Sumner Ives reported that all non-native English speakers at Tulane, unless "individually excused," were required to enroll in a special English course for non-native speakers before taking the required English course. This program was unique in that the status of the course was determined after the beginning of the semester. Based on a reading test during the orientation, the teacher would decide whether each student should move to a "regular section" or remain in the remedial course. When most of the remaining students had limited English proficiency, the course was taught as a remedial English language course, using the materials developed by the ELI at Michigan. The course became credit-bearing when a large number of students had reached advanced English proficiency and the textbooks for regular sections of composition courses were used (Ives 142–43).

The number of ESL writing courses continued to grow. In 1953, according to Harold B. Allen, about 150 institutions reported the existence of ESL programs for international students; by 1969, the number had nearly doubled. In addition, 114 institutions reported that they offered summer programs for international students (308). Initially, many of those courses were offered on a non-credit basis as preparation for a regular English requirement. These courses focused not only on writing but also on reading and oral communication skills. Non-credit English courses for non-native speakers offered at many institutions adopted the textbook series developed by the ELI at Michigan. Intensive language courses modeled after the Michigan ELI also became widespread, providing systematic instruction before second language writers were allowed to enroll in regular college-level courses.

Yet, a semester or two of extra language instruction was often not enough to help students fit the dominant image of students—after all, learning a second language is a time-consuming process, especially for adult learners—and they continued to bring language differences to college composition courses. For this reason, institutions began to develop a separate track of required composition courses for second language writers—courses that were designed to keep language differences out of the required composition course. In 1954, Michigan's Department of English Language and Literature in the College of Literature, Science and Art created one of the first credit-bearing ESL composition courses that paralleled the sections of English courses for native speakers of English (Klinger 1849). University of Washington followed suit with a three-credit composition course for second language writers, which emphasized purposeful cross-cultural communication with an audience rather than the language drills or linguistic analyses commonly used in intensive language programs at the time (Marquardt 31).

Embracing Language Differences as the New Norm

The assumption of linguistic homogeneity, which was more or less accurate in U.S. higher education institutions of the mid-nineteenth century, became increasingly inaccurate as linguistic diversity grew over the last two centuries. Yet, the growing presence of international students did not lead to a fundamental reconsideration of the dominant image of students in the composition classroom. It was not because the separate placement practices were able to eliminate language differences. For a number of reasons, none of these programs was able to contain language differences completely: because language learning is a time-consuming process, because students often come with a wide range of English language proficiency levels, and because developing placement procedures that can account for language differences is not an easy task. As Ives wrote, "Neither a frankly non-credit course for all, nor their [non-native English speaking students'] segregation into separate but parallel courses, nor their distribution throughout the regular courses is completely satisfactory" (142). Instead, the dominant image of students remained unchallenged because the policy of containment kept language differences in the composition classroom from reaching a critical mass, thus creating the false impression that all language differences could and should be addressed elsewhere. In other words, the policy of unidirectional monolingualism was enacted not so much through pedagogical practices in the mainstream composition course but through delegation of students to remedial or parallel courses that attempted to keep language differences from entering the composition course.

The policy of containment and the continuing dominance of the myth of linguistic homogeneity have serious implications not only for international second language writers but also for resident second language writers as well as for native speakers of unprivileged varieties of English. Many institutions place students into basic writing classes without distinguishing writing issues and language issues partly because underlying language differences are not easily discernible by observing student texts that seem, at least on the surface, strikingly similar to one another (Matsuda, "Basic" 74). As a result, basic writing courses often enroll many second language writers—both international and resident—although many basic writing courses, like the credit-bearing composition courses, are often designed for U.S. citizens who are native speakers of a variety of English (68).

By pointing out the problem of the policy of containment, however, I do not mean to suggest that these placement practices should be abandoned. On the contrary, many students do need and even prefer these placement options. As George Braine suggests, many—though certainly not all—second language writers prefer second-language sections of composition, where they feel more comfortable and where they are more likely to succeed. To deny these support programs would be to further marginalize non-native speakers of English in institutions of higher education where the myth of linguistic homogeneity will likely continue to inform the curriculum as well as many teachers' attitude toward language differences. Instead, composition teachers need to resist the popular conclusion that follows the policy of containment—that the college composition classroom can be a monolingual space. To work effectively with the student population in the twenty-first century, all composition teachers need to reimagine the composition classroom as the multilingual space that it is, where the presence of language differences is the default.

Works Cited

Allen, Harold B. "English as a Second Language." *Current Trends in Linguistics: Linguistics in North America.* Vol. 10. Ed. Thomas A. Sebeok. The Hague: Mouton, 1973. 295–320.

Bayley, Robert. "Linguistic Diversity and English Language Acquisition." *Language in the USA: Themes for the Twenty-First Century.* Ed. Edward Finegan and John R. Rickford. Cambridge, UK: Cambridge UP, 2004. 268–86.

Bennett, John W., Herbert Passin, and Robert K. McKnight. *In Search of Identity: The Japanese Overseas Scholar in America and Japan.* Minneapolis: U of Minnesota P, 1958.

Braine, George. "ESL Students in First-Year Writing Courses: ESL Versus Mainstream Classes." *Journal of Second Language Writing* 5.2 (1996): 91–107.

Brereton, John C. *The Origins of Composition Studies in the American College, 1875–1925: A Documentary History.* Pittsburgh: U of Pittsburgh P, 1995.

Connors, Robert J. *Composition-Rhetoric: Backgrounds, Theory, and Pedagogy.* Pittsburgh: U of Pittsburgh P, 1997.

———. "The Erasure of the Sentence." *College Composition and Communication* 52 (2000): 96–128.

Crusan, Deborah. "An Assessment of ESL Writing Placement Assessment." *Assessing Writing* 8 (2002): 17–30.

Dadak, Angela. "No ESL Allowed: A Case of One College Writing Program's Practices." Matsuda, Ortmeier-Hooper, and You.

Darian, Stephen G. *English as a Foreign Language: History, Development and Methods of Teaching.* Norman: U of Oklahoma P, 1972.

Gibian, George. "College English for Foreign Students." *College English* 13 (1951): 157–60.

Hamp-Lyons, Liz. "Rating Nonnative Writing: The Trouble with Holistic Scoring." *TESOL Quarterly* 29 (1995): 759–62.

Harklau, Linda, Meryl Siegal, and Kay M. Losey. "Linguistically Diverse Students and College Writing: What is Equitable and Appropriate?" *Generation 1.5 Meets College Composition: Issues in the Teaching of Writing to U.S.-Educated Learners of ESL.* Ed. Linda Harklau, Kay M. Losey, and Meryl Siegal. Mahwah, NJ: Erlbaum, 1999. 1–14.

Hartwell, Patrick. "Grammar, Grammars, and the Teaching of Grammar." *College English* 47 (1985): 105–27.

Horner, Bruce, and John Trimbur. "English Only and U.S. College Composition." *College Composition and Communication* 53 (2002): 594–630.

Institute of International Education. *Handbook on International Study: A Guide for Foreign Students and for U.S. Students on Study Abroad.* New York: Institute of International Education, 1955.

———. *Handbook on International Study: For Foreign Nationals.* New York: Institute of International Education, 1961.

———. *Open Doors: 1948–49*. New York: Institute of International Education, 1949.

———. *Open Doors 2004*. New York: Institute of International Education, 2005.

Ives, Sumner. "Help for the Foreign Student." *College Composition and Communication* 4 (1953): 141–44.

Kandel, Isaac Leon. *United States Activities in International Cultural Relations*. Washington, DC: American Council on Education, 1945.

King, Henry H. "Outline History of Student Migrations." *The Foreign Students in America*. Ed. W. Reginald Wheeler, Henry H. King, and Alexander B. Davidson. New York: Association Press, 1925. 3–38.

Klinger, Robert B. "The International Center." *The University of Michigan: An Encyclopedic Survey in Four Volumes*. Vol. 4. Ed. Walter A. Donnelly. Ann Arbor: U of Michigan P, 1958. 1843–49.

Kubota, Ryuko, and Kimberly Abels. "Improving Institutional ESL/EAP Support for International Students: Seeking the Promised Land." Matsuda, Ortmeier-Hooper, You.

Marquardt, William F. "Composition in English as a Second Language: Cross Cultural Communication." *College Composition and Communication* 17 (1966): 29–33.

Matsuda, Paul Kei. "Basic Writing and Second Language Writers: Toward an Inclusive Definition." *Journal of Basic Writing* 22.2 (2003): 67–89.

———. "Composition Studies and ESL Writing: A Disciplinary Division of Labor." *College Composition and Communication* 50 (1999): 699–721.

Matsuda, Paul Kei, Christina Ortmeier-Hooper, and Xiaoye You, eds. *Politics of Second Language Writing: In Search of the Promised Land*. West Lafayette, IN: Parlor Press, forthcoming.

Matsuda, Paul Kei, and Tony Silva. "Cross-Cultural Composition: Mediated Integration of U.S. and International Students." *Composition Studies* 27.1 (1999): 15–30.

Miller, Susan. *Textual Carnivals: The Politics of Composition*. Carbondale: Southern Illinois UP, 1991.

Norton, Bonnie, and Sue Starfield. "Covert Language Assessment in Academic Writing." *Language Testing* 14.3 (1997): 278–94.

Parson, A. B. "The Foreign Student and the American College." *The Foreign Students in America*. Ed. W. Reginald Wheeler, Henry H. King, and Alexander B. Davidson. New York: Association Press, 1925. 149–74.

Prendergast, Catherine. "Race: The Absent Presence in Composition Studies." *College Composition and Communication* 50 (1998): 36–53.

Rogers, Gretchen L. "Freshman English for Foreigners." *School and Society* 61 (1945): 394–96.

Russell, David. *Writing in the Academic Disciplines: A Curricular History*. 2nd ed. Carbondale: Southern Illinois UP, 2002.

Schueler, Herbert. "English for Foreign Students." *Journal of Higher Education* 20 (1949): 309–16.

Schwantes, Robert S. *Japanese and Americans: A Century of Cultural Relations.* New York: Harper and Brothers and the Council on Foreign Relations, 1955.

Shuck, Gail. "Combating Monolingualism: A Novice Administrator's Challenge." *WPA: Writing Program Administration* 30.1–2 (2006): 59–82.

Silva, Tony. "An Examination of Writing Program Administrators' Options for the Placement of ESL Students in First Year Writing Classes." *WPA: Writing Program Administration* 18.1–2 (1994): 37–43.

Smitherman, Geneva, and Victor Villanueva, eds. *Language Diversity in the Classroom: From Intention to Practice.* Carbondale: Southern Illinois UP, 2003.

Trimbur, John. "Peer Tutoring: A Contradiction in Terms?" *Writing Center Journal* 7.2 (1987): 21–28.

Valdés, Guadalupe. "Bilingual Minorities and Language Issues in Writing: Toward Professionwide Response to a New Challenge." *Written Communication* 9 (1992): 85–136.

5. "English Only," African American Contributions to Standardized Communication Structures, and the Potential for Social Transformation

Elaine Richardson

In examining "English Only" as it relates to the many language varieties in America, the model that surfaces is a center-periphery model. In this view, all official business of the U.S. government and courts, including proceedings and interactions (involving spoken and written language), will employ only English. The ideological force of English Only encourages public and private identities, wherein it does not matter if English is one's first, second, or third language; a certain hegemonic conception of what it means to be a thinking and acceptable American emerges. The standardized language ideologies underlying English Only run counter to the spirit of cultural, linguistic, and human diversity and reveal a preference for a certain type of "naturalization" of immigrants and an ideal type of assimilated African American and other "minority" American groups. It is in these ways that the ideologies of English Only relate to African American Language and African Americans. An important question that I would ask is: Can we afford not to abolish in its entirety the center-periphery model that has dominated education and the public sphere?

The English Only, center-periphery model's subordination and fracturing of the cultural identities of African Americans and other non-preferred groups and so-called language minorities and the model's push for the subordination or eradication of such people's language reveal the connection of the ideologies of English Only to the ideologies of colonialism (Macedo). Donaldo Macedo's quotation of Geralso Novas Davilla's definition of cultural colonialism is instructive:

> Culturally, colonialism has adopted a negation to the [native culture's] symbolic systems [including the native language], forgetting or undervaluing them even when they manifest themselves in action. This way, the eradication of [the] past and idealization and desire to relive the cultural heritage of colonial societies constitute a situation and a

97

> system of ideas along with other elements [that] situate the colonial
> society as a class. (16)

It is a fact that African Americans have had to fight to define ourselves against social identities that colonizers foisted onto us as subhuman jibberish-speaking slaves in need of domestication and civilization. In contemporary times, such blatantly racist views are shunned by most Americans; however, the colonial legacy is yet present, where we are constantly exposed to watered-down or "de-politicized" versions of Black history and Black educational and cultural aspirations. Towering intellects and educators such as Carter G. Woodson argued in the 1920s and 1930s that Black people were being trained to fit into the status quo and to comply in their own oppression. He called this miseducation—a form of training or socialization designed for the uplift of the dominant society, which inadvertently works to the demise of the oppressed people in the society. We can see the vehement opposition of the dominant society to the idea of African American Language or Ebonics as a method to enhance Black people's literacy education as one example of the subordination of Black people's language. Most any type of education or social exchange (barring commodified pop culture) that centers Black people in their own history and experience is regarded as un-American, separatist, or backward.

The ideas of naturalization and unity that underlie the English Language Unity Act of 2005 (also known as HR 997) seem to oppose the very diversity that is natural to humanity. The act reads as follows:

> A Bill to declare English as the official language of the United States,
> to establish a uniform English language rule for naturalization, and to
> avoid misconstructions of the English language texts of the laws of the
> United States, pursuant to Congress's powers to provide for the general
> welfare of the United States and to establish a uniform rule of natural-
> ization under article I, section 8, of the Constitution. (U.S. Congress)

One of the concerns taken into consideration with the proposal to change English from de facto to de jure status was practical application. Thus, the Congress declared that Official English applies to "all laws, public proceedings, regulations, publications, orders, actions, programs, and policies" but does not apply to

1. teaching of languages;
2. requirements under the Individuals with Disabilities Education Act;
3. actions, documents, or policies necessary for national security, international relations, trade, tourism, or commerce;
4. actions or documents that protect the public health and safety;

5. actions or documents that facilitate the activities of the Bureau of the Census in compiling any census of population;

6. actions that protect the rights of victims of crimes or criminal defendants; or

7. using terms of art or phrases from languages other than English. (U.S. Congress)

Congress had to acknowledge that its proposal to impose a standardized official version of English on its diverse public had important limitations. Points 1, 4, 6, and 7 are of special interest to the present argument. First, in order to teach what Congress refers to as "languages," forms other than English Only are needed. This very idea concedes that language is a socially constructed and contested phenomenon and therefore must be policed by those who want to keep a certain set of power arrangements in place. As Sinfree Makoni and Alastair Pennycook argue, "*languages, conceptions of languageness and the metalanguages* used to describe them are inventions. . . . [L]anguages were, in the most literal sense, invented, particularly as part of the Christian/colonial and nationalistic projects in different parts of the globe" (1; emphasis in original). Language is a medium of power and control. As such, teaching other languages has to align with our government's interests. And, so-called dialects of low-status speakers are not given serious consideration.

Point 4 gives the impression that the government or its representatives will make certain documents or communication events readily available in forms most accessible to its citizens to protect our public health and safety. From the government's perspective, it is not cost-effective to diversify forms, but it has to do so for matters of public health and safety. Education should be a public health and safety priority but is not viewed as such within this context. Point 6, regarding rights of victims and criminal defendants, raises a similar issue. Point 7 affirms the use of terms or phrases of other languages for art. This point illuminates our hypocritical American nature. We readily admit that cultural exchange and mixing is respectable in certain domains, but those domains are not seen as critically defining what we stand for as a nation, though we will claim that we are proud of our diverse heritage.

Ask any kid who has attended U.S. schools (public or private) if he or she knows of any African contributions to English. Who cares that some African terms (for example, tote, juke, gumbo, banjo, buckaroo, buckra, gorilla, okra, yam) have enriched American English (Turner)? And I won't even go into so-called popular culture items, where Black folks taught Americans how to be cool and hip and showed us all how to deal with life through the blues and identified America's obsession with bling. Although not all African Americans or Black Americans speak African American Language, Geneva

Smitherman estimates that at least 90 percent of African Americans use some forms of this language variety (*Talkin That Talk*). John Rickford and Russell Rickford observe that most African Americans speak differently than whites—or at least can when we want to. The ideologies underlying English Only trivialize Black American contributions to standardized American communication structures.

The contributions of all of America's languages to the country's development should be centralized and incorporated publicly into our national consciousness and education. In what follows, I give a brief overview of the Black contribution. In so doing, I hope to show why it is important to view people's language use as an important part of identity and knowledge-making that should not be taken lightly or marginalized by official policies.

Critical and multiple consciousnesses are built into the language acquisition process. When a group learns a language, its members make the new language fit, to the extent possible, the group's epistemological, ontological, and cosmological system. This is how we can say that there are uniquely Black versions of English, French, Dutch, and Portuguese, for example (Dalby), for which Robert Williams and associates coined "Ebonics." The concept and practice of Black discourse refers to the collective consciousness and expression of people of Black African descent. This consciousness reflects (unconscious and conscious) ancestral and everyday knowledge. In African American Language studies, Smitherman defines Black modes of discourse (call-response, signification, tonal semantics, and narrative sequencing) as a West African inheritance of African American Language speakers. Within the African American worldview, individuals are challenged to achieve balance and harmony with the universe while doing their own thing within the overall formulaic structure (Smitherman, *Talkin and Testifyin*). Broadly speaking, the diaspora of Black discourse(s) allows us to group a range of African, Neo-African, and Afro-American language varieties, expressive forms, and linguistic ideologies for comparative analysis of specific historical, political, sociocultural, and sociolinguistic features. Via slavery, colonization, neo-imperialism, migration, wars, global technological processes, and diasporic crossing, continental Africans and their descendants participate in the (dis)invention and global flow of Black discourse (Richardson, "(Dis) inventing Discourse").

Whether or not the Ebonic language has been brought closer to the language of its colonizer lexically and grammatically, the total systems of the language represent ways of being in the world. In *Talkin That Talk*, Smitherman demonstrates extensively that one must know not only words, how to pronounce them, or ritual stretches of discourse but also the cultural codes of a language to be considered proficient. What I want to emphasize here is that how one experiences the world is partly influenced by his or her language usage. The medium is at least partly the message. Language is not a neutral medium whereby a thought comes into my head, I open my mouth and make sounds that correspond to that thought, and I transmit them verbally to you. Language does not work like that. Language is structure and use. How people interpret words is based on vocal and gestural signs; the speech situation; the people present and their age, sex, and race; the familiarity between them; the history between them; everyday experience; background; the tone; the rhythm; the body—all of these are used systematically by human beings and are governed by our culture, social practices, and conditions under which we are communicating. When we talk about the written word, culture, identity, history, worldview, and context remain key for both reader and writer.

Let me give an example from *The Narrative of the Life of Frederick Douglass, an American Slave, Written by Himself* to illuminate the differential of the English language for African Americans. Young Frederick Douglass had made a habit of reading the *Columbian Orator* at every opportunity. In it, he read Sheridan's speeches on Catholic emancipation. As a youth, Douglass writes, these speeches spoke to his condition of "slave for life." His reading caused him to ponder deeply how he could escape that condition:

> While in this state of mind, I was eager to hear any one speak of slavery. I was a ready listener. Every little while, I could hear something about the abolitionists. It was some time before I found what the word meant. . . . If a slave ran away and succeeded in getting clear, or if a slave killed his master, set fire to a barn, or did any thing very wrong in the mind of a slaveholder, it was spoken of as the fruit of abolition. Hearing the word in this connection very often, I set about learning what it meant. The dictionary afforded me little or no help. I found it was "the act of abolishing"; but then I did not know what was to be abolished. . . . I did not dare to ask any one of its meaning, for I was satisfied that it was something they wanted me to know very little about. (279–80)

Certainly, the standardized definition of "abolition" did not include killing masters and burning down barns. In the sense that the dictionary or other official language/text does not speak to the experience of the Black person, Douglass's example is a revision of what literary scholars call the talking book trope (see Gates). Douglass's example demonstrates that until English words, concepts, and even events are infused with lived experiences and ideas that can be applied personally, they are not a part of the Black lexicon. The famous rhetorical question that Douglass asks in his "Fourth of July Oration" makes this point plain: "What to the American slave, is your Fourth of July?" (quoted in Hill 26). The importance of worldview and experience is crucial in grasping the development of African American Language and literacy practices. The American African use of the English language is fitted to our particular rhetorical situations (Richardson, *African American Literacies*).

Black discourse and rhetoric helped to evolve and revolutionize the meaning of equality in this country. So, we learn English. We look at the standard definition of words, and we understand them as they fit our reality. This is our legacy. We look at the Constitution, the Bill of Rights, the laws, and we say, "Hold up—what you are saying and what you are doing don't match up." We critically assess the terms so that they reflect the vision of freedom and equality that we have for ourselves, or so that they reflect our lives, so that what we know and what we say match up, so to speak.

Scholars of African American education have long argued that approaches to the language and literacy education of African American students should be informed by African American epistemology. African American epistemology involves using the social, economic, cultural, political, contemporary, and historical background and artifacts of African Americans to stimulate learning in all of the interrelated domains of human experience, including feeling (affective), knowing (cognitive), and acting (conative). Repeat after me and say "African American epistemology." *Webster's New World College Dictionary* defines "epistemology" as "the study or theory of the nature, sources, and limits of knowledge." "Episteeme" comes from the Greek meaning "knowledge." "Epistanai" is to understand or believe, originally "to stand before, confront" (458). In applying African American epistemology to language and literacy education, our goal should be to teach the unfamiliar through the familiar. Further, we must focus on the application of knowledge to reality, as we ask: How is this knowledge best applied to advance self, Black people, and society?

W. E. B. DuBois wrote:

> Work, culture, and liberty—all these we need, not singly, but together; for to-day these ideals among the [African] people are gradually coalescing, and finding a higher meaning in the unifying ideal of race,—*the ideal of fostering the traits and talents of the [African], not in opposition to, but in conformity with, the greater ideals of the American republic, in order that some day, on American soil,* two world races may give each to each those characteristics which both so sadly lack. We the darker ones come even now not altogether empty-handed: there are to-day no truer exponents of the pure human spirit of the Declaration of Independence

than the American [Africans]; there is no true American music but the wild sweet melodies of the [Black] slave. (43; emphasis mine)

Here we can see that DuBois held up the musical culture of Black people as a talent, as a Black way of knowing, of organizing our experience, of managing work, spirituality, and developing intellect. DuBois thought that our white counterparts could learn a lot from Black musical culture. He saw music as the universal language that could benefit the world for the "unifying ideal of race." DuBois's concept of unity is radically different than that espoused in the English Language Unity Act of 2005. What DuBois called "the wild sweet melodies" are the total culture of African American people, our desire to be free, to live, to love, to dance, to sing, to build, to live in harmony with humanity and nature. Our vernacular represents the historical and current survival strategies including vernacular arts, African-centered thought, literature, music, art, religion, and counter-linguistic practices that Black people have used and continue to use to achieve our goals of making lives better.

Because race has been used to justify the oppression of Black people, DuBois holds that we must prove ourselves a world-class people by exploiting our talents—not racial talents but cultural talents developed in response to our environment and through the continual interaction with "work" and "liberty" or working for freedom. Out of our despair and creativity, Black people created a way to both express and value ourselves. African American Vernacular expression is created, in part, by resistance to oppression. This resistance is "an assertion of humanity. . . . Collectively [these acts express] a need for self-identification, for a reality apart from the one being forced upon [us]" by the dominant culture (Wideman 34). Indeed, our words and melodies have helped to change this nation. It would seem that Black ways with words should be at the center of American education. Many African American thinkers have found ways to value and exploit the vernacular in their theory and praxis.

In his book *The Miseducation of the Negro*, Woodson argued that Black students should be taught their own linguistic history, not at the expense of "standard" English but as a way of positioning oneself and understanding oneself in relation to it. Woodson stated:

In the study of language in school pupils were made to scoff at the Negro dialect as some peculiar possession of the Negro which they should despise rather than directed to study the background of this language as a broken-down African tongue—in short to understand their own linguistic history, which is certainly more important for them than the study of French Phonetics or Historical Spanish Grammar.

. . . . The education of any people should begin with the people themselves. (14, 22)

Woodson wrote this in 1933. He dedicated his life to teaching, restoring, and
preserving Black history, of which Black language is a large part. Yet, no one
can deny that most African American students can go from kindergarten
through twelfth grade and even graduate from an institution of higher learning and not have a coherent understanding of African American Vernacular,
if only from a historical perspective, not to mention cultural or linguistic.
Smitherman's chapter "African Americans and 'English Only'" in *Talkin That
Talk* showed that although more Blacks than whites were opposed to English
Only, much "more need[ed] to be done to educate the Black community and
to activate the Black moral consciousness about language pluralism" (302).
Her study was interested in Blacks as social change agents in United States
political life.

At various times throughout the African sojourn in America, there have
been peaks in our quest for self-knowledge, to understand ourselves in relation to the world. For example, during the Harlem Renaissance, the "New
Negro Movement" had as its objective a cultural revolution. The main goal
of it was to change the stereotype that American Africans had no social or
cultural life worthy of study or admiration by the mainstream.

> The Renaissance brought attention to the central role of culture and
> artistic expression in the depiction of the new Negro. Its literary and
> artistic themes drew upon the Negro dialect as a unique and rich mode
> for expressing feelings, beliefs, values, and ideas. And it placed the
> American Negro in relation to his African heritage. . . . By restoring the
> connection with the cultures of Africa, *the new Negro* could legitimately
> claim a place in the New World as an authentic representation of the
> American experience. (Guy 211)

Moving closer to contemporary times, Smitherman is an example of an
African American thinker who has argued that language learning may be
accelerated if teachers build on the vernacular strategies that the student
brings to the classroom. Her *Talkin and Testifyin: The Language of Black
America* describes many of the African and African American ways of dis-
playing knowledge and the philosophy and history behind them. For nearly
three decades, Smitherman has been talkin and testifyin to language educators around the world about the social legitimacy of all languages. Her own
scholarly discourse is a mixture of standard and African American surface
and deep structures, demonstrating the kind of critical literacy that theoreti-

cally, if not practically, academia espouses for its students. Smitherman's work made a way for a cadre of African American Language and literacy scholars (Kynard; Ball and Lardner; Campbell; Kinloch; Cooks; Holmes; Kirkland; Moss; Gilyard; and many others).

Janice E. Hale-Benson is also an example of a contemporary African American educational theorist who has offered an illuminating view. In writing about the learning styles of some Black students, Hale-Benson argues that many Black youth employ a people-oriented, relational- and field-dependent learning style rather than an analytical style. Her work points us toward bridging the gap between Black ways of knowing and academic articulation of that knowing. One way to do this is through connecting the relational, people-oriented style to the academic through the Black vernacular tradition. This viewpoint shows the narrow conception of English promoted by English Only proponents.

African American Vernacular practices such as freestylin can be seen to function heuristically. Freestylin—"unrehearsed, stream of consciousness rap" (Westbrook 50); "to do yo own thang, wear your own unique style of [whateva]" (Smitherman, *Talkin That Talk* 137)—points us in the right direction. However, a broader view of freestylin that attends to its nature and function is necessary to avoid the practice of promoting the surface level or commercial version as the deep structure of Black cultural productions. Such an investigation of freestylin would lead us to see it as intellectual, verbal, and social dexterity—a discourse practice from the Black vernacular tradition of resistance arts. From a sociolinguistic point of view, language must be evaluated in the context of use and only makes sense when studied in the context of social and cultural (historical, political, and economic) practices of which it is but part (Gee 3). Because language is situated within context, language use is linked to and framed by something broader, linked to discourse, linked to ways of being a certain type of person, coming out of a certain historical situation. Freestyle (a form of improvisation) is a central vernacular epistemic form that has been influenced by (at least) two crucial historical factors: (1) the demand from dominant whites that all manner of behavior and communication of African people display their compliance with domination and supposed inferiority, and (2) African people's resistance to this demand "through the use of existing African [communication] systems of indirectness" (Morgan 24). As Marcyliena Morgan explains, "Indirectness includes an analysis of discourses of power" (24). Within the phenomenology of indirectness operating both within white supremacist encounters and African American culture and social encounters and interactions, words or phrases could have contradictory or multiple meanings beyond traditional

English interpretations. In this sense, freestyle is part of the Afrodiasporic tradition of jackin English cultural forms. "Jackin" is a riff off of "hijacking." It refers to a situation of contiguous juxtaposition of complex signs, borrowing, revising, and turning them to purposes for which they were not originally envisioned. "Freestyle" as it relates to African Americans' use of English, digital technology, and other commodities involves flow, layering, and rupture. In her study of rap music and Black culture, Tricia Rose writes:

> What is the significance of flow, layering, and rupture as demonstrated on the body and in hip hop's lyrical, musical, and visual works? Interpreting these concepts theoretically, one can argue that they create and sustain rhythmic motion, continuity, and circularity via flow; accumulate, reinforce, and embellish this continuity through layering; and manage threats to these narratives by building in ruptures that highlight the continuity as it momentarily challenges it. These effects at the level of style and aesthetics suggest affirmative ways in which profound social dislocation and rupture can be managed and perhaps contested in the cultural arena. (39)

Hiphop's discourse practices emanate from Afrodiasporic vernacular resistance arts, cultural productions, discourses, and literacies. These qualities of flow, layering, and rupture are evident in African American Language use. The Hiphop generations have continued the legacy of widening and evolving the English language, and because of Hiphop's positioning in the global order, it has become a global lingua franca, taking Black language and resistance practices around the world. I have observed African American Language/Hiphop language incorporated into Japanese, German, Estonian, French, and Dutch (Richardson, *Hiphop Literacies*). Again, it is not only the incorporation of the vocabulary that interests me, though I find that fascinating; it is the adoption of Black style and ideology that is very important.

Halifu Osumare explains that "African American music, dance, and style, at the epicenter of American culture, are not only part of . . . technology-mediated global youth culture, but are absolutely essential to it." Not only is Hiphop tied to the "global supply-and-demand capitalist marketplace," it simultaneously offers semiotic opportunity to identify connective marginalities, explained as "social resonances between black expressive culture within its contextual political history and similar dynamics in other nations" (171–72). In these ways, Hiphop proliferates even in places that have comparatively small Black populations.

Germany offers a case in point. For some Hiphoppas, such as Turkish German rappers, Hiphop offers semiotic identification of "connective marginalities." Some scholars acknowledge the major influence of resistance strategies of Afrodiasporic aesthetics in "global Hiphop." For example, Ayhan Kaya discusses a Turkish rap group's semantic inversion of the term "Kan-Ak" (usually spelled "Kanak" or "Kanake") as a parallel to the African American Hiphop redefinition of "nigga." Kanak, now a widely used label for second-generation migrants (mostly but not only Turks) who resist the discriminative and assimilationist views of dominant German society, though originally a term of abuse toward foreigners, has been reappropriated and upgraded by migrants themselves—hence the parallel to "nigga."[1] Such youth employ African American Hiphop as a means of imagining themselves as a part of a transnational/global Hiphop nation. Yasemin Yildiz discusses this phenomenon as it is exemplified in the book *Kanak Sprak* by the Turkish German writer Zaimoglu, containing monologues of twenty-four Turkish German youth. Yildiz writes:

> The English words, "breaker," "posse," and "peace," stem from the vocabulary of African American rap culture and in the speech of this [German Hiphoppa] provide an identity, a community, and a vision, respectively. Beyond the referential meaning of the words, they offer a mode of orientation and of making sense of the world, of one's own position within it as well as a "code" of conduct. This orientation and sense-making activity draws on a social analysis implicit in the terms themselves. Because of these implicit meanings, German words could not take their place. (328)

From this vantage point, freestyle is a culturally, historically, and socially influenced discourse practice that should inform our thinking about language equality and the role of African American Language in social transformation.

Macedo asks a critical question with regard to African Americans and English Only: "[I]f English-Only education can guarantee linguistic minorities a better future, . . . why do the majority of Black Americans, whose ancestors have been speaking English for over two hundred years, find themselves still relegated to the ghettos?" (16). My answer to Macedo's question is because our ways of learning, knowing, and being and our culture and humanity are marginalized. To acknowledge our language and experience and centralize it would affirm the need to transform society. As Macedo argues, the colonial legacy undermines our democratic aspirations.

African Americans and other historically excluded groups have a history of struggling to expand the discourse to include their voices, experiences, and rights. This is a point that is often marginalized in education rather than the center of inquiry for students, especially for students of African

American heritage whose language has been disrespected and marginalized. Historically speaking, Black folks didn't get their rhetorical training through the classroom. Ever since Blacks have encountered whites, one of the main principles that governed Black/white discourse was power. Signifying and a host of language strategies were adapted and developed in order to protect and advance the self and by extension African American culture. Investigation of Black folk forms and African American ways of knowing and being are ways to get at the principles underlying successful Black communication strategies. However, vernacular resistance arts and other African American epistemes are not often studied in this way. For the most part, African American students receive an incoherent understanding of their language and literacy traditions.

Henry L. Evans's discussion of the Afrocentric Multicultural Writing Project is very instructive on this matter. He writes:

> United States elementary, secondary, and higher education is essentially fashioned so that European Americans receive an education [that ensures the survival of their culture] and all other United States cultural groups do not. The frame of reference and the content of United States education are designed to promote knowledge and understanding of the European American by the European American. Other United States cultural groups are trained to support the European American cultural effort. . . . Inclusion theory . . . marginalizes students when conceptualizations and curriculum do not offer concrete means for centering the student in his or her culture or means to an enabling and emancipating situated self. For example, any paradigmatic shift by theorists of curriculum transformation that moves beyond contribution approaches or add-ons but does not provide students with access to the classical origins of their cultures and with a systematic understanding of their culture's developments becomes truncated, privileging the students' extant access to European American classical cultures and these cultures' systematic development. (273–74)

According to George G. M. James, Cheikh A. Diop, and Chancellor Williams, Greek philosophy, which dominates the intellectual landscape in classical rhetorical studies, began around 640 B.C.E. with the Persian conquests. In traditional accounts of rhetorical studies, there is only one "classical rhetoric" that is ever mentioned, and it refers to the Greek and Roman traditions. But if the genealogy of classical rhetoric begins in 640 B.C.E. and human civilization began on the continent of Africa in 4500 B.C.E., almost four thousand years of rhetorical innovations have gone largely unexplored by present-day rhetorical scholars. To add to this, African Americans' modern classical origins are rooted in African American Vernacular rhetoric, partially developed on American soil for purposes of survival.

In 1969, Smitherman suggested that teachers implement programs that expand on the Black student's existing linguistic abilities ("Comparison"). In general, proponents of bilingual education oppose English Only. They do so because they want to ensure that people who have not yet learned English will have proper instruction and an opportunity to learn English. But in order for education to move us forward in terms of democracy, we must embrace a multilingual and multicultural education and social future. African American scholars and thinkers have contributed much to the academy's understanding of language and rhetoric—W. E. B. DuBois, Carter Woodson, Frederick Douglass, Ida Wells, Lorenzo Dow Turner (the first African American linguist), and many others, including Arnetha Ball, Joycelyn Moody, Beverly Moss, Jacqueline Jones Royster, Shirley Wilson Logan, Keith Gilyard, Teresa Redd, Gwendolyn Pough, Denise Troutman, Margaret Lee, and Cornel West. According to Gilyard, "any educational course of action taken by African Americans, for African Americans, aimed toward the achievement of first-class citizenship, could not help but involve contemplation of the lessons of [the] courageous rhetoric [of Douglass, Walker, and Wells] and their amazing examples of language and literacy" (628).

Ideologies undergirding English Only continue the legacy of colonialism in that they devalue other languages and language varieties and by extension their speakers. Such ideologies promote a narrow conception of language, upholding a view of language that denies its role in power and domination. By relegating the role of Black language to pop culture, its identity as a language of critical resistance is subverted. By denying its usefulness and intellectual potential in schooling and official institutions, Black language continues to be marginalized and degraded in the mainstream. The fact of the matter is that we will have to discard the center-periphery model and our Band-Aid approaches to education and democracy if we are serious about equality.

Note

1. I am indebted to Jannis Androutsopolous for his knowledge of this topic and for turning me on to Yildiz's "Critically 'Kanak': A Reimagination of German Culture."

Works Cited

Ball, Arnetha, and Ted Lardner. *African American Literacies Unleashed: Vernacular English and the Composition Classroom*. Carbondale: Southern Illinois UP, 2005.

Campbell, Kermit. *Gettin' Our Groove On: Rhetoric, Language, and Literacy for the Hip Hop Generation.* Detroit, MI: Wayne State UP, 2005.

Cooks, Jamal. "Writing for Something: Essays, Raps, and Writing Preferences." *English Journal* 94.1 (2004): 72–76.

Dalby, David. *Black Through White: Patterns of Communication.* Bloomington: Indiana UP, 1970.

Diop, Cheikh A. *The African Origin of Civilization: Myth or Reality?* Trans. Mercer Cook. New York: Lawrence Hill, 1974.

Douglass, Frederick. *Narrative of the Life of Frederick Douglass, an American Slave, Written by Himself.* 1845. *The Classic Slave Narratives: The Life of Olaudah Equiano/The History of Mary Prince/The Narrative of Frederick Douglass.* Ed. Henry L. Gates. New York: Penguin, 1987. 243–331.

DuBois, W. E. B. "Of Our Spiritual Strivings." *The Souls of Black Folk.* 1903. Ed. David Blight and Robert Gooding-Williams. Boston: Bedford Books, 1997. 37–44.

Evans, Henry L. "An Afrocentric Multicultural Writing Project." *Writing in Multicultural Settings.* Ed. Carol Severino et al. New York: MLA, 1997. 273–86.

Gates, Henry Louis, Jr. *The Signifying Monkey: A Theory of Afro-American Literary Criticism.* New York: Oxford UP, 1988.

Gee, James P. *An Introduction to Discourse Analysis: Theory and Method.* New York: Routledge, 1999.

Gilyard, Keith. "African American Contributions to Composition Studies." *College Composition and Communication* 50 (1999): 626–44.

Guy, Talmadge C. "Alain Locke and the AAAE Movement: Cultural Pluralism and Negro Adult Education." *Adult Education Quarterly* 46 (1996): 209–23.

Hale-Benson, Janice E. *Black Children, Their Roots, Culture, and Learning Styles.* Provo, UT: Brigham Young UP, 1982.

Hill, Roy L. *The Rhetoric of Racial Revolt.* Denver: Golden Bell, 1964.

Holmes, David. *Revisiting Racialized Voice: African American Ethos in Language and Literature.* Carbondale: Southern Illinois UP, 2004.

James, George G. M. *Stolen Legacy: Greek Philosophy Is Stolen Egyptian Philosophy.* 1952. Trenton: African World, 1992.

Kaya, Ayhan. "Aesthetics of Diaspora: Contemporary Minstrels in Turkish Berlin." *Journal of Ethnic and Migration Studies* 28 (2002): 43–62.

Kinloch, Valerie. "Revisiting the Promise of 'Students' Right to Their Own Language': Pedagogical Strategies." *College Composition and Communication* 57 (2005): 83–113.

Kirkland, David. "Rewriting School: Critical Writing Pedagogies for the Secondary English Classroom." *Journal of Teaching Writing* 21.1–2 (2004): 83–96.

Kynard, Carmen. "'I Want to Be African': In Search of a Black Radical Tradition/African-American Vernacularized Paradigm for 'Students' Right to Their Own

Language,' Critical Literacy and 'Class Politics.'" *College English* 69 (2007): 360–90.

Macedo, Donaldo. "The Colonialism of the English-Only Movement." *Educational Researcher* 29.3 (2000): 15–24.

Makoni, Sinfree, and Alastair Pennycook. "Disinventing and Reconstituting Languages." Makoni and Pennycook, *Disinventing* 1–41.

———, eds. *Disinventing and Reconstituting Languages*. Clevedon: Multilingual Matters, 2007.

Morgan, Marcyliena H. *Language, Discourse and Power in African American Culture*. Cambridge: Cambridge UP, 2002.

Moss, Beverly J. *A Community Text Arises: A Literate Text and a Literacy Tradition in African-American Churches*. Cresskill, NJ: Hampton, 2003.

Osumare, Halifu. "Beat Streets in the Global Hood: Connective Marginalities of the Hip Hop Globe." *Journal of American and Comparative Cultures* 24 (2001): 171–81.

Richardson, Elaine. *African American Literacies*. New York: Routledge, 2003.

———. "(Dis)inventing Discourse: Examples from Black Culture and Hiphop Rap/Discourse." Makoni and Pennycook 196–215.

———. *Hiphop Literacies*. New York: Routledge, 2006.

Rickford, John, and Russell Rickford. *Spoken Soul: The Story of Black English*. New York: Wiley, 2000.

Rose, Tricia. *Black Noise: Rap Music and Black Culture in Contemporary America*. Hanover, NH: UP of New England, 1994.

Smitherman, Geneva. "A Comparison of the Oral and Written Styles of a Group of Inner-City Black Students." Diss. U of Michigan, 1969.

———. *Talkin and Testifyin: The Language of Black America*. Boston: Houghton Mifflin, 1977.

———. *Talkin That Talk: Language, Culture, and Education in African America*. New York: Routledge, 2000.

Turner, Lorenzo D. *Africanisms in the Gullah Dialect*. Chicago: U of Chicago P, 1949.

U.S. Congress. House. *The Official English Resolution or English Language Unity Act of 2005*. HR 997. Library of Congress. 17 Nov. 2007 <http://thomas.loc.gov/cgi-bin/query/z?c109:H.R.997>.

Webster's New World College Dictionary. 3rd ed. Ed. Victoria Neufeldt and David Guralnik. New York: Macmillan, 1997.

Westbrook, Alonzo. *Hip Hoptionary: The Dictionary of Hip Hop Terminology*. New York: Harlem Moon, 2002.

Wideman, John. "Frame and Dialect: The Evolution of the Black Voice in American Literature." *American Poetry Review* 5.5 (1976): 34–37.

Williams, Chancellor. *The Destruction of Black Civilization: Great Issues of a Race from 4500 B.C. to 2000 A.D.* Chicago: Third World Press, 1987.

Williams, Robert, ed. *Ebonics: The True Language of Black Folks.* St. Louis: Institute of Black Studies, 1975.

Woodson, Carter G. *The Miseducation of the Negro.* 1933. Trenton: Africa World Press, 1990.

Yildiz, Yasemin. "Critically 'Kanak': A Reimagination of German Culture." *Globalization and the Future of German.* Ed. Andreas Gardt and Bernd Hüppauf. Berlin: Mouton de Gruyter, 2004. 319–40.

6. Spanglish as Alternative Discourse: Working against Language Demarcation

Kate Mangelsdorf

The practice of segregating students in writing classes according to their language, which Paul Kei Matsuda has called "linguistic containment" (this volume), is based on the assumption that a clear line of demarcation can be drawn between the languages that people speak. This assumption is expressed in labels such as "first language," "second language," "native speaker," "non-native speaker," and so on. These binaries fail to describe the complexity of language use and also serve the ideological function of marking students according to their language practices. While this policy of linguistic containment might have had some benevolent results (such as supplying students with additional language study), it has also reified commonsense views of written language, such as the idea that language can be "right" or "wrong"—in other words, that there is such a thing as a standard, correct language. This belief has been described by James Milroy as "when there are two or more variants of some word or construction, only one of them can be right" (535). Because the belief in a standard written language is so widespread, writing professionals generally feel obliged to go along with this notion because of the assumption that so-called standard language can help students succeed in the mainstream culture. But by not challenging the notion of a standard language, we are passing along a naïve and even damaging view of language to our students.

The language policies of higher education are affecting more students in U.S. colleges and universities than ever before. The number of international students in higher education, which decreased after 9/11, is beginning to grow again so that in 2007, there were approximately 582,984 international students in higher education institutions in the United States (Chow and Marcus). These international students speak a variety of world Englishes, depending on their cultural and linguistic backgrounds. Thousands of other students—the so-called resident U.S. students or "Generation 1.5" students, who immigrated to the United States as children, as well as students born in the United States but who speak a language other than English—also take writing courses in college. According to the 2000 census data, 47 million Americans speak a language other than English at home (Crawford). As a result, many students with a variety of complex, creative, and constantly changing literacies enter higher education. For instance, many Generation 1.5 students have assimilated into the American popular culture and self-identify as native speakers. While their writing can contain grammatical markers commonly associated with so-called English as a Second Language students, English is not a second or foreign language to them—they have spoken English for many years. But they are not monolingual English speakers, either. When they are placed into writing courses, they are likely to be seen as deficient because they are evaluated according to an English language norm consisting of an idealized standard language used by "native" speakers that is demarcated from other languages.

Since students who enter writing classrooms don't simply leave their literacies at the door—they aren't empty vessels, in other words—classrooms are sites of what Gail E. Hawisher and Cynthia L. Selfe, among others, have described as the "cultural ecology of literacy," which is where there is "contestation between emerging, competing, changing, accumulating, and fading languages and literate exchanges" (this volume). Languages such as African American Vernacular English (AAVE) and Ebonics have been defended ever since the Conference on College Composition and Communication "Students' Right to their Own Language" statement in 1974, though there has been limited success in acknowledging, much less promoting, these languages in writing classrooms. Spanglish is another example of a so-called nonstandard language that many students speak (in fact, given current demographics, millions of people in the United States speak it), but it has been understudied in rhetoric and composition. In this chapter, I focus on Spanglish in order to demonstrate the effects on students of linguistic containment and standard language ideology. I also suggest how writing instructors, despite the best of intentions, play a role in promulgating a standard language ideology and discuss the challenges of changing that role.

Spanglish is part of what Ofelia García and Kate Menken refer to as the "dynamic plurilingual context" that many Latinos in the United States inhabit that goes beyond Spanish or English (173). My description of Spanglish that follows comes with a caveat: Spanglish is a living language that varies according to region. In the United States, different varieties of Spanglish are used in Puerto Rico, south Florida, Colorado, California, south Texas, Michigan, New York, Arizona, and New Mexico—wherever Spanish-speaking and English-speaking cultures interact. My reference point for Spanglish is El Paso, Texas, along the U.S.-Mexico border, one of the earliest sites of Mexican-influenced Spanglish in the United States.

Other varieties of Spanglish exist in Latin America wherever English and Spanish appear, especially in border areas such as northern Mexico. These regional differences are the result of the varieties of Spanish and English that are combined to form Spanglish (just as there are Englishes, there are Spanishes). Other terms for Spanglish include Tex-Mex, Chicano English, Chicano Spanish, Cubonics, Espanglés, Englanol, and Angliparla. *Pocho, pachuco,* and *caló* were originally derogatory terms for Spanglish; *pocho* has referred to Chicanos who have lost their connection to Mexico and who cannot speak so-called Standard Spanish, while *pachuco* and *caló* have at times referred to gang lifestyle and language. Each of these names for Spanglish reflects nuances of language, culture, and identity. For instance, in *Borderlands/La Frontera,* Gloria Anzaldúa wrote of the way that her identities shifted according to her languages, which she listed as Standard Spanish, Standard Mexican Spanish, Standard English, working-class English, Chicano Texas Spanish, regional variations of Chicano Spanish, north Mexican dialects, Tex-Mex, *pachuco,* and *caló* (55–58). Anzaldúa employs these multiple languages in what Damián Baca has called a "textual choreography" (132) as she works toward a mestiza consciousness that resists linguistic, cultural, and gendered borders.

There is disagreement among linguists about the status of Spanglish—is it a dialect, a variety, or an emerging language? The distinction between a language and a dialect is political; the aphorism "a language is a dialect with an army and navy" alludes to the connection between language demarcation and nation building. In particular, the assumption that languages were fixed entities connected to particular ethnic and cultural groups was a key tenet of colonialism (Pennycook 3). Accordingly, rather than use the terms "languages" and "dialects," Robert Phillipson uses "dominant" languages and "dominated" languages (39). Nonetheless, the language/dialect debate has been examined in linguistic terms. Peter Sayer notes that in some communities, "Spanglish is becoming more stabilized and 'grammaticized,'" characteristic of a language (99). Alfredo Ardila asserts that because of the regional variations of Spanglish, it lacks the unified lexicon and grammar of a language (63). Other scholars (Villa; Figueroa) consider Spanglish a variety of U.S. Spanish, with U.S. Spanish being one of many world Spanishes. In contrast, I refer to Spanglish as a language in the sense that Anzaldúa referred to it as a language—as "un lenguaje que corresponde a un modo de vivir" (55), a language in harmony with a way of living.

Spanglish has mistakenly been called a "linguistic mishmash," as Ana Celia Zentella has noted ("Introduction" 4), when in actuality it is a complex language that allows its speakers to strategically interact with their worlds. In Jaime Mejía's words, "rhetorical situations and strategies often include a tactical mixture of both English and Spanish" (52). Ardila differentiates between surface characteristics of Spanglish (such as word borrowings or code-switching) and "deep phenomena" at the lexical and grammatical level (68). Borrowings include English nouns that do not exist in Spanish, such as "laptop," as in "Mañana compraré un laptop" (Tomorrow I will buy a laptop), or English words that are simpler to say than their Spanish counterparts, such as *carro* instead of *automóvil*. Code-switching occurs when two languages are used within the same sentence, with one code as the base language (Sayer). In "para tener a good job necesito moviar a Nuevo York," Spanish is the base language. Spanglish contains alterations in the English word to accommodate Spanish spelling and/or pronunciation, as in *el cheque* (business check), *yarda* (yard), or *parkear* (to park). Spanish words take on English meaning; in Spanish, *carta* is a letter, while in Spanglish, *carta* is a supermarket cart (Stavans 91). The number and gender of a Spanish word is Anglicized, as in *la data* (data) in Spanglish instead of *los datos* in Spanish. Ardila also notes a process that he calls "equalization to English," when Spanish grammar becomes closer to English, as when verb tenses that exist in Spanish but not in English are not used in Spanglish (75–76). Conversely, Spanish syntax can replace English syntax, as in "the mother of her father" instead of "her father's mother." Rather than being random, the syntactic choices of Spanglish speakers are constrained by "intuitions . . . about how their two languages can and cannot be combined" (Sayer 98). Depending on their level of fluency, their sociocultural context, and their identity positions, Spanglish speakers can use mostly English with some Spanish influences, or mostly Spanish with some English influences. For example, the Spanish speakers in "Angelstown," the Mexican American community studied by Ralph Cintrón, used *pochismos*, or words in English, mostly when discussing their interactions with city officials (246). In contrast, for some speakers, Spanglish is not tilted toward either Spanish or English: it is truly an in-between language that represents their own cultural and linguistic in-between-ness. For many second-generation Latinos, Spanglish is the first language they learn (Zentella, "Afterward" 177).

The increasing use of Spanglish in the United States is an inevitable result of what happens when groups of people speaking different languages interact, most often due to conquest and colonization. English, for instance, developed as a result of the successive conquest of Britain by Germanic tribes and the Normans. However, in modern Western societies, language change has been resisted because it challenges standard language ideology, or the belief that language can be made uniform for the benefit of society. "Standard" language is a social rather than a linguistic construct. The standard norms are expressed in written forms of the language and as a result are based in educational settings, which "explains why one must go to school to learn one's 'native' language" (Wiley and Lukes 524). Milroy points out that the ongoing drive to standardize language has accompanied standardization of monetary systems and factory-made products as a result of the rise of capitalism and international trade (534). A tacit assumption of standard language ideology is that people must master the standard language norms in order to participate in the mainstream culture. In the United States, standard language ideology has also led to the assumption that English-language monolingualism is superior to and somehow more "American" than speaking other languages (with the exception of studying a "foreign" language in a school setting). This connection between speaking English and being an American was made explicit by President Teddy Roosevelt in 1917: "We must have but one flag. We must also have but one language" ("Roosevelt" 13). A standard language is seen as necessary for creating and maintaining national identity and power. The standard language ideology has led to laws banning bilingual education, such as Proposition 227 in California and Proposition 203 in Arizona, as well as to the movement to make English the official language of the United States. Because so many people who speak nonstandard forms of "English" or languages other than "English" are not white, these manifestations of the standard language ideology, for some, serve as coded expressions of racism.

Spanish-speaking countries have their own standard language ideology. In 1713, Phillip V established the Real Academia Española de la Lengua, which to this day still produces an "official" dictionary of the Spanish language. The RAE, as it's often called, established Castilian as the standard language for Spain and its conquered lands. Though recent editions of the RAE dictionary have accepted regional dialects of Spanish and some Anglicisms, "it is this one [the RAE dictionary] that is endowed with an aura of astonishing power to accept or deny the legitimacy of any given word" (Stavans 31). The development of the Spanish language is both a cause and effect of conquest. As Victor Villanueva writes, "The Latino's ways with words could not help but be influenced by the 400 years in which Spain dominated so much of the New World, and that those ways would have been influenced by the 700 years of Arab domination over Spain, and by the 200 years of Byzantium, with its rhetorical heritage going back yet another 700 years" (84). Because of the spread of English through colonization and the globalized electronic media, linguistic purity is still a major concern for many Spanish speakers (and others, such as French speakers). In addition to Castilian, the prestige varieties of Spanish are those spoken in the major capital cities of Mexico and the rest of Latin America. Of the twenty-eight recipients of the Premio Cervantes de Literatura, the equivalent of the Nobel Prize for Literature, all have used prestige Spanish varieties with the exception of three Cuban writers (Figueroa 48).

Spanglish is stigmatized in Mexico and the rest of Latin America just as much as in the United States. In one study of language attitudes, a middle-class Mexican family in Guanajuato reacted harshly to a native speaker of Chicano Spanish. The family was hosting several future Spanish teachers from the United States as they participated in a Spanish immersion program. One of the teachers was from Yuma, Arizona, on the U.S.-Mexican border, and self-identified as a speaker of Chicano Spanish. The host family expressed dismay at her language usage because they felt that a "'Mexican'" person (whether from Mexico or from the United States) who spoke Spanish in such a manner "was not really welcome in their home." In contrast, the family members were very tolerant of the language errors made by the teachers who were of British and/or northern European ancestry and who spoke Spanish as a second language (Riegelhaupt and Carrasco 4).

In El Paso, where I teach at the University of Texas–El Paso, Spanglish is a common spoken language. On campus, I hear Spanglish everywhere—on the pathways between buildings, in the union, in the library, in the parking lots, in the bathrooms, in the hallways. Students speak Spanglish on cell phones; they text-message in Spanglish; they use Spanglish on their blogs and on Facebook. But when they enter their English-language writing classes, they are careful to speak so-called Standard English. This is to be expected, considering the standard language ideologies of both English and Spanish that permeate the culture. They naturally assume that writing instructors expect only Standard English. For several years, in classes ranging from Basic Writing to graduate level, with students studying everything from business to art to nursing to rhetoric, I've asked my classes to write about their thoughts and feelings regarding Spanglish. I ask them to do this before we discuss any specific language topics so that I can learn about their attitudes before they might feel pressure from their peers or me to alter their attitudes.

Some students have embraced Spanglish because it is a part of their identity, it's a fun language to speak, and it helps them communicate:

> I speak Spanglish with my siblings. I write in my journal in Spanglish. I think in Spanglish. I speak Spanglish because I am a border citizen. I love Spanglish. I love to cross languages. I love to cross borders when I speak. Spanglish makes me unique. Languages should never have *fronteras*.

> Spanglish is cool because it demonstrates how inventive and creative the human mind is, especially when the mind plays with words.

Often, phrases in English and Spanish are joined because one phrase may have more emphasis and impact in Spanish than it would in English. And often, there are Spanish words for things which have no single word in English. For example, there's a Spanish word for the back of your knee, but there's no other way to describe this body part in English except for using medical terminology other than to say "the back of the knee."

Students have also noted that Spanglish is a way for them to show solidarity with other Spanglish speakers. It's an insiders' language, a way to determine the background and interests of others, to speak of matters close to them, to claim cultural identity. But when I asked students to elaborate on this idea in class discussions, they have been reluctant to say more. The classroom context gives them mixed signals. On the one hand, I encourage them to talk about and use Spanglish when they speak and write. On the other hand, I am an Anglo native-English speaker, I don't regularly speak Spanglish, and my limited ability to speak Spanish comes from having studied it as a foreign language. Furthermore, this is a class about writing in English, which automatically implicates it in the standard language ideology (of Spanish as well as English) that has surrounded them their whole lives. And as a living language, more commonly spoken rather than written, Spanglish resists the "permanence" of a written text.

Most students show a keen awareness of how Spanglish functions and is perceived in different contexts:

> Spanglish is a reality in the lives of people located in the border, one could even argue that it is associated with individuals living in northern Mexico and some locations of the southern United States. Thus, its use may be warranted and sometimes required in order to explain yourself in some settings.

> I believe it is not correct to mix two languages. We should either speak English or Spanish. On the other hand, I do know that in our region it is very easy for us to communicate in Spanglish and it is interesting that we can shift back and forth between the two languages during a conversation.

This student sees Spanglish as appropriate only with family and friends:

> I would not use Spanglish in a formal/academic/professional setting. I would rather not speak Spanish at all if it is not pure Spanish or formal Spanish with my employer, clients, or professors.

In contrast, Spanglish is sometimes necessary at this student's workplace:

> I sometimes speak Spanglish at work since it is difficult to translate technical words.... In my office, there are several coworkers who speak Spanish, so I communicate with them in Spanish. It is very common for us to have complete conversations in Spanish, but when it comes to explaining technical concepts, we have to shift to English since we learned those concepts in English.

This student's need to shift languages in her workplace contradicts one of the foundational beliefs of standard language ideology—that in order to communicate, people need to speak the same language. In actuality, the complex interactions that underlie many governmental and business transactions require that workers be able to shift languages according to their needs.

One tenet of a standard language ideology is that the boundaries drawn around idealized languages need to be protected from the contamination of other language practices. To the following students, combining English and Spanish harms the individual languages:

> I try not to [speak Spanglish], but some Spanish words have been corrupted into English words. Some people call it impure Spanish.

> In my point of view, Spanglish has made both English and Spanish weaker languages.

Two other students expressed the belief that the languages should be separated in order to facilitate language learning:

> I don't like it when people use "Spanglish." I think it sounds terrible and is improper. Those who use Spanglish start to use it all the time and don't even realize it. I believe you should either speak English or Spanish, but not both. If you use both, you won't learn either language properly and will be doing yourself and others a disservice.

> My first language was Spanish and when I learned English my mom would hit us if I would mix [Spanish] with English. The theory behind this is that if you spoke Spanglish you will never learn either language well.... I see [Spanglish] as a bastard language.

One student felt pressured by the stigma attached to speaking so-called nonstandard Spanish and nonstandard English:

> I actually feel ashamed of myself for not speaking Spanish better. This is probably due to the natives constantly criticizing either my Spanish

or English. It would sound terrible in a job interview. Maybe some of this is internalized racism.

Other studies of students' language attitudes show similar attitudes to Spanglish. In her study of the languages spoken by college students on the border between Mexico and south Texas, Michelle Hall Kells found that many students showed a "high degree of negativism that bilingual Mexican Americans exhibit toward Tex Mex as a language practice. It appears that many users adopt the attitudes of the dominant culture toward their language varieties" (189). In their study of Mexican American immigrants in Chicago, Marcia Farr and Elias Dominguez Barajas found that parents stressed the acquisition of Standard Spanish and Standard English as a way of maintaining and succeeding in both cultures (54). Similarly, in his ethnography of a Chicago Mexicano community, Juan C. Guerra noted that some parents disallowed Spanglish at home because children needed to speak "proper" Spanish (129–30). Robert Bayley and Sandra R. Schecter, who studied Mexican American families in San Antonio and San Francisco, reported that some parents actively discouraged their children from speaking Tex Mex (39). The ideology of linguistic purism, notes Norma González, makes some parents feel that the language that they speak is defective, leading to a sense of shame that is communicated to their children (168). She writes, "An ideology of linguistic purism and prescriptivism has engendered a generation of parents who feel that the Spanish they speak is substandard" (168). These attitudes toward Spanglish are understandable because in the United States, Spanish is a subordinate language to English, and Spanglish is subordinate to Spanish. Spanglish is also subordinate in Spanish-speaking countries outside of the United States. Thus, Spanglish speakers face a double stigma when speaking the language that for some of them is their first language, their home language.

Educational policies grounded in notions of demarcated languages will inevitably support linguistic containment and standard language ideology at the expense of students' lived languages. The Bilingual Education Act of 1968 had as it goal the development of bilingual students fluent in so-called Standard English and a standard home language. Instead of promulgating a deficit view of language, this act authorized an additive approach—English would be added to the language that students already knew. However, bilingual education is based on a notion of language demarcation in which contact between the two languages is discouraged, if not forbidden. The goal is to produce what François Grosjean calls an "ideal bilingual" who is equally fluent in both languages, someone who is the "sum of two complete or incomplete monolinguals" rather than someone whose language practices vary according to context and purpose (469). Bilinguals are compared to monolinguals and expected to achieve fluency almost equal to a "native" (that is, monolingual) English speaker (Valdés). English is the idealized Standard English, and the home language, usually Spanish, is also conceived as an idealized standard. Because of what Grosjean calls "a monolingual, fractional, view of bilingualism," a mixed language is considered interference or simply sloppiness. Because the languages are considered fixed, a unidirectional movement, from Spanish to English, is inevitable, and as a result bilingual education has become a unidirectional program with the sole goal of developing fluency in English (Flores and Murillo 198). Even these transitional bilingual programs were dismantled in 2002 when Congress, because of the No Child Left Behind Act of 2001, changed the Bilingual Education Act into the English Language Acquisition Act (ELA), which directed federal funding toward programs that emphasized only English (Mitchell 254). This educational policy, by conceptualizing language as fixed forms, renders students' languages invisible.

Also problematical are dual-language immersion programs in which English-speaking children are taught in classrooms with children from another language group. In most of these programs, the instruction is split equally between so-called Standard English and the other language. The goal is for both groups of children to develop proficiency in both languages. However, dual language programs maintain a strict division between the two languages, what Shanan Fitts has called a "parallel monolingualism": "The program design does not allow for any specific spaces in which the type of Spanish spoken by Spanish-English bilinguals in the United States, which might include codeswitching or borrowed words, is explored, honored, or officially allowed" (354). She found that students carefully monitored their language use in the classroom so that they wouldn't slip up and mix the two languages. Similarly, Sayer has noted that "the 'other' language of dual-language programs is not exactly the students' home language, but rather the standard variety of that language." He quotes an administrator who says that by the seventh grade, children feel too ashamed of their language (in this case, Spanglish) to use it in the classroom. According to Sayer, "If we take seriously the notion that we should honor kids' home language and even use it as a resource, then as educators we need to look for ways to validate and raise the status of the vernacular in the eyes of teachers, children, and their parents" (109).

How do we work against an educational culture that focuses exclusively on "Standard" English and a political culture in which twenty-eight states have declared English as the official language? Over the years, my response has been to make language a topic of the classroom—to study different texts and contexts that mix languages for specific rhetorical purposes. To this end, my students and I have studied graffiti art in El Paso, examining the English/ Spanish/Spanglish imagetexts in various neighborhoods. We have analyzed advertising that uses Spanglish to reach consumers, particularly military recruitment commercials and magazine ads. We've also examined the rhetoric of the farmworker movement in the 1960s and 1970s, in particular the speeches of César Chávez and the improvisational theater of El Teatro Campesino, to see when rhetors choose—and don't choose—to use Spanglish. In Chávez's published writings and audiotaped speeches, standard English and Spanish are separated; seeking to educate as many people as possible about the exploitation of farmworkers, his formal speeches were in English, with many of them later translated into Spanish in the farmworkers' newsletter (Jensen and Hammerback). In contrast, the actors in El Teatro Campesino, a guerrilla theater group that emerged to support the farmworkers' picket lines, mixed Spanish and English as they satirized exploitative business owners and encouraged farmworkers to continue the strikes. In their *actos*, performed in meeting halls or on flatbed trucks in the evenings after long days of farm labor and picketing, they depicted what Luis Valdez called "the reality of the *huelga* [strike]." In a scene dramatizing an encounter between a farm owner and farm laborer, the laborer would deliberately switch back and forth from English to Spanish in order to confuse and outwit the patronizing, arrogant *patroncito* (18–19). Spanglish in this context is a living language of resistance and critique.

Examining different rhetorical contexts for Spanglish has raised my awareness and my students' awareness of the power and creativity of this language, but for the most part it hasn't tempted them to use Spanglish in their own writing, despite my invitations. Referring to Min-Zhan Lu's notions of "sound bites," or our default assumptions about language, Anis Bawarshi has commented that "these sound bites are as likely to be operating on students as they are on teachers, with students often just as likely to resist invitations to produce alternative designs (when they can choose to do so) as teachers are to invite them" (652).

Students might resist my suggestion to resist because Spanglish is an insiders' language, and in many ways I am an outsider. Students for the most part speak Spanglish, creating and re-creating it spontaneously as they interact with others, so stabilizing it in writing may seem unnatural. And for the most part, I assign analytical essays, and though I emphasize the fluidity of this genre, students' previous experiences with school-based writing leads them to try to create an idealized Standard English.

It is ironic that Spanglish and other blended languages are valorized in literary studies, in particular postcolonial discourses, and in texts such as

Anzaldúa's that are frequently anthologized in composition textbooks. Yet our educational practices and terminology continue to be based on foundational notions of language. Even a seemingly benign term such as "English Language Learners" renders students' other languages invisible. I am not proposing that courses that support the development of students' languages be discontinued. Placement and curricular decisions need to be context-specific, which will result in a variety of policy decisions suited to particular settings. Instead, I'm proposing that we study and honor students' lived languages, such as Spanglish, in order to examine our own assumptions about language demarcation and containment. While I sit in my office writing responses to their essay drafts, my students are sitting in the student union speaking Spanglish and other languages, texting and chatting on cell phones, checking out the latest videos on YouTube, posting images on their Facebook sites—in other words, using the languages of the twenty-first century.

Works Cited

Anzaldúa, Gloria. *Borderlands/La Frontera: The New Mestiza*. San Francisco: Spinsters/Aunt Lute, 1987.

Ardila, Alfredo. "Spanglish: An Anglicized Spanish Dialect." *Hispanic Journal of Behavioral Sciences* 27 (Feb. 2006): 60–81.

Baca, Damián. *Mestiz@ Scripts, Digital Migrations, and the Territories of Writing*. New York: Palgrave/Macmillan, 2008.

Bawarshi, Anis. "Taking Up Language Differences in Composition." *College English* 68 (2006): 652–56.

Bayley, Robert, and Sandra R. Schecter. "Family Decisions about Schooling and Spanish Maintenance: Mexicanos in California and Texas." Zentella 31–45.

Chow, Patricia, and Rachel Marcus. "International Student Mobility and the United States." *International Higher Education* 50 (Winter 2008). 20 Mar. 2008 <http://www.bc.edu/bc_org/avp/soe/cihe/newsletter/Number50/p13_Chow_Marcus>.

Cintrón, Ralph. *Angels Town: Chero Ways, Gang Life, and Rhetorics of the Everyday*. Boston: Beacon, 1997.

Crawford, James. "Census 2000: A Guide for the Perplexed." *James Crawford's Language Policy Web Site and Emporium*. 20 Mar. 2008 <http://ourworld.compuserve.com/homepages/JWCRAWFORD/Census02.htm>.

Farr, Marcia, and Elias Dominguez Barajas. "*Mexicanos* in Chicago: Language Ideology and Identity." Zentella 46–59.

Figueroa, Neysa Luz. *"U.S." and "Them": A Study of the Language Attitudes of Speakers of High- and Low-Prestige Varieties of Spanish toward "World Spanishes."* Diss. Purdue U, 2004. Ann Arbor: UMI, 2004. DA3113798. *CSA Linguistics and Language Behavior Abstracts*. ProQuest. U of Texas-El Paso. 26 June 2008 <http://www.csa.com>.

Fitts, Shanan. "Reconstructing the Status Quo: Linguistic Interaction in a Dual-Language School." *Bilingual Research Journal* 29 (2006): 337–65.

Flores, Susana Y., and Enrique G. Murillo Jr. "Power, Language, and Ideology: Historical and Contemporary Notes on the Dismantling of Bilingual Education." *Urban Review* 33 (2001): 183–206.

García, Ofelia, and Kate Menken. "The English of Latinos from a Plurilingual Transcultural Angle: Implications for Assessment and Schools." Nero 167–83.

González, Norma. "Children in the Eye of the Storm: Language Socialization and Language Ideologies in a Dual-Language School." Zentella 162–74.

Grosjean, François. "The Bilingual as a Competent but Specific Speaker-Hearer." *Multilingual and Multicultural Development* 6 (1985): 467–77.

Guerra, Juan C. *Close to Home: Oral and Literate Practices in a Transnational Mexicano Community.* New York: Teachers College, 1998.

Jensen, Richard J., and John C. Hammerback. *The Words of César Chávez.* College Station: Texas A&M UP, 2002.

Kells, Michelle Hall. "Tex Mex, Metalingual Discourse, and Teaching College Writing." Nero 185–201.

Mejía, Jaime. "Bridging Rhetoric and Composition Studies with Chicano and Chicana Studies: A Turn to Critical Pedagogy." *Latino/a Discourses: On Language, Identity and Literacy Education.* Ed. Michelle Hall Kells, Valerie Balester, and Victor Villanueva. Portsmouth, NH: Boynton/Cook, 2004. 40–56.

Milroy, James. "Language Ideologies and the Consequences of Standardization." *Journal of Sociolinguistics* 4 (2001): 530–55.

Mitchell, Candace. "English Only: The Creation and Maintenance of an American Underclass." *Journal of Latinos and Education* 4 (2005): 253–70.

Nero, Shondel J., ed. *Dialects, Englishes, Creoles, and Education.* Mahwah, NJ: Erlbaum, 2006.

Pennycook, Alastair. "Performativity and Language Studies." *Critical Inquiry in Language Studies: An International Journal* 1.1 (2004): 1–19.

Phillipson, Robert. *Linguistic Imperialism.* Oxford: Oxford UP, 1992.

Riegelhaupt, Florencia, and Roberto Luis Carrasco. "Mexico Host Family Reactions to a Bilingual Chicana Teacher in Mexico: A Case Study Of Language and Culture Clash." *Bilingual Research Journal* 24 (2000). 21 May 2008 <http://brj.asu.edu/v244/articles/art6.html>.

"Roosevelt Demands Race Fusion Here." *New York Times* 10 Sept. 1917: 13.

Sayer, Peter. "Demystifying Language Mixing: Spanglish in School." *Journal of Latinos and Education* 7 (2008): 94–112.

Stavans, Ilan. *Spanglish: The Making of a New American Language.* New York: HarperCollins, 2003.

Valdés, Guadalupe. "Bilingual Minorities and Language Issues in Writing: Toward Professionwide Responses to a New Challenge." *Written Communication* 9 (1992): 85–136.

Valdez, Luis. *Early Works: Actos, Bernabe, Pensamiento Serpentino.* Houston: Arte Publico, 1990.

Villa, Daniel. "Languages Have Armies, and Economies, Too: The Presence of U.S. Spanish in the Spanish-Speaking World." *Southwest Journal of Linguistics* 19 (2000): 143–54.

Villanueva, Victor. *Bootstraps: From an American Academic of Color.* Urbana, IL: NCTE, 1993.

Wiley, Terrence G., and Marguerite Lukes. "English-Only and Standard English Ideologies in the U.S." *TESOL Quarterly* 30 (1996): 511–35.

Zentella, Ana Celia. "Afterward." Zentella 175–81.

———, ed. *Building on Strength: Language and Literacy in Latino Families and Communities.* New York: Teachers College, 2005.

———. "Introduction." Zentella 1–12.

7. There's No Translation for It: The Rhetorical Sovereignty of Indigenous Languages

Scott Richard Lyons

When Europeans arrived to the place they eventually named America, there were 300 indigenous languages spoken north of the Rio Grande, and these represented some 50 different language families. By contrast, Europe had only three language families: Indo-European, Finno-Ugric, and Basque. Linguists have since counted over 40 languages in the Athabaskan-Eyak-Tlingit language family, 30 in the Algonquian-Ritwan family, 30 in the Uto-Aztecan, and 23 in the Salishan. Other language families featured fewer tongues but had more speakers and covered vast geographical territory: Iroquoian in the Northeast and Southeast, Eskimo-Aleut in the Arctic, Muskogean in the Southeast. Some "isolates" like Cayuse and Zuni had/have only one variant and were/are subsequently more locally contained. Many of these languages are still spoken today. There are roughly 362,000 fluent speakers of the 154 Native languages surviving in the United States, with Navajo spoken by over 100,000. Canada has 60 active indigenous languages with Ojibwe, Cree, and Inuktitut featuring tens of thousands of speakers each. Mexico boasts the Western Hemisphere's greatest concentration of speakers, with 7.5 percent of its population speaking at least one of its 56 surviving indigenous languages. But it is the number of speakers in Central and South America that is most remarkable when compared to the situation in the "developed" North: 12 million speakers of Quechua, 3 million speakers of Guarani, and a million each of Maya, Nahuatl, and Aymara. Indeed, from the perspective of the North, it is the indigenous South that should be envied where language diversity is concerned.

That's not to say that any indigenous language is safe in our world today. On the contrary, all of these languages are in rapid decline and face serious threats of dormancy or extinction. Marianne Mithun argues that at present rates of decline, "all are likely to be gone by the end of the twenty-first century" (2). Norbert Francis and Jon Reyhner concur: "In the Americas, not a single exception exists to the overall tendency toward language displacement by either Spanish or English" (33). *USA Today* recently reported, "Of the estimated 7,000 languages spoken today, one vanishes every 14 days"; most endangered are those in five "hot spots": northern Australia, central South America, the Northwest Pacific plateau of the United States and Canada, eastern Siberia, and Oklahoma (Weise). Simply put, the languages of the world will be reduced by half by this century's end, and indigenous languages are winning this grim race toward linguistic oblivion. Why?

Some common themes obtain wherever language drift is an issue for indigenous peoples. First and by far most important, nearly all of these languages have at some point or another been explicitly targeted for extinction by colonizing powers. As only one example, from the latter nineteenth century until well into the twentieth, the federal off-reservation boarding school system in the United States actively sought to decrease indigenous language fluency as a matter of educational policy, as Brenda Child explains:

> All government boarding schools followed a strict policy that forbade Indian students from speaking tribal languages, the languages of their mothers and fathers. Former boarding school students remember being dealt with harshly for infractions of this rule. Beatings, swats from rulers, having one's mouth washed with soap or lye, or being locked in the school jail were not uncommon punishments. (28)

Sometimes backed by physical violence, these language prohibitions produced damaging effects: not just decreasing fluency but also shame. Students coming home on breaks quickly found themselves isolated from not only their communities but their families, and this was no matter of simple inconvenience but revealed a deeper emotional struggle. From the students' point of view, they had been taught that the language of their parents was inferior and savage, "a thing of the past," a sign of backwardness, and thus not the sort of thing to claim as one's own. At the same time, they felt different, excluded, and disabled from participating in home life—in some cases they were even teased—all on account of their poor Native language skills. So the shame cut both ways: I am bad because our language is bad, and I am bad because I can't speak it anymore.

Another reason for our present linguistic decline is the sheer power of the market. Even where explicit policies prohibiting Native languages are now illegal, the languages of colonizing, dominant cultures have become the tools of business and power. Schools, governments, the private sector, and the mainstream media do their business in dominant languages with predictable effects on indigenous ones. This unsubtle linkage of language and power can smack of racism. If states do not privilege minority languages to the point of mandating their use in some official capacity, there will be fewer political or economic incentives for people to perpetuate them. And that raises a third concern: an increasing fatalism or lack of will among Native peoples to revive their own languages, especially in the North. It is the rare tribal government that has funded its own language revitalization efforts to the point of much visible success, and while the occasional speakers produced by these programs are certainly worthy of praise, they really can't be taken as evidence of language revitalization. It is probably not helping matters any that Native intellectuals (in this case, literary critics) have lately taken to rationalizing indigenous language shift with slogans like "English is an Indian language" (Womack 120) and "Claiming English as an Indian language is one of the most important, if not the most important step toward ensuring Indian survival for future generations" (Weaver xviii). I would submit that the opposite is true: claiming English as an Indian language is tantamount to accepting one's own assimilation and colonization. Better to see the matter as White Earth Ojibwe elder Joe Auginaush sees it: "We're not losing our language, our language is losing us" (quoted in Treuer 5).

My critique of tribal governments and Native literary critics should not be taken as an attempt to blame the victim, however. Governments and intellectuals have power, and power is one thing the vast majority of Indians do not have. All told, the reason that increasing numbers of Native people do not speak their heritage languages today is due to old federal policies and new market logics, both of which are inseparable from the grand historical projects of imperialism and colonialism: the ultimate agents of language shift. Shame was a product of federal policy, fatalism a symptom of the market, and the loss of languages a logical result of the complex political system initiated in 1492. Don't blame Indians for that.

There are, of course, many grassroots language revitalization efforts underway in the Native world, and some have met with certain success. Different approaches abound: immersion schools, language apprentice programs, language camps and "nests" for kids, and others. It is not my purpose in this chapter to reflect upon these various programs and approaches; better minds than mine have been working on these initiatives for some time and deserve to be read for themselves (see Grenoble and Whaley; Hinton and Hale; and Hinton, Vera, and Steele). Rather, my subject here is a peculiar claim that is often made by language activists and speakers about why it is so important to learn and revitalize a language unfit for the market. As Ojibwe language activist Anton Treuer has put it, "At stake is the future of not only the language but the knowledge contained within the language, the unique Ojibwe worldview and way of thinking, the Anishinaabe connection to the past, to the earth, and to the future" (5). Treuer believes that the Ojibwe language comes with its own built-in worldview—it carries a culture—so losing the one means losing the other as well. "Culture and language are inextricably linked," Treuer writes, and by inextricably he means inextricably (5).

This is, of course, a restatement of the old Sapir-Whorf hypothesis that language determines thought. Edward Sapir and Benjamin Whorf claimed that different languages carried different ways of thinking about the world—about time, about matter, even about the number of words one might need to characterize various kinds of snow—promoting a view that some critics have called "linguistic determinism." In the sixties, linguists like Noam Chomsky challenged the Sapir-Whorf hypothesis and postulated the existence of a universal human grammar underlying all languages; Steven Pinker is the champion of that view now. For Pinker, it is not really the case that people think in languages at all but rather in something he playfully calls "mentalese," so he thinks it unlikely that languages would produce different and incommensurable worldviews lacking the prospect of rapid translation (60). The Sapir-Whorf hypothesis still has a respectable following, however, including, notably, cognitive linguist George Lakoff and anthropologist Peter Gordon. Most linguists today would probably position themselves in between the views of Sapir-Whorf and Chomsky-Pinker, assuming that language must influence—if not quite determine—thought at least to some degree. And if most of us can agree that language influences the thought of its speakers, then it would follow that cultures are influenced as well.

This debate, however, is not something that has inspired many fluent speakers or activists. From them you will hear simply this: "You can't think like an Ojibwe without Ojibwe." "Get the English out of your mouth—and out of your head." "I would like to give you the right to conduct that ceremony, but I cannot until you have mastered Ojibwe; the spirits won't understand you in English." I am obviously speaking from experience here. You will also hear statements like this: "I don't know how to say that properly in English, but it's close to this . . ." Or simply: "There's no translation for it." Sometimes you hear claims that seem to riff on the work of Chomsky and Pinker, only lacking the "universal" angle of their theories: "If you are an Ojibwe, you are hard-wired to learn this language and you will pick it up much quicker than non-Natives." These kinds of sayings, which are so common in language circles on reservations, are always intended to produce a desired result—the survival of the language itself—but they also impart a lesson or (dare we say it?) a worldview: namely, the speaker's understanding of language as a carrier of culture. This is the idea that I want to investigate further.

Ojibwemowin, the Ojibwe language, is spoken by some 60,000 people today in Minnesota, Wisconsin, Michigan, North Dakota, Manitoba, Ontario,

Saskatchewan, and Quebec (Treuer 5). On my reservation, Leech Lake in northern Minnesota, there are 100 or fewer speakers out of a local population of roughly 2,500, and most of them are over sixty years of age. There hasn't been a fluent speaker in my lineage since my grandparents' generation, many of whom attended off-reservation boarding schools in far-flung places like Flandreau, South Dakota, during the 1930s. As my father tells it, when he was a child in the 1950s, his parents' generation used Ojibwemowin to speak of matters they wished to keep secret from their children, a dynamic shared by many recent immigrant families in those days as well. I remember asking my grandfather to speak Ojibwe every so often—we kids loved hearing him rattle off the words for blueberry pie and crooked fence post, so long and complex those words were!—and he would oblige in a mysterious accent I now recognize to be perfect pronunciation. But beyond fulfilling the occasional wishes of his grandchildren, I do not remember him speaking Ojibwe out of anything we might call necessity. By the 1970s of my childhood, Ojibwe had become exotic and nostalgic.

In the 1990s—after Red Power and the Indian civil rights movement, the rise of a new gaming economy and institutions like our tribal college—I took Ojibwe classes in an effort to rebuild what had been so recently lost in my family. I wasn't the only one to do so; a whole generation ended up in those classes, at least for a time. What many of us discovered there was a language that is so different from English—so strange in its love of verbs and disdain of nouns, its contingency on social situation and cultural context—it immediately transformed us all into Sapir-Whorf hardliners. It also struck many of us as practically impossible to learn. We had too much English in our mouths and heads to get all of the verb conjugations and irregularities, and that's not even to mention the problem of pronunciation. Still, a few of us managed to become speakers—including a couple of my relatives (one of whom is Anton Treuer)—but not me. I was whisked away by the market to a job far away before fluency was possible: a decision I made then that I do sometimes question now. But even though I'm no fluent speaker, I did learn a few things about Ojibwe that make me take seriously the claim that the language carries a culture.

Consider, for example, the Ojibwe words that have been used to identify different groups of people. Ojibwes have long referred to themselves as *anishinaabeg*, meaning original or indigenous people. Beyond that basic identity, Ojibwes discerned different kinds of *anishinaabeg*, or what Europeans called "tribes," based upon observed cultural particularities. For instance, the word *ojibwe* means something puckered up, referring in all likelihood to the distinctive style of moccasins that Ojibwes wear, so the term seems to name those people who wear the puckered up moccasins: *anishinaabe ojibwe*. Sioux folks are also called *anishinaabeg*—because they are original people—but are further referred to as *bwaan* or burned: *anishinaabe bwaan*. The origin of *bwaan* is unclear, some insisting that it refers to the old Sioux practice of burning people alive and others suggesting it was actually the Sioux who ended up burned. But all such etymological questions aside, the point is that Ojibwe have long spoken of *anishinaabe ojibwe* and *anishinaabe bwaan*, identity markers classifying both Ojibwe and Sioux as original or indigenous people but different kinds. And the differences between the groups were based on cultural or ethnic observations, not biological notions like race, blood, phenotype, or even kinship.

The same logic holds in language used to describe non-Indians. The Ojibwe word for white is *waabishkaa*, but it has never been used to identify people of European origin. Rather, "white" people have long been called *gichimookomaanan* or big knives, signifying the swords the Ojibwe saw carried by the first Europeans they met. Since that moment of contact, there have been many different kinds of big knives to distinguish. *Wemitigoozhi* signifies a person of French descent, one who wears a piece of wood (*mitig*) like those cross-bearing Jesuits they encountered long ago. These people were different from those who are called *agongos* (chipmunk), which describes a person of Scandinavian ancestry. Why chipmunks? The sod houses the Scandinavian settlers lived in apparently struck the Ojibwe as similar to the dwellings of rodents. Both *Wemitigoozhi* and *agongos* are *gichimookomaanan*, but not all big knives are cut from the same cloth. A French person was one who lived with and like French people. A Scandinavian was one who lived with and like Scandinavians (and chipmunks). What made them different from each other was not biology but ethnicity: a way of living. Culture.

One of the best ways to capture this cultural, ethnic manner by which traditional Natives distinguished Indian, tribal, and non-Indian identities is to comprehend the words describing people of mixed origin, or those who are now typically called "mixedbloods." These words are instructive because they give us a clear sense of how new or ambiguous kinds of people were identified in cultural or ethnic terms as well. The Ojibwe word used to signify persons of mixed ancestry is *wiisaakodewininiwag*, or "diluted men." What is diluted is not specified. But it seems telling that in the Ojibwe language, one does not use the word *wiisaakode* when mixing something with water or any other liquid; that's called *ginigaawin*. What is diluted if not blood? One Ojibwe speaker I asked about this word, Bob Jourdain of Leech Lake, said he thought *wiisaakode* referred to a general dilution of "Indianness." When I pressed him about the possibility of blood being diluted in the use of the word *wiisaakode*, he laughed, shook his head, and said, "No, *wiisaakodewi-*

niniwag might be *deluded* but not *diluted*." A mixedblood would thus be a person whose identity is the product of mixed cultures or, more accurately, a diluted Indianness. This is quite a difference from non-Ojibwe descriptions of mixed ancestry. When Euro-Americans have described such people, they have typically used the language of breeding—mulatto, half-breed, and so forth—defining not only the mixed but by fiat circumscribing two locations of an ostensible purity. Speakers of Ojibwemowin have played a different language game regarding mixed identity, dealing in Indianness, not breeding or blood, when discerning one's degree of dilution.

These Ojibwe assessments of Indianness resonate with standards and words used by Lakota speakers as well. Lakota hails from a different language family (Siouan) than Ojibwe (Algonquin), but consider the logical similarities between *wiisaakodewinini* and the Lakota word for a person of mixed ancestry, *iyeshka*, which is typically translated to "talks white." Like Ojibwe's diluted man, "talks white" avoids defining identity in terms of blood and breeding and assesses something like Indianness instead—in this case, the manner in which a person speaks. Granted, on one level, *iyeshka* refers to the speaking of English. But as Lakota writer Elizabeth Cook-Lynn has noted, the phrase carries an additional connotation indicating which social group *iyeshka* has politically and culturally identified with. *Iyeshka* "is not generally regarded as a complimentary term," she writes, because people of mixed backgrounds "were and probably still are seen by native peoples as those who were already converts to the hostile and intruding culture" (35–36). "Talking white" is thus a sign of conversion or allegiance to the world of the whites. You are what you speak, and how you speak reveals your standpoint. It is a political statement.

Identifying different groups of people by the ways in which they live and/or their political allegiances—as opposed to viewing them in biological terms—can be taken as a cultural difference all its own, a worldview that is rather different from the meanings and methods of identity used in the dominant culture. To the extent that Indian nations have come to view and recognize tribal identities as primarily constituted by blood—and here we must note that fully two-thirds of America's federally recognized Indian nations today employ "blood quantum" as the sole means of granting tribal citizenship—Indian identity might be understood as assimilated into a new and dramatically different framework from what fluent speakers would understand and use. There's a world of difference between a "mixedblood" or "part-Indian" and *wiisaakodewinini* or *iyeshka*, and the difference would seem to be cultural.

But what of the concept of culture itself? How is the idea of culture addressed in the Ojibwe language? At first glance, it seems immediately meaningful that there is no word for "culture," at least nothing easily translatable like *miskwaa* and *makwa* for "red" and "bear." But there are words addressing certain practices, beliefs, and objects that we recognize in English as cultural in sensibility. As we examine these culture words, keep in mind that Ojibwe is, like most indigenous languages, driven by verbs, thus describing a world of actions more than a world of objects. That is, from the very beginning we can safely assume that Ojibwe senses of culture will conceive of processes more than things.

We begin with a sense of culture that speaks to ceremonial practice. *Izhitwaa* is an animate intransitive verb signifying having a certain custom or practicing a specific ceremony. In addition to being verb-driven, Ojibwemowin makes distinctions between animate and inanimate things, the difference being just what those words suggest: living and not living. *Izhitwaa* is a good example of how these significations work, as the word describes not just doing a ceremony or having a custom but characterizing ceremonial or customary objects and actors as alive. But there's another connotation built into *izhitwaa* as well, the sound of deep respect (*twaa*), which might be aptly understood as reverence. But *izhitwaa* speaks more than a reverent respect for life. There are many Ojibwe words employing the root word *izhi*, all of them expressing the basic idea of doing something meaningful in a certain way to produce a desired or expected outcome. *Izhitoon* is to cause something to happen; *izhiwebizi* to behave in an expected manner; *izhitigweyaa* to flow, river-like, to a specific place; and *izhise* to fly to a certain place, like the geese who never fail to follow their seasonal routes. *Izhitwaa* links up to these words insofar as ceremonial customs or religious practices are, like natural processes, designed to produce correct results.

Another Ojibwe culture word is *nitaa*. There's an explicitly pedagogical meaning built into *nitaa* as the word signifies being good or skilled at something, knowing how to do it, and doing it frequently. That is, one has to learn how to *nitaa*. But again, perhaps the most revealing meanings of *nitaa* are found in its cognate words. *Nitaawigi'* means to raise a child, and *nitaawigitoon* refers to the growing of something in general, like a crop. These words are actually interchangeable, placing on common ground the raising of both children and crops, which says something significant about the nature of *nitaa*: namely, that these things are not left to amateurs. The point of raising someone, whether kids or corn, is to ensure the healthy proliferation of life, and one does not accomplish that task without the skill acquired in what we would call a culture. But there's still more to this. Other *nitaa* words include *nitaawe*, signifying speaking or singing well, and *nitaage*, to properly kill game or to mourn. Yes, the killing of game is just like the raising of crops, both requiring substantial know-how in order to produce food, while proper mourning is considered an important aspect of living well. Similarly, *nita-awe* invokes the creative power of speech and song, two very highly valued practices pertaining to the substance and maintenance of life since they are the spirit of ceremonial discourse. Life is in fact what all of these *nitaa* words have in common; they all possess the sense of doing things well in order to bring about more life.

One Ojibwe word invokes a sense of culture resembling the old anthropological notion of a "whole way of life." *Inaadizi* signifies living in a certain way or with a particular character; its noun form *inaadiziwin* might be translated precisely to "way of life." Here, too, the cognates reveal a discernible pattern. *Inaabaji* means to use someone and *inaabadizi* to be useful (or employed), while *inaabandam* signifies an act of dreaming. So this way of life possesses connotations of certain use, to use or be used in a particular manner, even while unconscious and dreaming (for example, when visions are given and spiritual messages delivered). It posits, that is, the suggestion of practical utility. There is also a sense of the visual in these words, as *inaabam* suggests seeing someone in a dream and *inaabate* refers to watching smoke rise in a particular direction. In fact, *inaabi* means to look, or more precisely to peek, raising the question of who peeks at what when lightning (*inaabiwin*) strikes. Utility is linked to vision, as if one might see a good course of action and become useful through living this way of life. Finally, there is a judicial sense to the word, as *inaakonan* refers to deciding formally upon something and *inaakonige* means to make a judgment. Hence our word for law: *inaako-nigewin*. Seeing, using, being useful, judging, deciding: all of these notions inform the culture word *indaadiziwin* and suggest that our particular way of life is made up of certain values, namely utility, clear-sighted judgment, and visionary decision-making.

How do these various words and expressions add up? All of these Ojibwe senses of culture indicate, I believe, a single overarching concern: the desire to make more life. As rivers flow and birds fly, practicing religious ceremonies and other customs (*izhitwaa*) produces an intended result: more life. Behaving skillfully (*nitaa*) leads to more life, too, as evidenced by the proliferation of happy children and healthy crops. Living in a certain manner (*inaadizi*) allows a community to see, use, decide, and make clear judgments that are geared toward the production of more life. But perhaps the clearest indication of this goal is another phrase commonly used to describe Ojibwe life, *Anishinaabe bimaadizi*, or living as an Indian. *Bimaadizi* is a word used to describe the general state of someone being alive, and it possesses connotations of movement that are understood in a physical sense. Consider the cognates: *bimaashi* means to be blown along; *bimaadagaa*, to swim effortlessly, as if carried by a current; *bimaada'e*, to skate; and *bimaawadaaso*, to move along with a group, as in a school of fish. This flowing sense of living in sync with other lives, of going along with the ebb and flow of nature and never swimming upstream or cutting against the grain, suggests that Anishinaabeg are to live and move in concert with the rhythms of the natural world. Perhaps for this reason, Winona LaDuke has translated *anishinaabe bimaadiziwin*, the noun form of this expression, as "continuous rebirth" (4).

Another point must be made regarding the nature of these culture words. Ojibwe is a language of verbs rather than nouns, describing actions over objects, processes over things. As we see with *bimaadiziwin*, however, verbs can be turned into nouns by adding "-win" as a suffix. In this manner, *izhitwaa* can become *izhitwaawin*, *inaadizi* is made into *inaadiziwin*, and *bimaadizi* is transformed into *bimaadiziwin*. The difference in meaning when "-win" is affixed to a verb is the same difference between "living as an Indian" and "Indian life," or "doing something religious" versus "religion." What happens in the shift from verb to noun is the objectification of processes, the creation of concepts where once existed actions. It is out of concern over these meaningful differences that some Ojibwe speakers today will caution students of the language against using (or making) too many nounified "win"-words, finding their recent proliferation indicative of an increasing English influence and with it the adoption of a new and different system of thought. These same speakers would likely agree that in their minds there is a desire to "do cultural things" as opposed to having a "culture"—hence the absence of an easily translatable word. Maybe it wouldn't go too far to suggest that Ojibwe speakers don't have a culture at all. Rather, they spend their time "culturing."

Culturing would mean producing more life, living in a sustainable manner as part of the rhythms and flows of nature—never separate from them because any claim to live divorced from nature would likely be taken as a sign of mental illness, like the ones who have "gone windigo" or become cannibals. More life is the goal of Ojibwe culturing and the goal of nature itself, so how could it be otherwise? This is the cultural difference, the worldview built into these particular Ojibwe words, and obviously there are significant differences between these ideas, concepts, and expressions and those made in comparable English language terminology. One difference exists in the space between the noun and the verb, between culture as a thing and culturing. Another seems wedged between very different notions concerning the proper relationship between culture and nature—for one, there's a split; for the other, none possible. Other differences we could note would likely come down to these two basic sites of meaning: noun/verb, culture/nature. Therein lies a difference of cultures and worldviews, and perhaps incompatibility lies between them.

Ojibwe speakers have identified different human groups by observing the ways in which they cultured, and culturing was understood as the means of producing more life. When the world features fewer speakers of Ojibwe, and English inflects the language of most Indians, identity is increasingly understood in terms of blood, breeding, and race and decreasingly recognized by observations of particular kinds of culturing. Likewise, culturing is geared less toward the making of more life and more toward honoring the nounified notions of Culture or Religion. These are only a few small examples of the big differences that exist between Ojibwe and English as carriers of culture. A world lies between them. While some would characterize the transformations from one world to the next as no more than historical "adaptation" or "change"—sad, perhaps, but unavoidable—others experience them with a profound sense of loss and intimations of injustice. I see these shifts as a loss and not only to Indians. Does not the whole world suffer when humans stop thinking and acting for the primary purpose of producing more life?

One final example of cultural difference: the Ojibwe noun form of "stone" is *asin*, and it is animate, living. To be made of stone, however, is *asiniiwan*, inanimate. What is the difference between a stone and something made of stone? Life. Only humans have a power strong enough to kill a stone and transform it into a building material. Elders will tell you to be extremely careful, respectful, and above all thankful when taking the life of a stone. Actually, they are only commentators; it is Ojibwemowin that teaches the lesson.

I made a lot of funny mistakes when I was trying to learn Ojibwe, and sometimes speakers would play tricks on me. I'll never forget the time a Red Lake elder told a few of us that the Winnebago Indians were named by our ancestors *winniboogidag* or "dirty farts," a story we later told to a different group of fluent speakers who greatly appreciated the joke that had obviously been played on us, not the Winnebagos. Another time a white man who lived at Leech Lake for years told us about a most powerful word for respect, *manaadjetwaa*, which sounds like the French expression "ménage à trois." We thought for certain that somebody had played a trick on him, that the word wasn't real, and later we gleefully told some speakers about our funny discovery, only to learn that in fact the word was legit and furthermore the speakers weren't at all pleased by our interlinguistic reference. "What's so funny about that?" we were sharply asked. Those elders had far too much respect for the language to joke about a word, and especially that one. It was us and not the white man who lacked *manaadjetwaawin* and received a stern rebuke.

During those years, I learned a great deal about the mysteries of Ojibwemowin: its ability to communicate humor that more often than not translates poorly into English, its remarkable characterizations of the substances of the world and demarcations of them as living or not-living, and the entire story that a single word could tell about the subject of its reference. All of this metaknowledge is part and parcel of the language, and what else would we call it in English if not culture? Learning the language had a profound impact on my own sense of identity and belonging as well. Even with my limited capabilities, I found myself increasingly able to speak to people who knew the same words, concepts, and expressions that our ancestors knew. More dramatically, I found myself looking at and thinking about things in ways that I imagined they did. It meant a great deal to me, and it brought me into a community unlike any other to which I have ever belonged.

This same community, I hasten to remind you, is now endangered with extinction because its language is in rapid decline. The bodies will remain, but they will speak, see, think, act, and feel differently from before, because one worldview will be supplanted by another. As Mithun succinctly puts it:

> When a language disappears, the most intimate aspects of culture can disappear as well: fundamental ways of organizing experience into concepts, of relating ideas to each other, of interacting with other people. The more conscious genres of verbal art are also usually lost: traditional ritual, oratory, myth, legends, and even humor. Speakers commonly remark that when they speak a different language, they say different things and even think different thoughts. The loss of a language represents a definitive separation of a people from its heritage. (2)

I haven't even mentioned the realms of ceremony and song, important though they are. I expect the greatest sense of loss to be felt not so much in the sacred realms of religious life but even more in the simple and affirming spaces of everyday human community.

So what to do? Readers of this collection will doubtless want to know what role might be played by today's teachers of writing in the struggle to preserve Native tongues and linguistic diversity. Unfortunately, my answer is: probably very little. Composition is for all intents and purposes an assimilation program designed to bring speakers of other languages and/or nonstandard dialects into acceptable Standard English usage. To admit as much is not to suggest that the work of the writing teacher lacks honor. Far from it. Even during the height of the assimilation era, prominent Native intellectuals argued hard for the vital importance of the English language to be taught to Indians as a means of ensuring their survival. Such is no less true today, so if you have Native students in your class, go ahead and teach them what they need to survive: Standard English. Doing so does not make you like General Richard Henry Pratt, killing Indians to save men and all that. It would mean you are doing your job, and your job is definitely worth doing. It helps Indians to live.

That said, let us also admit that English is a global language, not an "Indian" one. Mark me as one detractor of the view famously expounded by Acoma Pueblo writer Simon J. Ortiz, who in 1981 wrote this about the connection between culture and language:

> Along with their native languages, Indian women and men have carried on their lives and their expression through the use of the newer languages, particularly Spanish, French, and English, and they have used these languages on their own terms. This is the crucial item that has to be understood, that it is entirely possible for a people to retain and maintain their lives through the use of any language. (10)

Retaining and maintaining "lives," okay. But cultures? I don't see how. Ortiz is a fluent speaker of his language who has built a successful career out of his simultaneous fluency in English, so perhaps for him this continuity is easier to recognize than it would be for most Indians: the ones who lack his fluency on either side of the equation. On the other hand, perhaps Ortiz should be our model for the future, an exemplar of bilingualism, but that would be a far different claim than the one he makes here.

For my part, I see the indigenous language revitalization movement happening around the world as an attempt by Native peoples to claim rhetorical sovereignty in the face of daunting pressures to assimilate linguistically. A few years ago, I tried to define rhetorical sovereignty as "the inherent right and ability of peoples to determine their own communicative needs and desires . . . to decide for themselves the goals, modes, styles, and languages of public discourse" (Lyons 449–50). That general vision could be pursued in English, Spanish, or indigenous languages, so I am not a fundamentalist on the issue. But I do believe that the historical languages of peoples should always be given priority when compared to settler languages like English or Spanish, not because they are "authentic" in some essentialist manner but because they are threatened. History made these languages indigenous and history is now threatening to take them away; one need not be essentialist to resist the present threats. Besides, as I've been saying all along, they do carry cultural knowledge and ways of being—a certain habitus, if you will—that are threatened right along with them. So let the language activists imbue them with all the authenticities that may be required to get their programs funded, functional, and filled, and let the rest of us see this work as an exercise of sovereignty and support it accordingly.

Writing teachers can help in this regard by acting as good citizens: combating the constant efforts to make "English Only" the law of the land, arguing for public financing of indigenous language revitalization programs (in large part because their endangerment was initiated by the federal government and not some "natural" process), and teaching the issues and initiatives behind Native language movements around the world. They can promote bilingualism by agitating for official recognition and uses of indigenous tongues and by supporting bilingual programs that already exist. And they can follow the leads of Hawaii and New Zealand and demand state financing of immersion schools; such schools have been the most successful revitalization efforts to date. Finally, they can think about their own investments in somebody else's language. These investments would include, at very least, the importance of diversity in any thriving ecosystem, medicinal and scientific knowledges embedded in Native words and understandings of habitats, the intrinsic value of recognizing human identities by observations of their culturing, and the imagination of a world where more life is actually the meaning of life.

Works Cited

Child, Brenda. *Boarding School Seasons: American Indian Families, 1900–1940.* Lincoln: U of Nebraska P, 2000.

Cook-Lynn, Elizabeth. *Why I Can't Read Wallace Stegner and Other Essays: A Tribal Voice.* Madison: U of Wisconsin P, 1996.

Francis, Norbert, and Jon Reyhner. *Language and Literacy Teaching for Indigenous Education: A Bilingual Approach.* Clevedon, Eng.: Multilingual Matters, 2002.

Grenoble, Lenore A., and Lindsay J. Whaley. *Saving Languages: An Introduction to Language Revitalization.* Cambridge: Cambridge UP, 2005.

Hinton, Leanne, and Kenneth Hale, eds. *The Green Book of Language Revitalization in Practice.* San Diego: Academic Press, 2001.

Hinton, Leanne, with Matt Vera and Nancy Steele. *How to Keep Your Language Alive: A Commonsense Approach to One-on-One Language Learning.* Berkeley: Heyday Books, 2002.

LaDuke, Winona. *All Our Relations: Native Struggles for Land and Life.* Cambridge: South End Press, 1994.

Lyons, Scott Richard. "Rhetorical Sovereignty: What Do American Indians Want from Writing?" *College Composition and Communication* 51.3 (Feb. 2000): 447–68.

Mithun, Marianne. *The Languages of Native North America.* Cambridge: Cambridge UP, 2001.

Ortiz, Simon J. "Towards a National Indian Literature: Cultural Authenticity in Nationalism." *MELUS* 8.2 (1981): 7–12.

Pinker, Steven. *The Language Instinct: How the Mind Creates Language.* 1994. New York: Harper Perennial Modern Classics, 2007.

Treuer, Anton. *Living Our Language: Ojibwe Tales and Oral Histories*. St. Paul: Minnesota Historical Society Press, 2001.

Weaver, Jace. "Preface." *American Indian Literary Nationalism*. Ed. Jace Weaver, Craig S. Womack, and Robert Warrior. Albuquerque: U of New Mexico P, 2006. xv–xxii.

Weise, Elizabeth. "Researchers Speak Out on Languages on the Brink of Extinction." *USA Today*, 18 Sept. 2007.

Womack, Craig S. "The Integrity of American Indian Claims (Or, How I Learned to Stop Worrying and Love My Hybridity)." *American Indian Literary Nationalism*. Ed. Jace Weaver, Craig S. Womack, and Robert Warrior. Albuquerque: U of New Mexico P, 2006. 91–177.

8. Discourse Tensions, Englishes, and the Composition Classroom

Shondel J. Nero

The thrust of much of the debate on what has been variously called "alternative discourse," "mixed forms," "hybrid language," or even my own term "academic interlanguage" (Nero) has been couched in terms of dilemmas, conflicting goals, or tensions. Lisa Delpit begins her essay "The Politics of Teaching Literate Discourse" as follows: "I have encountered a certain sense of powerlessness and paralysis among many sensitive and well-meaning literacy educators who appear to be caught in the throes of a dilemma. Although their job is to teach literate discourse styles to all of their students, they question whether that is a task they can actually accomplish for poor students and students of color" (285). A decade later, Janet Bean and her colleagues noted: "Lucile Clifton's poem[1] sets the essential dilemma not just for us but for an enormous amount of teachers: what someone from one culture is thinking may not be fully sayable in the language of another culture. By inviting home languages in classrooms dominated by standard English, we seem to be pursuing an impossible goal. What shall we do?" (38). In both cases, the tensions expressed have to do with how to validate students' vernaculars and teach them academic discourse at the same time. Both Delpit and Bean and her colleagues propose concrete strategies as possible solutions to the dilemmas discussed in their respective essays. Delpit argues for teaching the dominant discourse and making explicit the culture of power in the classroom while providing models of vernacular speakers who have succeeded in the mainstream. Bean and her colleagues, using a different approach, suggest inviting students to write in their home language in certain situations (such as freewriting, fiction, or memoirs), leaving the home language as the final product, while in other situations (such as formal academic essays), the home language can be used as the starting point, then revised into edited academic English.

In this chapter, I problematize the tension itself by arguing that two factors are at play here on the part of both educators and students: (1) the reality of evolving language and discourses defying our perceptions of, and desire for, fixed linguistic codes and discourses; and (2) the assumption that acquisition or affirmation of one discourse comes at the expense of another, which is related to the differential power attached to particular discourses. In the case of the first factor, I discuss the historical movement to "fix" or standardize English, especially in school, even as the language and its users continued to spread and change. In analyzing the second factor, I examine how the power and prestige attached to standard written English (SWE), particularly its grammar, coupled with the stigmatization of vernaculars in the classroom, perpetuate a sense of a linguistic trade-off. I then present the case of Caribbean Creole English (CCE) speakers as one group, among others, that challenges the notion of English as a fixed code. Examples of writing from CCE speakers illustrate the simultaneous use of vernacular and school discourse, defying the classroom impetus for a linguistic trade-off. I conclude by considering the implications of the foregoing for writing pedagogy.

A Brief Historical Perspective

Efforts to standardize the structure and use of the English language are by no means novel. They began in the late fifteenth century with the invention of the printing press in England and gained momentum in seventeenth- and especially eighteenth-century England. John Dryden, for example, had very fixed ideas about the "proper form of English," but it was quintessential language purist Jonathan Swift and his near obsessive concern with "ascertaining and fixing" the English language who led the failed attempt to create an academy to regulate English (akin to L'Académie française) (Svartvik and Leech 62, 64). However, Swift's efforts did spur public debate about the need for an authoritative source on the language, leading to a significant milestone in the history of English—the creation of Samuel Johnson's *Dictionary of the English Language* (1755) and, later in the United States, the publication of Webster's *American Dictionary* in 1828 (Svartvik and Leech).

The creation of dictionaries did not fix English but rather helped to codify it; that is to say, it provided a space for explaining the language in terms of rules and exceptions. The eighteenth century did also see the rise of Standard English (SE), the variety associated with power, prestige, and education. More important, the culture of linguistic prescriptivism that emanated from eighteenth-century language standardization debates found an institutional custodian in schools and colleges in both England and the United States. It manifests itself in the ongoing tension between efforts to prescribe language use, largely through schooling, in order to save SE from its putative decline and in the reality of dynamic language use and change.

Within the American academic tradition, concerns about the so-called decline of SE, the primary linguistic code through which academic discourse is instantiated, go back to the nineteenth century. Specifically, during the post–Civil War era, American colleges and universities introduced first-year composition as a kind of gatekeeping course to ensure that entering freshmen displayed the requisite proficiency in SE as their key to membership in academia (Berlin). Much later, in the latter half of the twentieth century, E. D. Hirsch, in making the case for what he called cultural literacy, argued that such literacy can be achieved only by requiring all students to master SE because of its status as the most "communicatively efficient" form of the language. Drawing on psycholinguistic research on memory and information processing, Hirsch suggests that the formal structure of the alphabetic system used in SE is more efficiently processed, leading to cognitive gains. Thomas J. Farrell extends the argument by asserting that Black English-speaking students' cognitive difficulties in academia (for example, scoring low on IQ tests) can be attributed to their primarily oral culture but can be remedied by teaching them SE, which would automatically enable them to think "literately," that is to say, in ways sanctioned by academic literacy.

In all of the cases cited, SE is generally assumed to be a highly prescriptive code expressed within strict adherence to Western essayist conventions. What is also assumed is that SE is an inherently superior code, as evidenced by the suggestions that it engenders cognitive gains and communicative efficiency. Finally, and perhaps most important, is the assumption that SE is a fixed code and that academic discourse, which primarily uses this code, remains relatively unchanged as well. Because of the common assumption of a fixed code, and by extension a fixed discourse, students whose language and discourse norms appear to be, as Patricia Bizzell notes, "at a relatively greater remove from the academic dialect" are deemed to be using an alternative discourse (*Academic* 238). But one might argue, alternative to what?

Alternative/Hybrid/Discourse/ Language: Teasing Out the Terms

In order to address the foregoing question, it might be helpful to begin with Paul Matsuda's distinction between some of the key terms in the debate. He sees the term "hybrid" as referring to the discourse itself (including the language and range of rhetorical patterns) and "alternative" as referring to the status of the discourse. By separating the discourse itself from its status, Matsuda is attempting to show the socially constructed nature of what is considered "alternative," echoing Jacqueline Jones Royster's argument that it's really about alternative assumptions about discourses. I would contend, then, that because language is used to index both discourse and assumptions about it, it is important to examine language in use.

The reality of language use defies the bifurcated premise underlying the term "alternative discourse"—that the standard language is the default code, largely unchanged, and that all other language use is alternative. This notion can be challenged if we begin with Bizzell's definition: "A discourse community is a group of people who share certain language-using practices" (*Academic* 222). To the extent that a community's needs, worldviews, and material realities change naturally over time, their language use will evolve accordingly. The academic community is no exception. Bizzell notes correctly, "Because academic discourse is the language of a human community, it can never be absolutely fixed in form. It changes over time, and at any given time multiple versions of it are in use" ("Intellectual" 1). Thus, what counts as normal or acceptable language use in the academic community, including use of SE, is constantly changing, albeit slowly. John H. McWhorter reminds us to take a diachronic view of language, asserting, "All languages are always in the process of gradually changing into new ones" (*Spreading* 1).

Why, then, do we hold so tenaciously to the view that the dominant language of the academic community—Standard English—remains unchanged, while all other dialects change in unpredictable and even unacceptable ways? McWhorter believes that part of the reason is that we view language use as frozen in time, as if the way we speak and write now is, and has always been, the only way of so doing. In fact, the opposite is true. Language change is both normal and inevitable. But, more important, McWhorter contends that it is the social associations we make with language that preclude us from seeing its variable nature. He writes, "It is very tempting to think that the speech of Rocky Balboa or of young Black inner-city teens is somehow a breach of grammar, a deformation of English. Yet these dialects are nothing but products of the same kind of gradual language change that elsewhere turned Latin into French" (*Spreading* 6), or similarly turned Old English into Modern English.[2] The point here is that we often link the assumptions we make about the people who speak a language to the language itself. The other reason that we hold on to a fixed view of English as only SE, in my view, is that it assures those who are proficient in it a position of dominance. It becomes a linguistic benchmark to which students as novices must always aspire in the hopes of obtaining membership to the academic club. Bizzell writes that proficiency with the standard language conveys an "educated ethos" (*Academic* 140).

Language, Power, and Linguistic Trade-Offs

Students, however, are not all equal novices in academia. Those who come to school or college fairly proficient in the written and spoken language varieties closer to the SE privileged in academia have an easier time reaching the benchmark and gaining acceptance. In the United States, those students who primarily speak and/or write varieties of English such as African American Vernacular English (AAVE), CCE, Tex Mex, world Englishes (WE), or English as a Second Language (ESL)—language varieties deemed alternative—tend to have a harder time meeting the benchmark. In many cases, "alternative" is a euphemism for "deficient" or "missing the mark." The reality is that the mark is constantly shifting by virtue of actual language use, as noted earlier. But many schools and colleges continue to subscribe to the humanist literacy scholars' narrowly defined aspects of grammar and rhetorical patterns of SWE as shibboleths, giving the impression that the mark is fixed. Only those students who have passed the test—that is, displayed mastery of certain linguistic and rhetorical forms of SWE (for example, being able to write a cogent five-paragraph academic essay)—can become legitimate members of the academic community and, ironically, earn the right to flout its linguistic rules. As Bizzell writes:

> If Standard English functions to unite the academic community, then, we can understand why novices are required to produce it more strictly in accordance with usage conventions than mature practitioners are. The novice is initiated into and bonded to the community through the process of her mastery of the community's language. The mature practitioner, on the other hand, more secure in her position, can afford to relax these elementary ties. (*Academic* 140–41)

A case in point: the success of Keith Gilyard's seminal work *Voices of the Self*, written in a combination of AAVE and SE, was certainly helped by the fact that Gilyard was already a professor at the time of its publication.

Peter Elbow is forthright about this phenomenon when he writes: "Most faculty won't accept from students many kinds of rhetoric and structure that they happily write and read from their colleagues. The term *academic discourse* doesn't really apply to student writing. We need a term like *school discourse* for what academics demand of students—as opposed to what they accept from peers" (128–29). For students, therefore, success in school is predicated on knowledge and mastery of such school discourse, which means the discourse carries real power. A. Suresh Canagarajah asserts that a normative attitude exists in which "the discourses of academic communities are not open to negotiation or criticism" ("Multilingual" 32), which gives them a kind of unquestioned power. In this environment, he contends, the cultural and discursive differences of multilingual/multidialectal students are treated as a "problem" for academic writing and are therefore the only discourses that may be criticized. Richard Ruiz refers to this as the "language-as-problem orientation." This means that school discourses are often framed in opposition to students' home discourses, particularly those discourses considered alternative. Students with marked vernaculars may then tacitly get the message that they must *give up* (the limitations of) their home discourses to *gain* (the social and economic benefits of) school discourses, creating the sense of a linguistic trade-off.

Fortunately, actual language use is neither that static nor dichotomous, and discourses are not that easily expendable. Most students—really, most people—do not readily submit to linguistic trade-offs. Students and their teachers live and interact within and across various discourse communities, including school. Their language use thus influences, and is influenced by, that of the various communities of which they are a part. Put another way, school and home discourses are neither fixed nor mutually exclusive. And students whose home discourses may be further removed from the school's may choose to live with and use multiple discourses, even if they are in creative tension with each other. Furthermore, many students have a strong desire to maintain in-group identity and solidarity through the use of their vernacular. A few examples: Delpit notes that many African American youth, even as early as fourth grade, begin publicly to use more elements of AAVE as a marker of in-group solidarity within and beyond the classroom while simultaneously using standardized forms of English with their teachers. Canagarajah gives the example of Sri Lankans "shuttling" between their ethnic language and Sri Lankan English ("Toward"). Hubert Devonish and Karen Carpenter describe the language used by school children in Jamaica as "peer group school language"—a variety that emerges out of the interaction between various home languages and the "levelling process of peer group pressure in school" (28). The peer group school language described by Devonish and Carpenter is part of a wide spectrum of language use among Anglophone Caribbean natives at home and abroad, broadly defined as Caribbean Creole English.

Caribbean Creole English

I have spent the greater part of the last eighteen years studying speakers of CCE, not only because they have been entering U.S. schools and colleges in steadily increasing numbers (Nero), especially in urban centers, but also because their public claim to being native speakers of English continues to complicate the ownership of the language and the definition of the language itself. CCE speakers thus present an interesting case for the composition classroom. Before discussing CCE speakers, it is necessary to first offer a working definition of Caribbean English.

In *The Oxford Companion to the English Language*, Lawrence Carrington provides a definition of Caribbean English as "[a] general term for the English

Language used in the Caribbean archipelago and circum-Caribbean main-land. In a narrow sense, it covers English alone; in a broad sense it covers English and Creole" (191–92). Carrington notes that the term is somewhat imprecise because of a long-standing popular classification of varieties of creole as dialects of English, sometimes called "creole dialects" or "patois"; because of the existence of a continuum of usage between English and creole (known as a creole continuum); and because of the use by scholars of the term "English" to cover both, as in the *Dictionary of Jamaican English*. By way of clarification, Carrington offers a list of meanings embraced in the term Caribbean English: (1) regionally accented varieties of the standard language (the acrolect), (2) localized forms of English, (3) mesolects between English and creole, as found in most communities, (4) kinds of English used in countries where Spanish is dominant (for example, English in Panama), and (5) varieties of English-based creole (the basilect) (quoted in Morris 19).

Today, there is still some debate in scholarly circles, and even in the Carib-bean community at large, about whether to consider English-based creoles dialects of English or separate languages. As Peter Roberts notes, "The wide spectrum in Jamaica challenges the definition of a language in that it calls into question the extent to which two speech varieties in a society can dif-fer and still be treated as belonging to the same language" (9). The debate is more political than linguistic, as has always been the case when discussions of language versus dialect are raised. Salikoko Mufwene offers an insightful discussion on what he characterizes as "an insidious naming tradition," not-ing that much of the debate about whether creoles and other new Englishes are labeled as separate languages or dialects of English has to do with who is setting the norms (in this case, "non-native speakers") rather than anything inherent to the varieties themselves (*Ecology* 108). Michel DeGraff takes the argument a step further by noting that linguists' construction of creoles as exceptional languages—that is, giving the impression that their formation is somehow different than the normal process of language evolution—has hurt their speakers in the educational system.

CCE Speakers in the Composition Classroom

Most CCE speakers publicly self-identify as native speakers of English[3]—Eng-lish, that is, as they have perceived, known, and used it. This is not a problem in and of itself except that (1) the dynamic language use of CCE speakers, spanning as it does a wide spectrum, as described above, is at once marked as different from what is typically perceived as English in North America, especially in school, and yet part of what Tom McArthur aptly calls "the Eng-lish languages" (13); and (2) composition classrooms, as observed by Matsuda, hold on to "the myth of linguistic homogeneity—the tacit and widespread acceptance of the dominant image of composition students as native speakers of a privileged variety of English" (Matsuda, this volume). CCE speakers/ writers, like others who don't fit the image, are therefore exceptionalized in the composition classroom—much to their surprise. Unlike traditional second language learners/writers such as speakers of Spanish, Japanese, or Russian, for example, who view English as a second language and expect to be framed as second language writers, CCE speakers/writers do not expect their English to be deemed exceptional or different or alternative because of their self-identification as native speakers of English. Thus, CCE speakers/ writers challenge not only the myth of a homogeneous composition class but also that of a homogeneous English. These speakers/writers reflect the fact that English is not a fixed code (as traditional schooling would have us believe), and so, as they use their variety of English to engage in academic discourse, they are in so doing changing academic discourse itself.

The following examples from the compositions of two Caribbean college students in New York (Nadine and Oscar[4]) whose language I have studied illustrate their varied language use in an undergraduate composition class. The first is an excerpt from an autobiographical essay by Nadine in which she describes the experience of her mother's emigrating from Jamaica to the United States, then returning later to bring her and her brother to the United States:

1   August 28, 1982 my mother left my brother and me. At the airport in Jamaica,
     I was very serious and not smiling. It was one week after my birthday. "Chu Chu,
     Mommy going away for two weeks. I'll bring back a lot of things for you."
     I stood there speechless and serious. I had always been a serious child.

5   In kindergarten, my teacher spank me.
     "Mommy, Miss Dunkan lick me and mi nuh trouble har."
     "Teachers always hit children in order for them to learn."
     "Mi nah go back a school, mi Nanny a fi teach mi a yard."
     My mother left Jamaica and four years later she returned.

10   It was November of 1986 that my life took a turn. It was a Monday, a regular
     school day for me. This particular day I walked home alone. I entered my yard.
     I began to notice that all my neighbors were staring.
     "What happened?"
     "Nothing [Nadine]."

15   As I stepped into the house, I noticed that there was a woman sitting at my dining
     table. The face was familiar but I was still puzzled. There was a picture above
     her. The picture was my mother. I looked at the picture, then I looked at the

woman.

"[Nadine], do you remember me?"

20 "Yes, Mommy." Then we hugged. A month later, my brother and I were brought to the United States. I was nine and my brother thirteen. (quoted in Nero 86)

In this excerpt, Nadine blends creole, CCE, and SE to create a piece that captures the range of emotions of a child who is left behind by her mother at the tender age of five (inferred from the dates and age references in the piece) and then reunited four years later. The reader is immediately drawn into Nadine's feeling of abandonment in the first three lines. In line 1, we are told that the mother left Nadine and her brother. The date, an emotional one for Nadine, is etched in the little girl's mind—August 28, 1982—hence, it is stated first. The preposition "on," which would normally be placed before the date in an SE sentence, is absent in this case. The vernacular discourse that is being enacted here does not require it. The reader is placed in time by the date itself. Nadine remembers clearly that it was one week after her birthday. Then she gives us a picture of her mother's language in lines 2–3: "Chu Chu, Mommy going away for two weeks. I'll bring back a lot of things for you." The use of the vernacular is appropriate to represent the mother's effort to bond with Nadine. "Mommy going away" is authentic CCE. The auxiliary verb "is" that would be required before "going" in SE is not required here. The term of endearment at the beginning of the mother's statement is an attempt to soften the blow. The mother knows fully well that she won't be back in two weeks. Many Caribbean children grow up hearing such lines. This is part of the home discourse—someone is always leaving and will return . . . some day. It's the reality of living in a migratory culture.[5] In this brief opening paragraph, Nadine effectively captures this emotional migratory phenomenon. Her sentences are short but poignant. In SE, she says, "I stood there speechless and serious. I had always been a serious child."

In lines 5–9, Nadine takes us back to her kindergarten years by simply placing us there and telling of her most vivid memory of the time and place—"In kindergarten, my teacher spank me." CCE requires no past tense inflection on the verb "spank." The context already tells us it is in the past. Then in line 6, Nadine contrasts her Creole speech—"Miss Dunkan lick me and mi nuh trouble har" (Miss Dunkan spanked me without my provoking her)—with her mother's SE response, "Teachers always hit children in order for them to learn," suggesting the mother's subtle disapproval of her creole speech by modeling an SE response. This entire sequence captures the ambivalent feelings toward creole speech among many Caribbean natives, even as they (paradoxically) continue to use the language as part of everyday home discourse.

When Nadine's mother returns to Jamaica four years later (November 1986), we learn by inference that her mother's promise to return in two weeks was not true. Nadine could barely recognize her mother after the four-year absence. Only when she looks at the picture above the dining table, then looks at the woman sitting below it, does she make the connection. The imagery here is powerful, and the reader is drawn into the emotion of the moment in lines 19–20: "'[Nadine], do you remember me?' 'Yes, Mommy.' Then we hugged."

In these twenty lines, Nadine made effective use of all the languages at her disposal (Creole, CCE, and SE), bringing home and school discourses to bear in a powerful piece. Such language may have been unimaginable in a college classroom fifty years ago, and, lest we get carried away, is still being relegated to certain "low stakes" genres of writing, such as journals or autobiographical pieces. But the writing illustrates the kind of multivocal approach (a fusion of students' vernacular discourses with academic discourse conventions) initially proposed by Canagarajah, which he argues allows students to engage with academic discourse while still inhabiting their own identities ("Challenges"). Canagarajah continues to advocate this kind of codemeshing in the composition classroom as a start toward expanding the use of multiple Englishes and discourses in the academy ("Place").

The second piece is an excerpt from a research paper written by Oscar on the life of internationally acclaimed Jamaican-born reggae superstar Bob Marley:

1   Bob Marley's interest in music was reflected at an early age when he took more
    interest in action songs than regular classwork. He was quoted in a television
    interview as saying, "The teacher say who can write, write, and who can sing,
    sing. So me sing." Bob Marley was described by his teacher and mother as a
5   bright boy but more meditative than aggressive when it came to learning. This
    shows the foundation which Bob Marley possessed and perfected to bring out his
    career as a world famous musician and speaker for the poor and Black people of
    the world. . . .
    Bob Marley was described by Frank Owen of the *New York Newsday* paper as a
10 "complex problematic figure in society." He became fabulously wealthy leaving
    from his career a large sum of $35 million for his children at the end of his life.
    He nevertheless lived a simple life observing the strict laws of his Rastafarian
    faith. He was also described by Owen as a gentleman who was a "reformed
14 rudeboy" who knew how to take care of himself in a fight. (quoted in Nero 110–11)

Because this is a research paper written in the third person, Oscar seems more detached from the writing than Nadine in her autobiographical piece.

Oscar is attempting a more "academic-sounding" piece by using the typical cues of formal writing, as expected in a research paper. For example, he uses the passive voice in several places: line 1—"was reflected"; line 2—"was quoted"; lines 4, 9, and 13 "was described." There are also longer sentences with more lexical density, which give the writing a more formal feel, such as lines 5–8: "This shows the *foundation* which Bob Marley *possessed and perfected* to bring out his career as a *world famous musician and speaker.*" Oscar's description of Marley in line 10 as "fabulously wealthy" strikes me as his own idiolectal superlative to capture the level of Marley's wealth. Oscar also includes secondary sources in his paper (another cue that it's a research paper). He quotes journalist Frank Owen's analysis of Marley from a newspaper article as a "complex problematic figure in society."

There are only two instances of Creole usage in this excerpt. In both instances, they serve to project Marley's identity. The first is from Marley himself in lines 3–4: "The teacher say who can write, write, and who can sing, sing. So me sing." It's appropriate that Oscar quotes Marley's Creole words verbatim. Marley made his name by speaking about the difficulties of his own poor upbringing and giving voice to the needs and struggles of ordinary people through his music. And that voice is a Creole voice. In the second instance, when Oscar makes reference to Owen's characterization of Marley in lines 13–14 as a "reformed rudeboy," the juxtaposition of the SE "reformed" with the CCE term "rudeboy"[6] captures Marley's complex identity as the ghetto boy who has come to be accepted in the mainstream.

In both Nadine's and Oscar's pieces, they write about topics that resonate with them as Jamaicans. Despite the very different genres—autobiography versus secondary research—they both draw on their repertoire of languages and discourses to reflect their investment in the subject and to attend to the requirements of the particular genre. In a sense, their writings are "acts of identity" (LePage and Tabouret-Keller). Yet, these two writers do not submit to a linguistic trade-off. In other words, they do not choose one language variety over another. They both utilize the range of languages necessary to do justice to the characters in, and the context of, the writing. They are both writing and rewriting school discourse.

Implications for the Teaching of Writing

I began this chapter by articulating what I perceive to be a state of affairs framed as a dilemma by Delpit and by Bean and her colleagues—that some writing teachers are struggling with ways to affirm students' vernacular and teach them school discourse at the same time. The writing samples above suggest that students like Oscar and Nadine come to the composition class already knowing and using a range of discourses that include their vernacular and varying levels of the standardized variety, and they do not necessarily perceive such dynamic language use as alternative or as a dilemma. The dilemma, therefore, seems to be more in the mind of the writing teacher, who might feel that validating students' vernaculars would get in the way of his or her professional and moral obligation to ensure that all students leave the writing class competent in school discourse and with the requisite proficiency in SE to be able to pass college exams, write acceptable term papers, and function successfully in the world beyond college. This suggests three underlying issues: (1) the vernacular is framed as a problem; (2) the perception is that allowing the vernacular in class delays, or interferes with, the acquisition of the standardized school discourse, which is seen as more powerful and useful; (3) the teacher may feel uncomfortable publicly correcting his or her students' vernacular.

Ruiz reminds us that language-as-problem has been the most dominant orientation underlying pedagogy for vernacular speakers, and it has been harmful to them. It assumes that their language should be fixed, ignored, or eradicated altogether. This orientation leads to the second issue stated above. Jeff Siegel's review of the research on teaching vernacular and second-language speakers, however, has shown that there is no evidence that use of the vernacular or first language interferes with the acquisition of SE. In fact, the opposite is true—enhancing the use of the first language has consistently led to gains in both languages for bidialectal and bilingual speakers.

The third issue above is also a function of the first. To the extent that a teacher feels that the vernacular is a problem, he or she is more inclined to correct it. The teacher is likely aware, however, that excessive correction of vernacular features, especially highly stigmatized ones, can be demeaning to students and ultimately counterproductive.

A more effective way of teaching writing, especially to vernacular speakers, would have to start from a different orientation—language-as-resource (Ruiz). Marcia Farr and Harvey Daniels list first among their fifteen key suggestions for effective writing instruction that students should have "teachers who understand and appreciate the basic linguistic competence that students bring with them to school, and who therefore have positive expectations for students' achievements in writing" (45). Without this starting point, writing pedagogy can become narrowly prescriptive. In addition, composition instructors in the twenty-first century classroom are likely to be more responsive to their students if they do the following:

- Have training in language diversity, including the history, spread, and use of Englishes and related creoles around the world. Such training will introduce and/or enhance understanding of the complex linguistic identities and language use of speakers of diverse varieties of English and creoles, such as CCE speakers, and would address the similarities and differences of traditional second language speakers/writers. Such training would begin to debunk the myth of linguistic homogeneity in the classroom and beyond.

- Introduce language diversity as an object of study in the writing classroom so that students come to appreciate the variable nature of English and all languages and the notion that writers adapt their language to genre, purpose, and audience. An honest discussion of language diversity must also include a critical examination of the differential power (material and symbolic) accorded certain language varieties and discourses and the ways in which language minority students might engage and shape those discourses.

- Invite students to write in the vernacular where it's appropriate to the genre, as Bean and her colleagues suggest. Nadine's autobiographical piece discussed above, written in a mixture of creole, CCE, and SE, seems more authentic because of the judicious inclusion of the vernacular. It not only reflects accurately the range of language of a typical CCE speaker but also rejects the notion that SE is the only medium acceptable for writing. In fact, giving students a choice in the written medium is more likely to make them want to experiment with the standard variety without having to give up their vernacular. Canagarajah is forthright on this issue when he writes, "We satisfy the desire of minority students to engage with the dominant codes when they write, and make a space for their own varieties of English in formal texts" ("Place" 599).

- Attend to the vernacular influence in writing (organizational style, grammar, and mechanics) in explicit and sensitive ways within the context of the writing (Adger, Wolfram, and Christian).

- Include vernacular literatures in class readings to provide models of language diversity in the canon. From Mark Twain's *Huckleberry Finn* to Sapphire's *Push*, students should see that use of the vernacular has a long history in great works of literature.

- Provide opportunities for "regular and substantial writing practice, aimed at developing fluency" (Farr and Daniels 45). Such writing should be, of course, coupled with regular and constructive feedback from the instructor and from peers.

Teaching writing in the twenty-first-century composition classroom is, and will continue to be, about coming to terms with linguistic diversity as the norm rather than the exception. As the myth of linguistic homogeneity continues to be debunked by the very presence of who is in our writing classrooms, so too will dissipate the notion that school discourse is fixed. Linguistically diverse students are already rewriting English. The tension between vernaculars and SE will be a moot point, as SE itself is changing, albeit slowly.

Notes

1. The poem being referred to here is Clifton's "defending my tongue," which includes the following lines:

> what I be talking about
> can be said in this language
> only

2. McWhorter's more recent work takes a radically different, less sympathetic view of language change in America (*Doing Our Own Thing*). He now likens what he describes as a national shift from a written to an oral culture to language degradation and laments that "the new linguistic order compromises our facility with the word and dilutes our collective intellect" (*Doing* xxiii).

3. Svartvik and Leech list the Caribbean, along with Ireland and South Africa, as part of the Inner Circle of English in addition to the five traditionally mentioned countries—the United Kingdom, the United States, Canada, Australia, and New Zealand—an acknowledgment, not often made in past configurations of Braj B. Kachru's concentric circles, that English use is widespread in former British colonies in the region (3).

4. The names of the students are pseudonyms.

5. There's a long history of Caribbean parents who migrate to North America in the hopes of improving their lives economically, leaving their children behind in the care of relatives. Eventually (often years later), the parent is able to sponsor the child, returning home to bring them to the United States or Canada—a process known as staggered migration.

6. A "rudeboy" is a term developed in Jamaica during the 1960s to refer to a disaffected young man growing up in a poor urban ghetto who often became involved in crime.

Works Cited

Adger, Carolyn Temple, Walt Wolfram, and Donna Christian. *Dialects in Schools and Communities*. 2nd ed. Mahwah, NJ: Erlbaum, 2007.

Bean, Janet, Maryann Cucchiara, Robert Eddy, Peter Elbow, Rhonda Grego, Ellie Kutz, Rich Haswell, Patricia Irvine, Eileen Kennedy, Al Lehner, and Paul Kei Matsuda. "Should We Invite Students to Write in Home Dialects or Languages? Complicating the Yes/No Debate." *Composition Studies* 31.1 (2003): 25–42.

Berlin, James. *Writing Instruction in Nineteenth-Century American Colleges.* Carbondale: Southern Illinois UP, 1984.

Bizzell, Patricia. *Academic Discourse and Critical Consciousness.* Pittsburgh: U of Pittsburgh P, 1992.

———. "The Intellectual Work of 'Mixed' Forms of Academic Discourses." Schroeder, Fox, and Bizzell 1–10.

Canagarajah, A. Suresh. "Challenges in English Literacy for African American and Sri Lankan Tamil Learners: Towards a Pedagogical Paradigm for Bidialectal and Bilingual Minority Students." *Language and Education* 11.1 (1997): 15–36.

———. "Multilingual Writers and the Academic Community: Towards a Critical Relationship." *Journal of English for Academic Purposes* 1.1 (2002): 29–44.

———. "The Place of World Englishes in Composition: Pluralization Continued." *College Composition and Communication* 57 (2006): 586–619.

———. "Toward a Writing Pedagogy of Shuttling between Languages: Learning from Multilingual Writers." *College English* 68 (2006): 589–604.

Carrington, Lawrence. "Caribbean English." *The Oxford Companion to the English Language.* Ed. Tom McArthur. Oxford: Oxford UP, 1992. 191–93.

Clifton, Lucille. *Quilting: Poems 1987–1990.* Rochester, NY: ROA Editions, 1991.

DeGraff, Michel. "Linguists' Most Dangerous Myth: The Fallacy of Creole Exceptionalism." *Language in Society* 34 (2005): 533–91.

Delpit, Lisa. "The Politics of Teaching Literate Discourse." *Freedom's Plow: Teaching in the Multicultural Classroom.* Ed. T. Perry and J. W. Fraser. New York: Routledge, 1993. 285–95.

Devonish, Hubert, and Karen Carpenter. "Full Bilingual Education in a Creole Language Situation: The Jamaican Bilingual Primary Education Project." Occasional Paper No. 35. Society for Caribbean Linguistics, 2007.

Elbow, Peter. "Vernacular Englishes in the Writing Classroom? Probing the Culture of Literacy." Schroeder, Fox, and Bizzell 126–39.

Farr, Marcia, and Harvey Daniels. *Language Diversity and Writing Instruction.* New York: ERIC Clearinghouse on Urban Education; Urbana, IL: ERIC Clearinghouse on Reading and Communication Skills, 1986.

Farrell, Thomas J. "I.Q. and Standard English." *College Composition and Communication* 34 (1985): 470–84.

Gilyard, Keith. *Voices of the Self: A Study in Language Competence.* Detroit, MI: Wayne State UP, 1991.

Hirsch, E. D. *The Philosophy of Composition.* Chicago: U of Chicago P, 1977.

LePage, Robert Brock, and Andrée Tabouret-Keller. *Acts of Identity: Creole-Based Approaches to Language and Ethnicity.* Cambridge: Cambridge UP, 1985.

Matsuda, Paul. "Alternative Discourses: A Synthesis." Schroeder, Fox, and Bizzell 191–96.

McArthur, Tom. *The English Languages.* Cambridge: Cambridge UP, 1998.

McWhorter, John H. *Doing Our Own Thing: The Degradation of Language and Music and Why We Should, Like, Care.* New York: Gotham Books, 2003.

———. *Spreading the Word: Language and Dialect in America.* Portsmouth, NH: Heinemann, 2000.

Morris, Mervyn. "Is English We Speaking." *English Today* 36.9 (1993): 18–26.

Mufwene, Salikoko. *The Ecology of Language Evolution.* Cambridge: Cambridge UP, 2001.

———. "Language Birth and Death." *Annual Review of Anthropology* 33 (2004): 201–22.

Nero, Shondel J. *Englishes in Contact: Anglophone Caribbean Students in an Urban College.* Cresskill, NJ: Hampton, 2001.

Roberts, Peter. *West Indians and Their Language.* Cambridge: Cambridge UP, 1988.

Royster, Jacqueline Jones. "Academic Discourses or Small Boats on a Big Sea." Schroeder, Fox, and Bizzell 23–30.

Ruiz, Richard. "Orientations in Language Planning." *Language Diversity, Problem or Resource? A Social and Educational Perspective on Language Minorities in the United States.* Ed. Sandra Lee McKay and Sau-Ling Cynthia Wong. New York: Newbury House, 1988. 3–26.

Schroeder, Christopher, Helen Fox, and Patricia Bizzell, eds. *ALT DIS: Alternative Discourses and the Academy.* Portsmouth, NH: Boynton/Cook, 2002.

Siegel, Jeff. "Keeping Creoles and Dialects Out of the Classroom: Is it Justified?" Nero 39–67.

Svartvik, Jan, and Geoffrey Leech. *English: One Tongue, Many Voices.* New York: Macmillan, 2006.

9. A Rhetoric of Shuttling between Languages

A. Suresh Canagarajah

The dominant approaches to studying multilingual writing have been hampered by monolingualist assumptions that conceive literacy as a unidirectional acquisition of language competence, preventing us from fully understanding the resources multilinguals bring to their texts. According to the monolingualist assumption, writing in a second language mimics the process of writing in the first language. Therefore, the processes by which native speakers of English develop proficiency in writing English can be applied to explain the routes multilinguals should take to become proficient writers in English. This process of development is assumed to take place (or expected to take place) without any involvement from the other languages one speaks. At best, the competence of the multilingual is considered additive—that is, one language competence added to competence in another, each remaining distinct and whole.

However, research in second language acquisition points to the possibility that the relationship between one's languages is multilateral and generative. Through the notion of multicompetence, Vivian Cook theorizes the ways in which a multilingual simultaneously works with diverse languages of proficiency even as he or she communicates in one. Furthermore, the competence is more than the sum of its parts, going beyond the resources provided by the individual languages. In other words, a bilingual person's competence is not simply two discrete monolingual competencies added together; instead, bilingual competence integrates knowledge of two languages and is thus qualitatively different from monolingual competence. François Grosjean captures this possibility in an early psycholinguistic article with a telling title: "Neurolinguists, Beware! The Bilingual Is Not Two Monolinguals in One Person." This changing view, well underway in psycholinguistics and second-language acquisition, has yet to transform literacy and composition studies. Despite this, multilingual writers have drawn on personal and traditional resources (sometimes in surreptitious and subversive ways) to develop as competent writers of English (see Canagarajah, "Safe Houses"; *Resisting*). This chapter is part of a larger project to learn from the strategies of successful multilingual writers as they shuttle between languages and discourses (see Canagarajah, "Place"). After illustrating the complex writing proficiency of a multilingual writer in the textual study informing this chapter, I attempt to change the questions and frameworks of composition studies in order to develop a rhetoric that addresses the possibility of shuttling between languages and discourses.

Dominant Approaches to Explaining Multilingual Writing

How do teachers and researchers of English writing orient themselves in relation to linguistic and cultural difference in the essays they read? In what I will call the inference model, if they see a peculiar tone, style, organization, or discourse, many teachers instinctively turn to the first language (L1) or "native" culture (C1) of the writer for an explanation. This was the model and practice of some early versions of contrastive rhetoric (see Kaplan). Even now, sympathetic scholars in our field seek explanations from L1 or C1 for what they perceive as difficulties multilingual writers have when composing an essay in English (see Fox). Among other problems with this model, the writer is treated as being conditioned so strongly by L1 and C1 that even when he or she writes in another language, those influences are supposed to manifest themselves in the new text. Apart from this determinism, there is also the misleading assumption that one can unproblematically describe the traditions of L1 literacy by studying the English essay of a multilingual writer (even if the writer is a student in a developmental writing program). The model fails to acknowledge the different types of mediation that can complicate the realization of texts in different languages. For example, in addition to language, the writer's purposes, audience expectations, topic, and rhetorical and social contexts can contribute to textual differences.

In recognition of some of these limitations in the inference model, some scholars have now slightly modified their approach in what I call a correlationist model. They study the texts in L1 descriptively before they relate this information to explain the writer's peculiarities in L2 (see Indrasuta; Kubota, "Investigation of Japanese").[1] However, here again, we must be careful not to consider texts written in any genre, by any author, to any audience in L1 as suitable to produce generalizations about a language, and then apply them to explain problems in texts of any genre, author, audience, and proficiency level in English. How these different variables will create different realizations of the text is often not taken into consideration. This is in accord with a monolingualist orientation, which assumes that each language has an invariable discourse that will express itself in texts written by any author in any genre or context. Though there are a few rare cases where researchers have been able to study the same multilingual authors writing college-level essays in a classroom setting but in different languages, the important variable is still considered to be language rather than the many other mediating factors and negotiation strategies. Marjorie Cook, H. Dunkelblau, Gehan Wahid Kamel, and Ryuko Kubota ("Investigation of L1-L2") have each published studies that compare the writing in L1 and L2 of the same set of students. However, the large subject pool and quantitative modes of analysis don't permit these researchers to ask questions related to specific strategies of negotiation that I pose in this chapter. The model I am proposing, the negotiation model, considers how multilingual writers move *between* texts (see figure 9.1).

This third model is different from the first two in many respects: identity, agency, discourse, and competence of multilingual writers are not conflated or reduced to the characteristics we see within a single text or language. Instead, rather than studying multilingual writing in a static manner, locating the writer within a language, we would study the movement of the writer between languages; rather than studying the product for descriptions of writing competence, we would study the process of composing in multiple languages; rather than studying the writer's stability in specific forms of linguistic or cultural competence, we would analyze one's mobility (that is, life between multiple languages and cultures); rather than treating language or culture as the main variable, we would focus more on the changing contexts of communication, perhaps treating context as the main variable as writers switch their language, discourse, and identity in response to this contextual change;

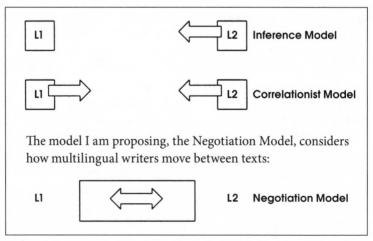

Fig. 9.1. Inference, correlationist, and negotiation models of multilingual writing.

and rather than treating writers as passive, conditioned by their language and culture, we would treat them as agentive, shuttling creatively between discourses to achieve their communicative objectives. As a precondition for conducting this inquiry, we have to stop treating every textual difference as an unconscious error. We must consider it as a strategic and creative choice by the author to attain his or her rhetorical objectives.

To adopt this analytical orientation to multilingual writers, we have to study the same writer composing in multiple languages, shuttling between one language/context/discourse and the other. Ideally, we should study the author writing in relatively the same genre though for different audiences and languages. This methodological approach would enable us to refrain from generalizing across subjects or contexts and address the ways in which individual writers negotiate their rhetorical challenges as they write in different languages. Needless to say, to conduct such a study, the researchers themselves have to be multilingual. Only scholars who are proficient in both (or all) the languages an author is using will be able to undertake this kind of study meaningfully. In those cases in which English is the researchers' only language, the best that they can do is to compare some other researcher's description of one person's writing in one language (other than English) with their study of that or some other author's writing in English, leading to the limitations of the first two models described above.

Background to This Analysis

In the following discussion, I compare writing samples from the same writer in the same genre (research articles, or RAs) in two different languages (English, or L2, and Tamil, or L1) in three different rhetorical contexts: RA in L1 for local publication (text 1); RA in L2 for local publication (text 2); and RA in L2 for foreign publication (text 3). The writing samples are from a senior scholar in Sri Lanka. Professor K. Sivatamby[2] has considerable exposure to the scholarly communities in the West. He obtained his doctorate in drama at the University of Birmingham and has held fellowships in foreign universities, including Berkeley. At the time of this writing, Sivatamby was a faculty member of the departments of Tamil and drama at the University of Jaffna in Sri Lanka. It is fortuitous that the writing samples I collected from Professor Sivatamby deal with the same subject: his attempts to analyze the ideological character of Jaffna Tamil society. Sivatamby is perhaps the only local scholar who has written extensively on this subject. The similarity of subject across the articles thus aids in controlling this analysis for topic as well. The question for us is: How does a single author present the same topic in the same genre in different languages for different audiences and publishing contexts? We are thus able to analyze how a multilingual writer shuttles between discourses without having to rely on essentialized notions of genre, subject, or language. In order to keep this discussion within a manageable level, I want to focus mainly on the introduction in the RA. The introduction is the most widely studied and described section in the RA genre (see Swales; Mauranen). This is also the section that receives the most rhetorical effort and composing time, as it emerges from ethnographic studies (see Knorr-Cetina). The introduction is the most discursively sophisticated and strategic section in the article, as the methodology and results sections have become more impersonal and stereotypical. I will invoke John Swales's typology of opening moves here, in what he calls the Create a Research Space (CARS) model. I use this model only for heuristic purposes, bearing in mind that RA discourse conventions vary across disciplines and communities. Swales's model for introductions is illustrated in figure 9.2.

Acts of Representation

The first article for analysis (text 1) was published in Tamil in a series for research monographs at the University of Jaffna. The following is the introduction:

> One of the features about Jaffna culture that is always visible but never discussed is a realistic depiction of the society. We don't speak or even attempt to speak about culture, which is always in front of our eyes besides regulating and controlling our social practices.
>
> Since this silence hampers the healthy development of this society, I am undertaking this analysis to fill this lack at least academically. At a period when our community is facing a serious crisis in its history, and when it is undergoing radical changes, it is the duty of the social sciences to at least provide some preliminary thoughts and data on our community's fundamentals and assumptions.
>
> Research relating to Jaffna society from anthropology and sociology are poor indeed. There are only a few foreign scholars working in this field (Bryan Pfaffenberger, Kenneth David, Skjonberg). Tamil scholars who have earned international prestige in these disciplines—like S. J. Tambiah—themselves do not give full attention to anthropological and social scientific research relating to the concerns of Tamil Eelam people.
>
> In a situation like this, doing research on the nature of the social changes taking place here is the duty of academics at the University of Jaffna. I have been drawn to this subject from the experience of reviewing the tradition of Tamil literature from the disciplinary perspectives of social history, sociology, and anthropology. This article is being written from that academic background. (Sivatamby, "YaaLpaaNa")[3]

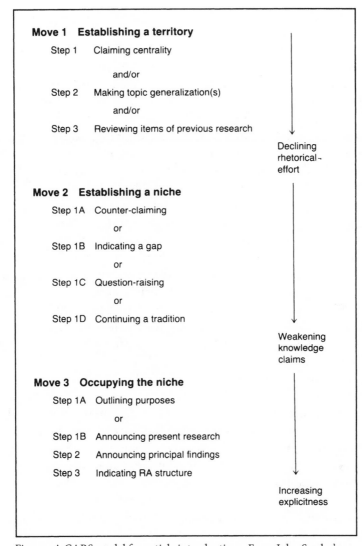

Move 1   Establishing a territory

Step 1   Claiming centrality

and/or

Step 2   Making topic generalization(s)

and/or

Step 3   Reviewing items of previous research

Declining
rhetorical –
effort

Move 2   Establishing a niche

Step 1A   Counter-claiming

or

Step 1B   Indicating a gap

or

Step 1C   Question-raising

or

Step 1D   Continuing a tradition

Weakening
knowledge
claims

Move 3   Occupying the niche

Step 1A   Outlining purposes

or

Step 1B   Announcing present research

Step 2   Announcing principal findings

Step 3   Indicating RA structure

Increasing
explicitness

Fig. 9.2. A CARS model for article introductions. From John Swales's *Genre Analysis: English in Academic and Research Settings* (Cambridge: Cambridge UP, 1990), 141. Copyright © 1990 Cambridge UP.

For readers of Western scholarly communities, Sivatamby's article in Tamil will be striking for the casual and relaxed opening. The author seems to be under no pressure to create a niche for this paper in the scholarship relating to this subject (move 2 in Swales's CARS typology, after the opening move of "establishing a territory"). This peculiarity can be explained by the fact that one doesn't have to market a scholarly paper aggressively in the local academic community. There is no urgency to fight for publishing space, earn academic credit, or attract reader interest here, which are the reasons why Western scholars adopt in their opening a "marketing discourse" (in Anna Mauranen's apt terminology). In the local context, academic publications are few and oral construction of knowledge—in colloquia and public lectures—earns as much credit (see Canagarajah, *Geopolitics*). Furthermore, material considerations such as the lack of good library resources and access to the latest publications also hinder local authors from creating a niche for their research. Without a sufficient awareness of the current state of academic conversation on a subject, one can't confidently say what is original about one's research.

What local scholars must adopt, instead, is what I have called a "civic ethos." Scholars must show what important service they are performing for their community by writing this paper and/or constructing this knowledge. One doesn't write papers simply to develop an original viewpoint and earn professional or personal credit. Scholarship has to be socially responsible. Therefore, Sivatamby opens by arguing that it is unwise and unhealthy not to discuss the ideological character of our society—controversial though the subject may be—as Tamils are living in a time of ethnic conflict and identity politics that demands a reflexive understanding of their own social formation. In fact, the author uses the word "duty" at least twice to emphasize that he is fulfilling an urgent community need.

This opening is significant also for certain other omissions of RA introductory conventions. The article doesn't announce the findings (or the author's thesis) in advance (move 3, step 2, in the CARS model). The author also doesn't indicate the structure of the article or the organization of his argument (another obligatory feature: move 3, step 3). Here, again, the author may be deferring to local expectations. In the local community, there is a preference for embedded modes of argumentation that respect the reader's involvement in deciphering the threads of reasoning in the paper. Being too explicit and calculated about the structure or argumentation would project an image of the author as pompous and the reader as ignorant.

The third paragraph appears to fulfill a literature review of sorts (an important step in the move of niche creation), but the names of certain authors are simply mentioned. There is no citation either here or at the end of the article. Also, the theses or important findings of these scholars are not discussed. This peculiarity is probably because local scholars often know the names and texts of those who have published on a topic but don't have the publications handy to do a close reading or to cite references (because of working conditions I discuss later). At any rate, the reason these names are mentioned here is to fulfill the civic ethos. The author is not interested in discussing their work in detail but only in pointing out why it is important for local scholars to address this subject. He intends to show that only foreign scholars have dared to address the subject, even though they too are few. It is possible also that these names serve to boost the authority and credibility of the author in the eyes of the local reader. The mention of these names shows that Sivatamby has the necessary background knowledge to discuss this topic intelligently. Therefore, the citation of names in this text functions rhetorically quite differently than in the West.

Another section that is not very prominent in this article is the description of methodology. Though this is a separate section that follows the introduction in Swales's typology, the statements in the final paragraph of the opening section seem to serve as a declaration of research approach and disciplinary orientation in Sivatamby's article. As a professor of drama, Sivatamby notes that his observations are primarily based on a study of literary texts (although from the analytical perspective of social sciences). There are many reasons why local readers/scholars don't expect in RAs any statement of narrowly conceived research with sophisticated instruments for extended periods of time. The work conditions in local educational institutions don't permit research of that nature. As long as one has an earned doctorate and possesses the relevant academic credentials, even informal, intuitive, and impressionistic observations are valued as scholarly knowledge.

At the end of the introductory section, most Western readers would usually ask: What exactly is the author arguing in this paper? We don't find any statements pertaining to the thesis in Sivatamby's article. Researchers have found that in articles where the thesis is not clearly spelled out in the beginning of the text, scholars tend to state it at the end. Scandinavian scholars adopt an end-weighted development, where they state their thesis after letting the reader work out their own conclusions from the proffered data in the body of the text (see Mauranen). However, instead of providing the thesis or a summary, what Sivatamby chooses to do at the conclusion of the paper is to humble himself: "If I have troubled anyone's mind with the manner in which I have presented this subject or the data, I ask for your pardon." Then he quotes a religious verse that acknowledges his limitations and invokes God to use him as an instrument for knowledge and human progress. He includes such an apology, perhaps because he has made many critical comments on competing ideologies that are sometimes held with religious zeal in the local community. This is also a very conventional speech act in local public speaking. Called *avai aTakkam* (humbling oneself before the court), this act may have connections to the rules of speaking in feudalistic times or before royalty. This is still the preferred opening move in public speaking. In local academic writing, I call this the display of a "humility ethos" (see Canagarajah, *Geopolitics*). As for the argument of the paper, it remains completely implicit. In some genres of local discourse, even to offer to tie all the threads at the end of the article is to insult the intelligence of the reader by not letting him or her do the interpretive work. This is perhaps another reason why the author chooses not to state his position or summarize his argument in the concluding section. The humility ethos is also revealed in his introduction. It is understandable that Sivatamby projects there an ethos that involves less self-display, agonistic tone, or claims to originality as stipulated by the CARS opening.

The second writing sample (text 2) by Sivatamby shows how an essay to the local community is written in English. This article appeared in a collection of essays by local bilingual scholars, featuring diverse disciplinary perspectives on the Jaffna society. Though there are some changes in tone and discourse in recognition of the English-speaking (and bilingual) audience, there are still many similarities with the previous text as both the English-dominant and Tamil-dominant scholars belong to the same community with related RA expectations. This is how the article opens:

> The Tamils of the Jaffna peninsula of Sri Lanka constitute the dominant Tamil group in the island. It is largely their experience at the national level and their perceptions of the Sinhalese and their motivations that have defined the Tamil grievances and decided the pattern of the struggle to redress them.
>
> An attempt is made here to understand the Jaffna man in relation to two of the most important ideological perceptions he has of himself: a) the preserver of the great Saiva-Tamil tradition, and b) the heir to the liberal traditions of the West and the reformist tradition of Gandhi symbolized by the Jaffna Youth Congress Movement.
>
> The Sri Lankan image of the Jaffna Tamil [is that of] . . . The relevant census figures of the Jaffna district for 1971 were . . . [more background information follows]. (Sivatamby, "Towards")

As in the previous article, there is no effort to create a scholarly niche for this paper, no announcement of thesis or main findings, and a lack of an anticipatory mention of the article's structure. What the author does achieve in the opening move resembles his rhetorical priorities in the earlier paper. There is an invocation of a civic ethos as he alludes to the current ethnic conflict in the island between the Tamil and Sinhalese communities. The author argues that it is important to understand the ideological character of Tamils if we are to understand the reasons for their resistance against Sinhala language.

However, there are slight differences in the introduction that indicate that the author recognizes the changed audience and is trying to fulfill their expectations. Note the formulation of the "problem" in the second paragraph. The author provides a formal statement of the research question discussed in this paper: "An attempt is made here to understand the Jaffna man in relation to two of the most important ideological perceptions he has of himself." The author lists the two perceptions separately. Though this is the same ideological tension that is analyzed by the author in the earlier paper, it is presented more succinctly here. We therefore see a more formal and explicit orientation to the research subject. This change of tone is further confirmed in this text's concluding paragraph:

> The quantitative and qualitative changes that have taken place in the evolution of Tamilian nationalism, should be seen in the perspectivity of the liberal Youth Congress tradition. That would provide the nationalist ideology with a continuity and possibility of development on social democratic lines.

There is no pronounced expression of a humility ethos in this conclusion, but there is a distinct academic ethos invoked with a suitable researcher-like language (for example, "quantitative," "qualitative," even the neologism "perspectivity"). Furthermore, the contradictory ideological strands introduced in the beginning of this paper are reconciled in a subtle and unobtrusive way. The author suggests that the liberal traditions of the West, introduced by the Youth Congress, will modify in a healthy way the chauvinistic streak in the religion-based Saiva-Tamil ideology. I believe that this shift to greater formality, explicitness, and impersonality is in recognition of the English-educated ethos of the readers of this article.

In the third rendition of the same subject (text 3), this time in a paper published in an international journal based in Sweden, we find even greater rhetorical shifts in the discourse in recognition of the foreign audience:

> The current ethnic crisis . . . has brought about an overall unity and solidarity among the Tamils of Ilankai [an indigenous name for Sri Lanka]. However, in terms of social formation—the social structure and relationships, the modes of production at the peasant level—we could easily see that there are three discernible Tamil formations. . . .
> [Brief historical introduction follows.]
> So, any study of the history of the Tamil demands within the Ilankai context should necessarily focus on the nature and role of the importance of Yalppanam [an indigenous name for Jaffna] Tamil society, the

type of problems it faced, how it expressed and formulated them as its political grievances, and the type of solutions it put forward. . . .

Amidst the social and political challenges which it had to confront, the Yalppanam Tamil society developed two ideologies which have been the main source of its social, intellectual, cultural, and political sustenance. Those are:

a) the Saiva Tamil ideology propounded by Armuka Navalar, and
b) the reformist liberal ideology of the Youth Congress.

They are in fact contradictory to each other, but in the manner they have been coalesced into that society and its political articulations, one finds the specific characteristics of the Yalppanam society emerging. A full-scale intellectual history of Yalppanam would be the apt academic way one could see how these two strands have been woven into one whole. [A footnote refers to another article by the author titled "An Ethnography of the Sri Lankan Tamils."]

In this paper an attempt is made to present in a preliminary manner the formation and the subsequent history, in outline, of the continuity of the Saiva Tamil ideology. (Sivatamby, "Ideology")

Though the civic ethos is thinly evoked in the opening line of the introduction (with the reference to the ethnic conflict), the author quickly moves on to show the academic significance of his analysis. The introduction presents in an even more explicit way the centrality of this subject (move 1, step 1, in the CARS model). The author methodically lists four issues that are important for analysis—the role and importance of the Tamil society, the type of problems it faces, how it expresses and formulates them as its political grievances, and the type of solutions it puts forward. Furthermore, the research "problem" is formulated even more rigorously and tautly (with both strands of ideology blocked separately for consideration): the Saiva Tamil ideology propounded by Armuka Navalar and the reformist liberal ideology of the Youth Congress. Also, the potential contradiction behind this dialectic and the evolving paradox are articulated with greater complexity. In fact, this paradox points indirectly to the thesis the author is developing in this paper (as we will find again in the concluding paragraph), which is that the religio-linguistic ideology may limit the egalitarian social changes unleashed by the youth movement. Finally, in this introduction, the author fulfills an important step in the CARS model—announcing the present research (move 3, step 1b)—in a very formal and direct way: "In this paper an *attempt* is made to present in a *preliminary* manner the formation and the subsequent history, in *outline*, of the continuity of the Saiva Tamil ideology" (emphasis mine). The language is significant for the care with which it is chosen. Note the hedges in at least three places within a single statement. The author projects a very objective and restrained researcher-like ethos here. However, the strategy might also be a paradoxical display of the humility ethos. I will discuss later how Sivatamby accommodates Western conventions on his own terms and sometimes finds ways of merging diverse discourses to develop a hybrid rhetoric.

What is fascinating about text 3 is that it was published about two years before the more informally and implicitly developed introduction of the first article discussed (text 1). Even the second article (text 2) was written eight years before the local publication in Tamil (text 1). In other words, the chronology is as follows: text 2 was published first in 1984, text 3 in 1990, and then text 1 in 1992. This fact suggests that the more rigorous formulation of the thesis and research problem in text 3 is not an effect of time (that is, attributable to the extended period of gestation Sivatamby may have enjoyed to sharpen the argument). If the author chose to open text 1 in a less explicit and direct way, this is not an act of omission or failure but rather an act of choice. The indirectness of the thesis in text 1 doesn't result from inability; it is a conscious strategy for specific rhetorical reasons. The author is leaving aside the tight formulation of the research problem (which he had already published eight years before this paper) in deference to the preference of local Tamil readers who expect a more implicit and subtle development of research findings. In fact, the author seems to even make a distinction between the English-based and Tamil-based readership in the local academic community. He is relatively more objective and explicit for the English readers in text 2, which too was written before the Tamil paper.

It is also interesting that there is an explicit development of ideas in text 3, written for the foreign audience. The conclusion shows that the author is conscious of a progression in the argument through the paper:

> But to say that the Saiva Tamil ideology has been weakened or is no more effective is to run to hasty conclusions. It should be remembered that the social base of this ideology at the place where it really rises—the rich peasantry—has not yet been changed in any effective sense. The possibilities of this ideology slowing down the social radicalization of the militants is [sic] not improbable.

The author assumes that the reader would have come to one possible conclusion while reading his analysis: "that the Saiva Tamil ideology has been weakened or is no more effective." However, he wants to nudge the reader toward another conclusion that is also implicit in his analysis—that the character of the peasantry, which sustains this ideology, has not changed. Furthermore, he projects a possible ideological development for the future—that the militant ideology of contemporary youth may get modified as the conflicting ideological strands play themselves out. This is a concession to the alternate argument. It provides a more qualified and balanced stance for the author. Such a complexly formulated conclusion shows that the author can adopt the CARS model or a more front-weighted writing typical of Western RAs if he wants to. He has his thesis, findings, and the different strands of argument carefully worked out for himself. But he is not choosing to present his argument in the CARS model in texts 1 and 2 as he prefers a different mode of presentation in his writing for the local readership.

Though the thesis is not explicitly developed in the body of the essay in text 3 (in fact, the author adopts a narrative approach as he recounts important stages of the community's history), he expects the reader to have followed the progression of his argument. This ending suggests a teleological progression for the paper. The paper displays an end-weighted thesis development. This observation would help us realize that while the author does make a shift to a slightly different discourse in this third paper, he hasn't changed his rhetoric wholesale. There are many features in this paper that are similar to the paper written for the local Tamil audience (texts 1 and 2). We find that even in text 3, there is no explicit niche creation, no literature review, and no advance statement of the findings, the structure of the article, or the evolving argument. These features are thus consistent across all three papers. I submit that the author is not giving in completely to the dominant discourses of Western scholarly readers, although he is aware of their preferences and accommodates them partially. He chooses, however, to retain certain other features of his preferred discourse even as he writes to the Western audience. We must wonder whether this is an act of rhetorical resistance, in which he is nudging the reader to shift to his discursive preferences even as he shifts to theirs. If this is indeed the case, what the author is attempting in text 3 is a multivocal discourse that merges the strengths of local scholarly discourse with the dominant conventions of mainstream academic discourse. This is an example of an author gaining voice and agency despite, alongside, and even through the dominant rhetorical conventions by skillfully inserting his preferred strategies in the text.

What gives credence to this subversive reading of the author's strategy is the enigmatic nature of two moves in the introduction of text 3. First, we have to wonder why the author fails to mention any literature at all here when he did perform a literature review of sorts in the first article. After all, that move is more important in the third text as the Western audience considers it almost an obligatory feature of RAs. However, the author probably realizes that this move has to be performed very thoroughly in order to satisfy an audience that has ready access to scholarly literature and expects an agonistic stance toward other texts as one builds one's own argument on a topic. I know from my life in Jaffna that because local libraries are not equipped to enable them to do a thorough literature search or find complete bibliographical information, many local scholars feel that they can't perform this move effectively. To provide an exhaustive literature review on the subject or even to cite completely the few publications referred to is impossible. (Note that even though the author refers to certain publications in the introduction to the first paper, they are not cited at the end of the paper. Nowhere in the paper are the complete bibliographical references provided.) Because of such limitations, local scholars adopt certain coping strategies (see Canagarajah, *Geopolitics*, for more documentation). They adopt what I have called "the less said the better" strategy. They prefer to start with a straightforward announcement of their research and get into their analysis rather than perform an incomplete literature review that would attract unnecessary attention to their limitations, generate criticism from the referees, and jeopardize their chances of getting published.

The second move that is puzzling in text 3 is the mention of a methodology—another obligatory move in Western scholarly publishing. The author claims an academic treatment of this subject by performing an "intellectual history" of Jaffna. To back this claim, he provides a footnote that refers to an article based on ethnography that he has previously published. The implication is that a similar methodology has been used for text 3, or that the discussion here is based on the ethnography he has already conducted. But when I consulted the paper he refers to in the footnote, I found that there was no mention of a sustained fieldwork having been conducted. That paper is an article on culture, based on literary sources—and perhaps on the author's informal observations as an insider in the Jaffna community. Since local scholars find it difficult to conduct extensive research with sophisticated instruments and resources, they fear that their findings may be construed as informal, intuitive, or impressionistic by Western scholarly circles. Therefore they are under pressure to find other ways of validating their "findings." Ethnography is a low-budget, "low-tech" method that can easily be adopted. The informal observations the author may have conducted are still justifiable as an impressionistic/anecdotal ethnography. At any rate, most readers do not inquire into the details of the research procedure. The author skillfully adopts an eminently useful academic convention—that is, footnoting—to make a claim without having to offer a full substantiation of it. The methodology, like the literature review, is a rhetorical act that makes a gesture toward fulfilling a move important for Western readers. This appears to be another coping strategy.

Local scholars sometimes thus parody Western conventions they don't strongly favor. They seek creative ways of fulfilling the requirements when they don't have the resources to do so satisfactorily. They may in fact exploit the academic conventions to their advantage, using one convention to negotiate another (in this case, using footnoting to deal with methodology). They also know that given the brevity of the research article, not all the information can be given in the body of the paper. Therefore, many moves in the RA are already rhetorical gestures even for Western authors. Local authors thus know that it is possible in a paper to make claims or drop hints to satisfy certain obligatory conventions without going through exhaustive scrutiny by the readers or reviewers of a journal. It is possible that this awareness gave Sivatamby the confidence that he would get published in refereed journals in the West. Furthermore, he probably knew that as papers on the subjects he was writing about are rare in Western journals, he had a greater chance of getting published, even if he didn't perform an exhaustive literature review or a methodology description. This article is at least newsworthy. Moreover, he would know that in the broad areas of social sciences and humanities, there is less importance attached to discussing methodology than in the natural sciences.

What I am suggesting here is that the author is not only being creative in shuttling between communities but also being critical in choosing the terms in which he wants to represent himself. The critical practice in his writing expresses itself in many different forms. There is a subversive side in finding surreptitious ways of fulfilling certain Western conventions, a satirical and parodying act of fulfilling certain mainstream expectations without total involvement. There is an appropriative function of finding spaces within the dominant conventions to insert one's own voice and preferred conventions. The author performs these strategies in a rhetorically satisfactory manner in order to get published in a refereed Western journal. This success, for me, proves the agency of multilingual writers. These authors are not conditioned by discourses to use them passively. They negotiate with them to use the competing literacy conventions on their own terms. They may very well be using a critical resource that multilingual and postcolonial subjects are specially endowed with. These are the benefits of the "double vision" or "in-betweenness" that is engendered in the interstices of discourses (Bhabha). As these authors move between languages and discourses, they use the conventions of one to orient critically to the conventions of another. The fact that Sivatamby could get published in a Western journal, despite choosing not to fulfill all the established moves of RAs, and in fact adopting certain atypical moves, shows that oppositional or alternative forms of writing are not impossible in the academy.

Is it possible to prove that Sivatamby was conscious of the strategies and resources he was using in his writing? In my informal telephone interview with him, I found it difficult to obtain concrete evidence that he had a well-considered opinion about his writing approach. It appeared that these were intuitive choices and strategies in his writing repertoire, no doubt developed over time through his multilingual writing experience. The lack of a conscious awareness of one's writing strategies is not uncommon. I received a similar response when I asked Geneva Smitherman about her similar strategies of merging African American Vernacular English and standard written English into her academic writing (see Canagarajah, "Place"). She said: "Would like to help this important work you're doing, it's badly needed, [so-and-so] was saying to me not too long ago that I should try to do some kind of conscious, meta-linguistic, outta body or whatever to figure out just how and when I do this code switching. Something I need to try to do." She in fact implied that it is the duty of other scholars to perform an objective analysis and help authors understand these strategies. Such strategies might even be unacknowledged by the authors themselves, as radical appropriation of textual strategies has questionable and risky status in the academy.

The intuitive strategies of multilingual writers don't necessarily come from a vacuum in the brain. There are powerful traditions of textual hybridity that these writers might be drawing from. It is interesting to consider the influences on Sivatamby's texts from the *manipralava* (mixed code) writing tradition from precolonial times in Tamil communities. At a time when Sanskrit was the language of religion and philosophy, Tamils mixed it with their vernacular when they started using Tamil language for such purposes (see Viswanathan). Through such mixing, they challenged the elite and sacred status of Sanskrit while upgrading Tamil as a language suitable for discoursing on such subjects. After the encounter with British colonialism, Tamils have adopted the same strategy of code-mixing in their postcolonial academic and literary writing. Even popular magazines fluidly move between English and Tamil, without translations or glosses, assuming a veritable bilingual reading. There are other literacy traditions in non-Western communities that are similarly multilingual and multimodal (see de Souza on the literacy practices of the Kashinawa in Brazil). The mode of writing valued in the Western communities, on the other hand, is graphocentric (see Mignolo; de Souza). According to this tradition, what are valued are texts that are monolingual and unimodal (that is, texts using written words from one language at the exclusion of other symbol systems and modalities). It is this graphocentric tradition that still appears to influence the monolingualist assumptions dominant in composition.

Developing a Multilingual Rhetorical Orientation

As we consider the implications of Sivatamby's writing practice to develop a rhetorical orientation that would do justice to the resources and strengths of multilingual writers, we must first note an important textual comparison in the examples above. There are greater similarities in discourse between text 1 and text 2, although they are written in different languages. On the other hand, though text 2 and text 3 are both in English, the discourse is very much different as the author is writing these papers to different communities. This comparison should show us that language doesn't determine the difference in the texts of multilingual authors; rather, it is context or audience that motivates the difference in discourse. Sivatamby's first two texts are roughly similar in their implicit thesis development and invocation of civic ethos and humility ethos. This similarity can be explained by the local audience he is addressing in these papers. In other words, it is not language or culture but rhetorical context/objective that is the main variable in multilingual writing. Whatever language authors choose to use, they can vary their style and discourse depending on the rhetorical context. This finding should be a corrective to composition teachers who perceive multilingual writers as always conditioned by their native language or culture.

The comparison also shows that there are multiple genres of English writing for multilingual writers. Using English language doesn't mean a single way of writing. The same language may be used to construct different texts if the language is used for different contexts and communities. This should show us the limitations of thinking of a specific language as endowed with a specific culture or a specific mode of writing. Equating one language with one discourse (the usual practice of contrastive rhetoric) is terribly limited. For Sivatamby, the same language holds very diverse possibilities—that is, different textual realizations. Furthermore, both English and Tamil have multiple realizations in the same genre of RA writing. They provide possibilities for the author to adopt different discourses for the same genre, motivated by different linguistic and cultural preferences. Moreover, within the same text, Sivatamby finds ways of accomplishing diverse rhetorical acts. The text thus becomes hybrid. If we want to address constraints in writing, it is more relevant to think about the repertoire of a writer than about the repertoire of a language or culture. The author can choose from the different options available to him or her as a multilingual.

This textual comparison illustrates the agency of multilingual writers. They are not linguistically or culturally conditioned to write only in one particular way. They can be rhetorically creative. In fact, it is their very multilingualism that may account for their creativity. Their multilingualism provides that magical "double vision" that enables them to understand the possibilities and constraints of competing traditions of writing and to carve out a space for themselves within conflicting discourses. This realization should show the limitations of thinking of writers as coming with homogeneous identities. Multilingual writers, like everyone else, come with multiple identities. What they choose to display varies according to diverse contexts in order to achieve their interests.

The shifts in rhetorical perspective can be represented as follows:

Monolingual Orientation	Multilingual Orientation
focus on language/culture	focus on rhetorical context
language = uniform discourse/genre	language = multiple discourses/genres
repertoire of the language/culture	repertoire of the writer
texts as homogeneous	texts as hybrid
writer as passive	writer as agentive
writer as linguistically/culturally conditioned	writer as rhetorically creative
writer as coming with uniform identities	writer as constructing multiple identities

Pedagogical Implications

How will the above orientations motivate a writing pedagogy of shuttling between communities? The shifts in pedagogy can be represented as follows:

Monolingual Orientation	Multilingual Orientation
deficiency/errors	choices/options
focus on rules/conventions	focus on strategies
texts as transparent/objective	texts as representational
focus on text construction	focus on rhetorical negotiation
written discourse as normative	written discourse as changing
writing as constitutive	writing as performative
texts as static/discrete	texts as fluid
texts as context-dependent	texts as context-transforming
compartmentalization of literacy traditions	accommodation of literacy traditions
L1 or C1 as a problem	L1 or C1 as a resource
orality as a hindrance	orality as an advantage

We must keep in mind that not every textual or linguistic difference is an error (as I noted at the beginning of this chapter). Many of the presumed errors can be choices made by authors from a range of different options in order to achieve their communicative purposes. For this reason, we must encourage students to orient to strategies of communication and de-emphasize a strict adherence to rules and conventions. The rules and conventions can be negotiated for one's purposes with suitable strategies. Though Sivatamby is aware of the dominant conventions in each context, and in fact accommodates them on occasion, he also modifies them slightly for his purposes. We have to teach our students strategies for rhetorical negotiation so that they can modify, resist, or reorient to the rules in a manner favorable to them. While there is a school for learner strategy training in English for Speakers of Other Languages (see Wenden), we also have descriptive studies of favorable strategies that multilingual writers may use in order to negotiate competing discourses effectively (see Leki; Canagarajah, *Critical* 118–21). Furthermore, we must encourage students to stop focusing on writing as a narrowly defined process of text construction. Writing is rhetorical negotiation for achieving social meanings and functions. In other words, writing is not just constitutive, it is also performative. We don't ordinarily write simply to construct a rule-governed text except in English composition courses. Although it is important for texts to be constructed sensibly in order to be meaningful, we write in order to perform important social acts. We write to achieve specific interests, represent our preferred values and identities, and fulfill diverse needs. Sivatamby is writing because he wants to help the local community understand its political conflicts, encourage scholars to pay more attention to the political crisis, and develop a rhetoric that represents his social values and personal interests. Furthermore, students should understand that texts are not objective and transparent, written only to reveal certain viewpoints or information. Texts are also representational. They display our identities, values, and interests. It is advisable, therefore, for students to engage with the text to accomplish their preferred interests rather than let the dominant conventions represent their values according to their choosing. The pedagogy should make students critically aware of their interests in writing, values motivating their rhetoric, and identities constructed by their texts.

In order to fulfill these expectations in writing, we should encourage multilingual students—in fact, all students—to look at the text/context connection in a different way. Texts are not simply context-bound or context-sensitive; they are context-transforming. It is for this reason that students should not treat rules and conventions as given or predefined for specific texts and contexts. They should think of texts and discourses as changing and changeable. Students can engage critically in the act of changing the rules and conventions to suit their interests, values, and identities. In other words, we are interested in developing not only competent writers but also critical writers. Therefore, though we should make students sensitive to the dominant conventions in each rhetorical context, we must also teach them to critically engage with them. We should help students demystify the dominant conventions behind a specific genre of writing, relate their writing activity to the social context in which it takes place, and shape writing to achieve a favorable voice and representation for themselves.

In such a multilingual pedagogy of writing, we would treat the first language and culture as a resource, not a problem. We would try to accommodate diverse literacy traditions—not keep them divided and separate. If we invoke differences in communities, it would not be to discount their value but to engage with them in order to find a strategic entry point into English. Similarly, we should reconsider the place of orality in writing. Oral discourse and oral traditions of communication may find a place in writing as they provide useful resources for narrative and voice for students from multilingual backgrounds. They can also help deconstruct the values behind literate traditions and expand the communicative potential of writing. Sivatamby's affinity to the orality-dominant local academic community and Tamil knowledge-making practices (such as the *manipralava* tradition) help him to draw from their resources to deconstruct mainstream texts and critique the conventions of literate communication.

Conclusion

The methodology and analytical orientation adopted in this study are important not only for second language writers. For all of us, literacy in the context of globalization involves shuttling between diverse languages and modalities of communication. The term "multiliteracies" captures the new need for all of us in writing (Cope and Kalantzis). Even first-language students of English have to shuttle between diverse communities and contexts in their professional, social, and personal lives. The dominant monolingualist orientation to composition cannot address the needs of our students today. The multilingual orientation provides a more robust paradigm that accommodates the literacy needs of postmodern citizens in globalization. Compositionists have to turn their attention to developing pedagogies of shuttling between languages and communities. If we truly want to reinvigorate English composition and make it relevant for the increasingly multilingual communication of globalization, it is important to learn from the writing practice of expert multilingual writers and traditions of multiliteracies in non-Western communities.

Notes

This is an expanded and revised version of an article that appears in *College English* (see Canagarajah, "Toward.") I thank Professor K. Sivatamby for encouraging me to study his writing strategies and for permitting me to quote from his articles.

1. Kubota ("Investigation of Japanese") demonstrates the advantages of this approach by comparing Japanese students writing in Japanese and Canadian students writing in English. Similarly, Indrasuta compares Thai students writing in Thai and American students writing in English.

2. I am using the real name of the author as I am discussing articles that are already published.

3. The translation of the title is the author's own. The rest of the text has been translated from the original Tamil to English by me.

Works Cited

Bhabha, Homi K. *The Location of Culture.* New York: Routledge, 1994.

Canagarajah, A. Suresh. *Critical Academic Writing and Multilingual Students.* Ann Arbor: U of Michigan P, 2002.

———. *A Geopolitics of Academic Writing.* Pittsburgh: U of Pittsburgh P, 2002.

———. "The Place of World Englishes in Composition: Pluralization Continued." *College Composition and Communication* 57 (2006): 586–619.

———. *Resisting Linguistic Imperialism in English Teaching.* Oxford: Oxford UP, 1999.

———. "Safe Houses in the Contact Zone: Coping Strategies of African American Students in the Academy." *College Composition and Communication* 48 (1997): 173–96.

———. "Toward a Writing Pedagogy of Shuttling between Languages: Learning from Multilingual Writers." *College English* 68 (2006): 589–604.

Cook, Marjorie. "The Validity of the Contrastive Rhetoric Hypothesis as It Relates to Spanish-Speaking Advanced ESL Students." Diss. Stanford University, 1988. *Dissertation Abstracts International*, 49/9, 2567A.

Cook, Vivian. "Going Beyond the Native Speaker in Language Teaching." *TESOL Quarterly* 33.2 (1999): 185–209.

Cope, Bill, and Mary Kalantzis, eds. *Multiliteracies: Literacy Learning and the Design of Social Futures.* New York: Routledge, 2000.

De Souza, Lynn Mario. "A Case among Cases, a World among Worlds: The Ecology of Writing among the Kashinawa in Brazil." *Journal of Language, Identity, and Education* 1.4 (2002): 261–78.

Dunkelblau, H. "A Contrastive Study of the Organizational Structure and Stylistic Elements of Chinese and English Expository Writing by Chinese High School Students." Diss., 1990. *Dissertation Abstracts International*, 51/4, 1143A.

Fox, Helen. "Being an Ally." *ALT DIS: Alternative Discourses and the Academy.* Ed. Christopher Schroeder, Helen Fox, and Patricia Bizzell. Portsmouth, NH: Boynton/Cook, 2002. 57–67.

Grosjean, François. "Neurolinguists, Beware! The Bilingual Is Not Two Mono-linguals in One Person." *Brain and Language* 36 (1989): 3–15.

Indrasuta, C. "Narrative Styles in the Writing of Thai and American Students." *Writing across Languages and Cultures: Issues in Contrastive Rhetoric.* Ed. Alan C. Purves. Newbury Park, CA: Sage, 1988. 206–26.

Kamel, Gehan Wahid. "Argumentative Writing by Arab Learners of English as a Foreign and Second Language: An Empirical Investigation of Contrastive Rhetoric." Diss. Indiana University of Pennsylvania, 1989. *Dissertation Abstracts International* 50/3, 677A.

Kaplan, Robert B. "Cultural Thought Patterns in Intercultural Education." *Language Learning* 16 (1966): 1–20.

Knorr-Cetina, Karin D. *The Manufacture of Knowledge: An Essay on the Constructivist and Contextual Nature of Science.* Oxford: Pergamon, 1981.

Kubota, Ryuko. "An Investigation of Japanese and English L1 Essay Organization: Differences and Similarities." *Canadian Modern Language Review* 54 (1998): 475–507.

———. "An Investigation of L1-L2 Transfer in Writing among Japanese University Students: Implications for Contrastive Rhetoric." *Journal of Second Language Writing* 7 (1999): 69–100.

Leki, Ilona. "Coping Strategies of ESL Students in Writing Tasks across the Curriculum." *TESOL Quarterly* 29 (1995): 235–60.

Mauranen, Anna. *Cultural Differences in Academic Rhetoric.* Frankfurt am Main, Germany: Lang, 1993.

Mignolo, Walter D. *Local Histories/Global Designs: Coloniality, Subaltern Knowledges, and Border Thinking.* Princeton: Princeton UP, 2000.

Sivatamby, K. "The Ideology of Saiva-Tamil Integrality: Its Sociohistorical Significance in the Study of Yalppanam Tamil Society." *Lanka* 5 (1990): 176–82.

———. "Towards an Understanding of the Culture and Ideology of the Tamils of Sri Lanka." *Commemorative Souvenir: Jaffna Public Library.* Jaffna, Sri Lanka: Catholic Press, 1984. 49–56.

———. "YaaLpaaNa camuukaTai viLanki koLLal—aTan uruvaakkam asaiviyakkam paRRiya oru piraarampa usaaval" [Understanding Jaffna Society: A Preliminary Inquiry into Its "Formation" and "Dynamics"]. Prof. S. Selvanayagam Memorial Lecture 8, University of Jaffna, Sri Lanka, June 1992. Mimeograph.

Smitherman, Geneva. E-mail to the author. 10 Feb. 2004.

Swales, John. *Genre Analysis: English in Academic and Research Settings.* Cambridge: Cambridge UP, 1990.

Viswanathan, Gauri. "English and Literate Society." *The Lie of the Land: English Literary Studies in India.* Ed. R. S. Rajan. Oxford: Oxford UP, 1993. 29–41.

Wenden, A. *Learner Strategies for Learner Autonomy.* New York: Prentice Hall, 1991.

Two

Responses to Struggling with
"English Only" in Composition

10. Ownership of Language and the Teaching of Writing

Shirley Wilson Logan

Language is dynamic, fluid, ever changing. Attempts to regulate it and fix it in time will always fail. Attempts to disparage certain language dialects or the users of those dialects and to privilege users of others have all too often succeeded. Electronic communication has further erased linguistic borders and exposed the absurdity of projects to mandate and legislate national languages. So what's a twenty-first-century writing teacher to do? The chapters in the first section provide a variety of answers to this question, all linked to the recognition that language is a tool of communication shaped to fit the purposes of those who use it. In this response, I consider how these answers have reaffirmed and redirected my still-evolving understanding of what writing teachers can do to develop their students' rhetorical and digital sophistication—as in the experiences Gail E. Hawisher and Cynthia L. Selfe with Yi-Huey Guo and Lu Liu chronicle—to communicate in a variety of situations and to learn to appreciate the linguistic dialects they encounter in the process.

In his chapter "A Rhetoric of Shuttling between Languages," A. Suresh Canagarajah observes the tendency to attribute linguistic variances to first-language interference (my term). The practice is based on the belief that a writer's first language will always affect and even overdetermine his or her ability to communicate effectively in English. This inference model (his term) for explaining multilingual writing fails to take into account other factors—purpose, context, audience—that could account for textual differences. By comparing an experienced multilingual writer composing a research article in his first and second languages within three different rhetorical contexts, Canagarajah makes the point that we need to adopt a multilingual orientation to composition, one that recognizes that what we often misinterpret as second language interference is in fact accommodation to different audiences and different purposes. Relatedly, often implied in explanations of peculiarities in the English essays of multilingual writers is a lack of intelligence on the part of the writer or speaker, especially if the first language is based in an already marginalized culture or a so-called third world culture. Enslaved Africans in America, already literate in other languages, were one such group. William D. Piersen noted as a corrective that slaves "were not speaking English like idiots, but like Africans" (40).

This tendency is closely related to what John Trimbur in his chapter refers to as "a now familiar gesture [in which] language and race become proxies for each other." Elaine Richardson, in her chapter, also expands upon the damning characterizations of "subhuman jibberish-speaking slaves in need of domestication and civilization." Such characterizations were necessary to support the purposes of American slavery, based on the belief in an inferior race, speaking an inferior version of the oppressor's language.

Trimbur argues for the use of multiple languages in American culture and against the "English Only" movement and even against linguistic tolerance. He points out that instead of adopting a laissez-faire attitude toward language use, the American Founding Fathers—in particular, Thomas Jefferson—adopted an attitude based on expedience rather than a belief in the equality of languages. Jefferson's denunciation of the Louisiana Remonstrance of 1804, which decreed that only English should be used in territorial transactions, was based not on a concern for the residents' rights to their own language but on the belief that it would not be expedient to require a new language so soon. This argument reveals the extent to which an English Only mentality informed the making of America from the outset. Such an embedded resistance to multilingualism helps to explain why attitude change is so difficult to accomplish in this English Only environment.

Kate Mangelsdorf's chapter critiques the practice of sorting students according to their English language abilities and reminds us that "'standard' language is a social rather than a linguistic construct." The chapter brought to mind an article in *Wired* on the growing popularity in China of what is often called "Chinglish," a variation of English developing on its own and often without the benefit of native English speakers. The author of the article makes the point that "by 2020, native speakers will make up only 15 percent of the estimated 2 billion people who will be using or learning the language. Already, most conversations in English are between nonnative speakers who use it as a lingua franca." When I first read the title of the *Wired* article— "How English Is Evolving into a Language We May Not Even Understand"—I braced for another lament on the decline of Standard English. Instead, the author takes the sensible view that "Chinglish" may actually turn out to be more efficient than current versions of English, even suggesting that native speakers and writers of English may find it necessary to learn this variation of their own language to communicate broadly (Erard). In using the term "native speakers" here, I borrow Mangelsdorf's definition, which includes both monolingual and multilingual speakers and writers. Mangelsdorf says that we must be conscious of this distinction between monolingual writers and their multilingual counterparts, who are often evaluated against an imagined, idealized Standard English norm. Conversations in our writing classrooms about such trends and distinctions could serve to promote new ways of understanding the openness of language and the need to decenter our own versions of English.

Related to this issue for me is that an increasing number of international graduate students are enrolled in my English 101 teacher preparation classes, having been awarded departmental teaching assistantships. These are multilingual future first-year writing instructors, whose first language is not English and whose experiences are not based in U.S. culture. Many are concerned about a loss of credibility once their students hear them speak with what they understand to be a "foreign accent," even though the information they provide will comport with programmatic requirements in all respects. They are worried that they will not be able to draw as many examples from U.S. popular culture, especially from television shows, as their U.S. peer teachers. I generally say to them that the kinds of engagements they can have with the students will be mutually beneficial in that their students will have the opportunity to experience more completely the wide array of cultural and linguistic experiences out of which their own versions of English develop. Likewise, approaching English as a second or third language gives the international TA a more nuanced vantage point from which to view the difficulties students often have in grasping some of the arbitrary conventions of written English. It could be argued, in fact, that such teachers are better equipped to develop students' ability to navigate the complexities associated with learning those conventions, whether the students are monolingual or multilingual English writers and speakers.

These engagements could also then facilitate discussions, led by writing instructors regardless of linguistic backgrounds, on the many versions of English already present in the classroom to make the point articulated in Shondel J. Nero's chapter. She argues that the writing classroom's fluidity of Englishes should not be thought of as a problem nor as a loss of an established stable tradition of English writing, which is, in fact, always changing. Nero reminds us that past and current attempts to discipline or regulate English and to serve as individual or institutional custodians of English in order to save it from "decline" ignore this central characteristic of a dynamic language. Those who make such attempts even claim that this monolithic Standard English enables more intellectually rigorous cognitive processes. These claims, in turn, are linked to assumptions of the general superiority of those thought to speak this allegedly unadulterated English. They are motivated by more than the desire to preserve a certain kind of English; they are rooted in the desire to maintain power, control, and privilege. Our own teaching practices reflect these desires, particularly when we tell our first-year writing students that in order to succeed in the academy, they must learn the "academic discourse." I have not yet been able to determine just what this term means in a general sense that would hold across the academy, and since the meaning will vary according to the context, it seems more useful to teach students how to adapt their writing to those various contexts rather than create the impression that there is this mysterious discourse to which they must be initiated before they can become bona fide members of the academy. As Nero suggests, perhaps a better term might be "school discourse," and even that term should not imply one particular way of communicating but should be understood as a rhetorical stance one takes toward writing in various academic situations. I found myself writing "Yes!" all along the margins of Nero's chapter, especially in the last section where she considers implications for the teaching of writing.

Min-Zhan Lu's description of the practice of tongue surgery in China and South Korea to reduce first-language accents and to improve economic advancement in English-speaking contexts is compelling. Lu encourages a move away from what she calls "standardized" English to appreciate more fully the value of a richer figurative language. Chinua Achebe's comparison of his original passage from *Arrow of God* with a "standardized" version supports the claim that discourse is enriched by use of this mixture of figurative and literal language, although I suspect that no one really communicates in this literal manner, one that has been stripped of nuanced meaning. The important point this comparison reinforces is that since no one actually uses language in this bare-bones way, every user is always already employing his or her own version of language. As Richardson observes, language users adapt language to fit their worldview. Whether the version is acceptable or not often depends upon metalinguistic factors that take us back to Trimbur's point about the conflation of language and social position. Further, this recognition of unique adaptation also echoes Paul Kei Matsuda's chapter, where he argues persuasively for recognition of the heterogeneity of language practices in our already multilingual higher education writing classrooms.

I found especially useful Lu's foregrounding of James Baldwin's distinction between "imitating" and "using" a language and how that distinction moves us to consider the extent to which we should promote not only our students' rights to their home languages but also their rights to use—and in the process to transform—languages of wider communication. Thus, it is not enough to insist on the value and usefulness of the languages our students bring to the classroom; as we teach other dialects in which to communicate for various purposes, we need to consider the possibilities for using them in new ways, adapting them, inhabiting them, and enriching them. Perhaps the best way to reduce what Michelle Hall Kells refers to as "linguistic shame" is to bring to light the ways in which language is always and already collectively owned (133). This approach to language learning is indeed different from one that insists on a kind of linguistic code-switching according to purpose and context that does not affect the codes themselves. I suspect those who are most comfortable in "using" a variety of linguistic contexts have in fact come to own some portion of all the variants in which they communicate.

Scott Richard Lyons's piece on the importance of multilingual approaches to languages and of preserving indigenous languages—always deeply embedded in culture—offers another answer to the question as to what a writing teacher can do. Lyons points out that South America has far more living indigenous languages than North America, many threatened with extinction. His firm assertion of the intricate link between language and culture caused me to wonder again about the cultural knowledge loss when Africans, brought to the United States, soon lost facility with their native languages and, after a few generations, even knowledge of it. Most compelling is his admonition that we all need to think more clearly about what we lose when somebody else's language is lost. This for me is a critical point of entry for class discussions—not just that we need to protect everyone's right to language but that by not doing so we endanger what Lyons calls "the importance of diversity in any thriving ecosystem."

While most of the activities suggested by these chapters involve students directly, we must also pay attention to the preparation we provide graduate teaching assistants, who, at many higher education institutions, teach most of the first-year writing courses. Although we recognize that this reality is itself a problem, it is not one this chapter was written to address, but it must be noted. Many of these TAs enroll in courses designed to prepare them to teach 101, never having themselves taught anything nor taken a 101 course. Many are primarily interested in literature. Some are frequently creative writing majors who often hope to maintain a clear distinction between "creative" writing and the writing of 101 classes. Now, I need to inject here that most students in all these categories develop into fine first-year writing teachers, but they approach the task with a great deal of anxiety. When I teach the University of Maryland's version of this preparatory course, I like to open our discussion of language ownership, Standard English, and correctness by asking, "How many of you speak a dialect of English?" A few raise their hands right away, recognizing immediately the point I hope to make; some raise them slowly and tentatively, looking furtively around the seminar room; and the rest sit in silent and motionless superiority. Those in this last group are almost always the traditional literature majors.

Correcting some of the misconceptions about language use among these inexperienced but influential future first-year writing teachers may be one of the most important ways to advance change. These instructors can influence the attitudes about language ownership of first-year students when they are most impressionable. For example, instructors can reinforce a broader understanding of linguistic diversity, shaped as much by location as identity, by putting eighteen-year-olds to work collecting examples of the range of Englishes they encounter over the course of a week—in their living quarters, in their classrooms, at social events, and in the media. Their findings could be shared and discussed for their appropriateness to the rhetorical situations. A revealing conversation might develop around relationships between the socioeconomic locations of the various sources as well. Students could also be encouraged to include some of their own linguistic formulations among the examples. Because they are impressionable, their instructors must model the right kinds of attitudes and approaches to language, like the ones suggested by the chapters in this collection. Chapters from the first section should certainly be on the required reading lists of writing teacher preparation courses. I certainly intend to add them to mine.

Works Cited

Erard, Michael. "How English Is Evolving into a Language We May Not Even Understand." *Wired* 16.7, 23 June 2008 <http://www.wired.com/culture/culturereviews/magazine/16-07/st_essay>.

Kells, Michelle Hall. "Leveling the Linguistic Playing Field in First-Year Composition." *Attending to the Margins: Writing, Researching, and Teaching on the Front Lines.* Ed. Michelle Hall Kells and Valerie Balester. Portsmouth, NH: Boynton/Cook, 1999. 131–49.

Piersen, William D. *Black Yankees: The Development of an Afro-American Subculture in Eighteenth-Century New England.* Amherst: U of Massachusetts P, 1988.

11. Why Don't We Speak with an Accent? Practicing Interdependence-in-Difference

LuMing Mao

As I was thinking of how best to begin this response, I came across, almost serendipitously, this story reported in the 17 July 2008 on-line issue of *USA Today*. Manuel Castillo, a California truck driver and a permanent U.S. resident, was headed back to California from picking up onions in Glennville, Georgia. He was stopped in west Alabama for a routine inspection and fined, with a maximum penalty of $500, for violating a federal law requiring that anyone with a commercial driver's license speak English well enough to converse with police. He wasn't speeding, and the inspection and computer check turned up no offenses. Mr. Castillo, a trucker of twenty years, was literally ticketed for "speaking with an accent." As reported by Jay Reeves, Mr. Castillo understood what the trooper was asking of him and responded to him in English as well, albeit "with an accent." And he planned to pay the $500 fine instead of returning to Alabama to contest the charge.

Many questions sprang to my mind as I was processing what I was reading. Why would Manuel Castillo be penalized for no other reason than that he didn't speak the type of English that this federal law seems to have called for? Why is it that people continue to be hung up on the notion that some do and some don't "speak with an accent" and that some accent is more privileged than other accents? Is this not the case that those who are supposed to be "accent-free" actually have no less of an accent—except that their accent has been sanctioned by "an army and a navy"? What, if anything, does speaking English "with an accent" have to do with safety on the road—especially if one considers that the inspection and computer check turned up no offenses by Mr. Castillo? Although it might be helpful to require truckers to be able to communicate with state troopers in English, is it reasonable at all that they have to speak a particular kind of English that is "standard" and "accent-free"? Is this brand of English more correct, superior, or necessarily more adaptive to the needs and wants between truckers and troopers? Why can't other varieties of English be accepted so long as they are understandable and so long as they are communicative? I cannot help but wonder why powers-that-be continue to treat other Englishes spoken in the United States as inferior, less American, and thus unacceptable. Is it possible anyway for one single variety of English to represent our myriad ways of knowing and speaking?

My profound disappointment in this law, however, was somewhat mitigated by the realization that our profession has lately taken a lead in responding to these questions, in exposing and challenging the misconceptions or misguided beliefs that have informed our policies and our writing classroom practices (Matsuda, this volume). I was even more pleased when I realized that many of the answers I was searching for are being developed and articulated by my colleagues whose work is featured in this collection. I became anxious to learn more from their timely contributions and to add to this important conversation a bit of my own voice, however incomplete or limited it may have to be.

What undergirds the law requiring truckers to speak English well enough to be able to converse with police officers is this Standard English ideology that the first nine chapters vigorously engage with and critique in their own respective contexts. The Standard English ideology sees only one variety of language—which is always privileged and prescribed—as correct, as not susceptible to the whims of time or the influence of individual users, and as "accent-free." This ideology is further predicated upon the belief that Standard English is simply a better fit for communication than are the rest of Englishes and that naturalization or assimilation of ethnic minorities and immigrants into the American melting pot "naturally" calls for these individuals to abandon their native or home languages and to master Standard English. Such an ideology entails serious material and symbolic consequences. One can see this ideology, for example, written all over the tragic fate of indigenous languages in America, nearly all of which have been targeted for eradication by colonizing powers (Lyons, this volume), and over the subordination and fracturing of many minority languages, including African American Vernacular English (Richardson, this volume). Not to mention the tongue surgery inflicted upon Asian children so that they can supposedly turn themselves into fluent English speakers (Lu, this volume) and, most recently, the humiliation and monetary loss suffered by Mr. Castillo.

However, language is fundamentally a social process requiring joint authorship and the complex and complicated process of securing one another's uptake; it is not a mental, interiorized phenomenon as linguists of a certain persuasion have advocated in the past. That is to say, language is always used in particularizing situations and for specific purposes, and it is always tied to what Judith Butler calls "historicity of ideas" in the sense that language use "has a history that not only precedes but conditions its contemporary usages, and that this history effectively decenters the presentist view of the subject as the exclusive origin or owner of what is said" (227). Language use, therefore, can never be divorced from its occasions of use and its users. To suggest otherwise is to perpetuate this Standard English ideology and to contribute—symbolically, if not literally—to penalizing people like Mr. Castillo for speaking English "with an accent."

Efforts to codify Standard English and to remove it from particularizing contexts and situations have a long history (Nero, this volume). Such efforts not only help to maintain the status quo but also serve to create a social and discursive divide. This kind of divide relegates or subjugates ethnic minorities and immigrants into speaking lesser Englishes or compels them to take extreme measures, such as "cleansing" themselves of their home languages or taking the surgical route to repair an alleged accent-inducing impediment, in hopes of joining this exclusive language club. A corollary to this divide is a persistent tendency to trivialize or dismiss altogether occasions of use that are considered "outside of the mainstream" or simply "non-representative."

But if truth be told, language cannot be kept away from its concomitant social and cultural situations of context. Whenever two or more languages or varieties of language are in close contact with one another for an extended period of time, they are bound to compete to be heard on their own respective terms. Such discursive copresences are always historically conditioned and interwoven with highly asymmetrical relations of power, and they are characterized by creative and dialectical significations or by what I call "interdependence-in-difference." It is our responsibility, as teachers of writing and rhetoric, to guide our students to trace and analyze how such discursive copresences have been historically formed and how they are being currently manifested. In other words, we must study and promote words, concepts, categories, and discourses that can debunk the Standard English ideology and that can reveal relationships of subordination, resistance, and re-presentation. It is encouraging to note that the first nine chapters of this book have carried out this important undertaking with considerable success.

And my colleagues probably would agree that these complex relationships embodied in our linguistic acts have now taken on a new dimension brought on by a global economy and a technological revolution, both of which have in many ways redefined the self, the other, and the nation. If the contact zone conceptualized by Mary Louise Pratt focuses on the creative aspects of colonial and colonizing discursive encounters, I submit that we have entered, and in fact have already constituted, a new contact zone where our linguistic acts emerge, intermingle, and secure their uptake under conditions of contact and collision and within and across the borders of the nation-state. This new contact zone in fact calls on us to focus on how such acts or practices are being shaped by "cultural, social, and economic interconnectivities" (Hesford and Schell 465) or by what Gail E. Hawisher and Cynthia L. Selfe with Yi-Huey Guo and Lu Liu call "a cultural ecology of literacy" (this volume).

One question kept coming back to me in the wake of Mr. Castillo's story: What exactly can we do as teachers of writing and rhetoric to combat this Standard English ideology and to confront this discursive and cultural divide? Or, what would it take to bring people to accept that no accent is more equal than others so that future Castillos will not be ticketed for speaking English "with an accent"? And, in a related issue, how can we fully mobilize this new transcultural and transnational contact zone in order to promote discursive copresences and to cultivate interdependence-in-difference? In other words, how can we collectively tear down this ideology and close up this divide?

Min-Zhan Lu in her chapter proposes pursuing "living-English work." That is, she suggests that we address how individuals use English to express themselves against globalization and how their use reveals their dynamic relations with diverse languages, including English. I cannot agree more, but I also cannot help but think of the challenges and complexities embedded in this kind of undertaking.

In her chapter, Kate Mangelsdorf tells us that she often asks her students to reflect on the role of Spanglish in their lives and to analyze a wide variety of texts that mix languages for specific rhetorical purposes. This kind of critical engagement, which echoes A. Suresh Canagarajah's effort to teach our multilingual students rhetorical strategies to negotiate between diverse literacy traditions, enables both Mangelsdorf and her students to experience how individual language users employ Spanglish for expressive and symbolic purposes. It further helps them raise their critical awareness of the power and creativity of Spanglish and, I might add, of different layers of interpretation that would not be available without this kind of discursive mixing or entanglement.

At the same time, we simply cannot underestimate the impact of historical and new forms of power as we participate in this new contact zone. Copresences or interdependence-in-difference will not make power asymmetry any less palpable, any less persistent, or any less pernicious. If my own experience is any indication, critiquing Standard English and developing critical language awareness work within schools and other educational institutions can face resentment and resistance, either of which can come even from our own students who have taken Standard English as the norm or as the language of choice and who are fearful of the alleged "cognitive dissonance" that practicing cross-language writing could potentially engender. Therefore, we must develop strategies and practices that encourage and inspire representations "that go against the grain of the cultural and discursive frames in which language [Standard English] is lodged" (Pennycook 263) and that mark interdependence-in-difference "as the most legitimate area of inquiry, where multiple voices speak out from history to dialogue with each other, and where difference is not only acknowledged but cultivated in the acts of mixing" (Lam 387).

Lu further calls on us to treat these multilingual practices as "critical resources" (this volume; also see Nero, this volume). I want to take her call a step further. That is to say, as critical resources, individual users' discursive practices and their socially and historically conditioned occasions of use are as much a contested site as a means for representation and interpretation. Otherwise stated, they become places of contact where struggles over meaning are fought out and where new forms of interdependence-in-difference coalesce and emerge. In the words of Lydia H. Liu, such practices "register a meaning-making history that cuts across different national languages and history" (32).

Using such practices as sites of contact, we can then begin to guide our students and ourselves to examine our own cultural and linguistic histories and to open up both opportunities and limitations made possible by our discursive copresences. Instead of worrying about what trade-offs or pay-offs our practices may or may not effect, and instead of focusing too much on the differences between "the norms" of Standard English and "the breaches" that characterize other varieties of English or other languages, we can begin to teach our students to practice interdependence-in-difference by using these discursive copresences to express their own needs and wants and to write themselves back into the American imaginary.

For Scott Richard Lyons, there is not much that today's teachers of writing and rhetoric can do to preserve indigenous languages and linguistic diversity (this volume). What we can do, on the other hand, aside from teaching Native students the English language to ensure their survival, is to encourage them to pursue cross-language work and to explore how such linguistic copresences as, say, the togetherness of verbs in the Ojibwe language and nouns in the English language may make it possible to challenge the norms of the English language and to help them claim what Lyons calls "rhetorical sovereignty" that, if I might add, may very well be teeming with instances of interdependence-in-difference.

Similarly, it is paramount, as Elaine Richardson has rightly argued in her chapter, that we learn to know the cultural or epistemological codes of African American Vernacular English, or any other language for that matter, so that we can fully treat African American vernacular practices such as "freestylin" as critical resources. At the same time, it is no less paramount for us to further provide our African American students with rhetorical strategies and agency to juxtapose freestylin with Standard English so that they can learn to dislodge the latter from the center of the academic world and to turn it to serve purposes for which it was not originally intended. Such practices once again constitute, in my view, a powerful form of interdependence-in-difference or, to quote cultural anthropologists John Comaroff and Jean Comaroff, "a historically situated, historically unfolding ensemble of signifiers-in-action, signifiers at once material and symbolic, social and aesthetic" (quoted in Lam 387).

Let me add an example of my own here. I have lately drawn upon the work of Asian American spoken word and Hiphop artists as a contested site where participants negotiate and construct new meanings and new identities. For example, i was born with two tongues, a Chicago-based, pan-Asian spoken word troupe, has developed a highly inventive, heterogeneous form to confront racism and to legitimate Asian American experiences. *Broken Speak*, their premiere album, represents a hybrid of spoken poetry, music, and political empowerment. Filled with emotion, musical experimentation, and metaphorical language, each of the sixteen tracks on this album draws upon the oral traditions of the Black and Caribbean communities and the Hiphop stylistics to create an "Asian rap." Such a rhetorical mixing radically collapses the boundaries of different discursive practices by making what is familiar unfamiliar and by turning "this foreign talk" (read as "Standard English") into a song of celebration with distinctively jarring and unsettling affect. In so doing, *Broken Speak* signifies that Asian Americans have come out of their silence and out of speaking in the background. While their speech may still be "broken" or they may still "speak with an accent," Asian Americans have reasserted themselves into the larger American narrative by practicing their distinctive forms of interdependence-in-difference.

In a way, practicing interdependence-in-difference is in part to re-member what has been erased or displaced, recovering traces of other Englishes, other languages (see Trimbur, this volume), and other accents. But more important, it is to invent and further legitimate new Englishes, new languages, and new accents and bring them into our ways of knowing, speaking, and writing. In so doing, we can begin to ensure that we will never forget what Manuel Castillo went through on that eventful summer day in 2008 in west Alabama. We can begin to view "speaking with an accent" not as a liability but as an asset, as a contact-zone experience that deserves not censure but celebration. Consequently, "speaking with an accent" can then serve as an accentuating synecdoche for promoting discursive copresences, for practicing interdependence-in-difference—so much so that we all can ask ourselves, not a moment too soon, "Why don't we speak with an accent?"

Works Cited

Butler, Judith. *Bodies That Matter: On the Discursive Limits of "Sex."* New York: Routledge, 1993.

Hesford, Wendy S., and Eileen E. Schell. "Configurations of Transnationality: Locating Feminist Rhetorics." *College English* 70 (2008): 461–70.

i was born with two tongues. *Broken Speak.* San Francisco, CA: Asian Improv Records, 2002.

Lam, Wan Shun Eva. "The Question of Culture in Global English-Language Teaching: A Postcolonial Perspective." *Tokens of Exchange: The Problem of Translation in Global Circulations.* Ed. Lydia H. Liu. Durham, NC: Duke UP, 1999. 375–97.

Liu, Lydia H. *Translingual Practice: Literature, National Culture, and Translated Modernity—China, 1900–1937.* Stanford: Stanford UP, 1995.

Pennycook, Alastair. *The Cultural Politics of English as an International Language.* London: Longman, 1994.

Pratt, Mary Louise. "Arts of the Contact Zone." *Profession 91.* New York: MLA, 1991. 33–40.

Reeves, Jay. "Feds May Tighten English Fluency Law for Truckers." *USA Today* 17 July 2008. 18 July 2008 <http://www.usatoday.com/news/nation/2008–07–17-truckers_N.htm>.

12. The Challenges and Possibilities of Taking Up Multiple Discursive Resources in U.S. College Composition

Anis Bawarshi

In announcing the theme for the 2008 Conference on College Composition and Communication, "Writing Realities, Changing Realities," program chair Charles Bazerman called on participants to "inquire how writing reveals our histories, inscribes facts, and makes realities available for thought and deliberation." Similarly, in her 2004 Braddock Award–winning essay, "An Essay on the Work of Composition: Composing English against the Order of Fast Capitalism," Min-Zhan Lu calls on scholars and teachers of writing to be more attentive to students' "discursive resources," which she defines as "the often complex and sometimes conflicting templates of languages, englishes, discourses, senses of self, visions of life, and notions of one's relations with others and the world" (28) that emerge from, respond to, reflect, and communicate language users' lived realities. These resources, as the chapters in this collection attest, are acquired over time (through schooling, in part, but also significantly—and strategically—through historical and cultural experiences, sociopolitical positioning, relations and affiliations, participation in various communities, and so on) and can be inextricably connected to one's sense of self and the world. As the authors in this collection remind us, linguistic and discursive resources are not simply set aside or exchanged when we encounter new contexts; rather, we carry them with us, consciously or unconsciously, and they come to bear on the way we can access, experience, and participate in various contexts, including college composition courses.

Within composition studies, as across higher education, there is increased attention to outcomes—to defining and assessing what students will learn and be able to do at the end of their first-year composition (FYC) courses. At the same time, there is also increasing concern among composition researchers about being able to identify and demonstrate what skills and knowledge developed in FYC courses transfer to other contexts and enable students to succeed in those contexts that they negotiate in school and beyond. While research on outcomes and transfer has begun to shed some light on the challenges students face as they negotiate disciplinary and professional writing contexts after FYC, there has been less attention to incomes—to what linguistic and discursive resources students bring with them to FYC and, more important, to how they can use these resources within academic writing contexts. If the ability to seek connections between contexts and to abstract from and draw on prior resources are all preconditions supporting effective writing transfer across different contexts (as research on knowledge transfer suggests), then how do students negotiate between and make use of their varied linguistic and discursive resources? What resources do they feel permitted to draw on? What resources do they feel excluded from using? And what effects do these constraints have on students' abilities to communicate successfully?

Thus far, research in U.S. composition studies has generally neglected the repertoires of linguistic and discursive resources students bring with them. The authors in this collection alert us to what is at stake in maintaining this neglect, calling on us who teach and administer college composition courses to recognize these multilingual and multidiscursive resources as "multilateral and generative" (Canagarajah) rather than competing and interfering and to help students make use of these resources both to adapt to and adapt standardized academic English so that it can reflect and express the varied experiences of its increasingly multilingual and multiliterate users. In this response, I examine some of the obstacles we face and outline some pedagogical possibilities for encouraging students to take up their multilingual and multidiscursive resources in college composition.

As teachers and administrators of FYC, we likely know from our experiences and, certainly, from the authors in this collection that students increasingly bring a wealth of discursive and linguistic resources to our courses. These resources are not randomly acquired, static "tools" but rather examples of what Lu in this collection calls "living-English work"—the work done by language users to make English, in its varieties, reflect and express their situated experiences, relations, and identities. As every author in this collection attests, the history of any language, dialect, or form of discourse is the history of the uses it has been subjected to by its users to limn their various, uniquely situated cultural experiences. At the same time, the history of any language, dialect, or form of discourse is the history of its uses within asymmetrical relations of power. As such, nonprivileged varieties of English emerge not only as ways to negotiate peripheralized experiences and identities but also, as John Trimbur explains in this volume, as attempts by their users to seek "some linguistic traction in relations of drastically unequal power." The tacit policy of "English Only" monolingualism and "the myth of linguistic homogeneity" (Matsuda, this volume) that drives the exclusion of nonprivileged varieties of English, as well as other languages, from FYC thus excludes all students from encountering examples of living-English work. At the same time, it also denies an increasing number of multilingual students the opportunity to develop as assets and to use strategically the full range of their linguistic and discursive resources to accomplish their communicative goals.

In this collection, A. Suresh Canagarajah, Gail E. Hawisher and Cynthia L. Selfe with Yi-Huey Guo and Lu Liu, Kate Mangelsdorf, Shondel J. Nero, and Elaine Richardson all provide examples of how individuals do not exclusively demarcate language differences but rather use them strategically to accomplish specific communicative goals. Such examples support the argument, sustained throughout the collection, against linguistic containment (see Paul Kei Matsuda's chapter for a discussion of linguistic containment, especially in terms of the practice of separating ESL and FYC courses) and offer instead some form of what Canagarajah identifies as "a rhetoric of shuttling" between languages and discourses. Such shuttling mirrors on a local, individual level what Trimbur, Lu, Richardson, Nero, and Mangelsdorf describe as happening on a macro-, historical level as living-English work. That is, a policy of linguistic containment and segregation underestimates (and works against) the extent to which successful multilingual writers deploy their range of linguistic and discursive resources strategically in order to create identification and establish authority in different rhetorical situations. By demonstrating how multilingual writers exercise agency over and negotiate the multiple resources they deploy, Canagarajah's, Hawisher and Selfe's, and Nero's case studies help counter the assumption that "acquisition or affirmation of one discourse comes at the expense of another" (Nero). At the same time, a policy of linguistic containment also underestimates (and works against) the extent to which the strategies of linguistic shuttling used by multilingual writers can serve as examples for all students of how to use their own various discursive resources strategically for rhetorical purposes.

Before we can successfully implement a rhetoric of shuttling between languages and discourses in FYC, however, we need to confront some of the factors that discourage such work. In her chapter, Lu argues that one of the challenges teachers and students face involves delaying our default reactions, what Lu refers to as "our learned distaste for non-idiomatic English lexicons and grammar—*our learned inclination* to view them as either exotic or downright stupid, nonsensical, incorrect" (emphasis mine). Such learned inclinations guide our assumptions and help us make sense of our encounters. They are also just as likely to be operating on students as they are on teachers, with students often just as likely to resist invitations to produce alternative or hybrid discourses (when they can choose to do so) as teachers are to invite them (recall, for example, Mangelsdorf's students at the University of Texas–El Paso, who use Spanglish everywhere on campus but their English language writing courses). To confront this challenge, we need not only to delay these learned inclinations but also, as the chapters here urge us to do, to historicize them and make them a site of critical examination and intervention in our classrooms.

In the context of a laissez-faire U.S. language policy described in Trimbur's chapter, learned inclinations become especially important sites of language regulation and standardization, making such regulation more difficult to challenge because it is maintained and distributed through everyday social interactions. What this means, I think, is that even if writing programs were to institute a language policy that is responsive to language differences, this overt policy will still need to contend with the covert, learned inclinations that manage, execute, and maintain the dominance of unidirectional monolingualism. Yet it is these very learned inclinations that we must confront if we as teachers and administrators want to develop pedagogies that are more attentive and hospitable to language differences and if we want to encourage our students to deploy them more safely and strategically.

To historicize and examine the learned inclinations that regulate our interactions with language differences, we (teachers and students) need to interrogate what rhetorical genre theorists have come to call our "uptakes," the complex, often habitualized, socio-cognitive pathways that mediate our interactions with others and the world. Within speech act theory, uptake traditionally refers to how an illocutionary act (saying, for example, "It is hot in here" with the intention of getting someone to cool the room) gets taken up as a perlocutionary effect (someone subsequently opening a window) under certain conditions. Recently, Anne Freadman has brought uptake to bear on genre theory, arguing that genres are defined in part by the uptakes they condition and secure. For example, in a classroom, some genres function mainly within intra-classroom relations, such as when the assignment prompt creates the conditions for the student essay, while other genres function directly and indirectly in relation to genres outside of the classroom, such as the way that class rosters and grade sheets connect students in the classroom to a system of genres, including transcripts, at the registrar's office and, beyond that, to genres such as résumés and letters of recommendation that draw students into larger economic relations. Together, these inter- and intra-generic relations maintain the conditions within which individuals identify, situate, and interact with one another in relations of power and perform meaningful, consequential social actions—or, conversely, are excluded from them. Uptake helps us understand how systematic, normalized relations between genres coordinate complex forms of social action—how and why genres get taken up in certain ways and not others and what gets done and not done as a result.

As Freadman is careful to note, uptake does not depend on causation but on selection. Uptake, she explains, "selects, defines, or represents its object. . . . This is the hidden dimension of the long, ramified, intertextual memory of uptake: the object is taken from a set of possibilities" (48). Uptakes, Freadman tells us, have memories. What we choose to take up is the result of learned recognitions of significance (akin to what Lu calls "learned inclinations") that over time and in particular contexts become habitual. Knowledge of uptake is knowledge of what to take up, how, and when, including how to execute uptakes strategically and when to resist expected uptakes. Such knowledge is often tacitly acquired, ideologically consequential, deeply remembered, and quite durable. In much the same way, the linguistic memory of U.S. English that Trimbur describes reveals the extent to which such memory selects, defines, or represents its history by way of systematically displacing other languages. In this way, uptakes are as much habits of remembering as they are what Trimbur has called "habits of forgetting" (579).

The kinds of interventions the chapters in part 1 are asking us to make in the work of composition are challenging precisely because they require critical engagement with our uptakes. And this is particularly difficult because uptakes, as learned inclinations that mediate our encounters with language differences, are less textually, materially "visible" and more deeply held as attachments. Yet uptakes are what we have to contend with as we work to create classroom environments that are hospitable to language differences and that make strategic use of students' various discursive resources.

In her chapter, Nero observes that students come to the composition course "already knowing and using a range of discourses," an observation supported by a research study my colleagues and I conducted into how FYC students use prior resources, namely prior genre knowledge, when they encounter new writing tasks.[1] In the study, we surveyed and interviewed students about their prior writing experiences in school, in work, and outside of school and work. Our findings indicate that students have a wealth of prior genre knowledge and that they write these genres in different domains: school, work, and other. Although students have an expansive repertoire of genre knowledge and report using these genres in all three of the domains we supplied—school, work, and outside of school and work (but most extensively in school and outside of school and work)—their writing did not tend to cross domains. In other words, the students' discursive resources were generally domain-specific and were demarcated in such a way that these resources tended not to traverse domains. When we analyzed students' writing in FYC and conducted discourse-based interviews with students following the survey, again we found that despite the fact that they have a wealth of genre knowledge and have written in a number of different domains, students tended not to draw on the full range of their experiences and resources when confronted with a new writing task in college.

Here, I think, we see students' uptake memories at work, as they habitually select from a set of possibilities and, in the process, exclude a range of others that might serve them just as well, if not better. These learned and self-limiting inclinations, I argue, work against the rhetoric of shuttling between languages and discourses, and if we want to encourage such shuttling, we as teachers of writing need to help students critically examine and intervene in the uptakes that guide their inclinations.

Lu's chapter helps us understand how we can reveal differences masked by dominant uptakes and make productive use of the ambivalence produced by the presence of alternative uptakes. Such a "thick" attention to uptakes allows students to identify the meanings, relations, and experiences that are "dismissed or trivialized" by dominant uptakes. Lu's chapter offers specific strategies for intervening in uptakes. Such strategies involve "using" (appropriating) rather than "imitating" (being appropriated by) uptakes. Submitting uptakes to different uses invites students to experience and confront what uptakes allow to be said and not said and their consequences. Likewise, submitting uptakes to different uses invites students to take up alternative uptakes, both in terms of having students analyze what alternative uptakes offer to the making of meaning (a practice suggested by Mangelsdorf as well, where students analyze the uses of standardized and mixed languages to gauge their rhetorical effectiveness) and in terms of having students strategically deploy alternative uptakes in order to experience the ways these uptakes position them and produce affiliations with which they may or may not be comfortable.

The key is to delay and, as much as possible, interrupt the habitual uptakes long enough for students to examine critically their sources and motivations, as well as for students to consider what is permitted and what excluded by these uptakes. For example, when we assign a writing task, rather than begin with some kind of traditional invention activity, including asking students to do primary or secondary research on a topic, we can instead ask students to tell us what they think the task is asking them to do, what it is reminding them of, and what prior resources they feel inclined to draw on in completing the task. Because uptake represents its object, how students recognize the task at hand is shaped by and shapes how they take it up, so it becomes crucial to ask students to consider how they come to recognize a task. Such a metacognitive process is, itself, an invention strategy, but it serves to help students interrogate their default inclinations to act in certain ways and not others. This becomes an important first step in encouraging a rhetoric of shuttling between languages and discourses. At the same time, we also need to design assignments that invite students to use a wider range of their linguistic and discursive resources, assignments for example that invite students to mix genres and modalities from different domains and then to reflect afterward on the experience of shuttling between discourses and domains.

The chapters in this collection help us to see uptake both as a site of instantiation and regulation of power and as a site of intervention. At the same time, they help us imagine what such interventions can look like and do: from the work that historicizes linguistic memory (and forgetting) and traces its political trajectories in U.S. language policy, to the work that reveals the relations between language standardizations and structures of injustice, to the work that seeks to historicize and contextualize the many different uses of English in the United States and across the world, to the close reading of writers' discursive resources as matters of design that resist normalized uptakes. Part of the work of intervening in uptakes involves recognizing contradictions in what uptakes promise and what they actually deliver: in this case, what the acquisition of standardized Englishes promises by way of opportunities and what it actually delivers. It is in these and other ways that the chapters reveal the possibilities of intervening in uptakes and the possibilities that such interventions offer for more responsive and responsible uses of English. The stakes are significant. Given the multidiscursive, multilingual conditions in which all language users (L1, L2, L3, and so on) participate, the persistence with which we who teach and administer composition courses in the United States adhere to the myth of linguistic homogeneity not only renders us complicit in sanctioning and reproducing standardized English usages and the hegemony such usages support but also artificially denies all students (again, L1, L2, L3 . . .) access to the varied resources that allow users of a living language to participate in and achieve consequential meanings and actions.

Note

1. The study, titled "Accessing Academic Discourse: The Influence of First-Year Composition Students' Prior Genre Knowledge," is a cross-institutional study that was carried out at the University of Washington and University of Tennessee in 2006–2007. The co-investigators at UT were Mary Jo Reiff and Bill Doyle, and at UW they were Cathryn Cabral, Sergio Casillas, Rachel Goldberg, Jennifer Halpin, Megan Kelly, Melanie Kill, Shannon Mondor, and Angela Rounsaville. To learn more about the study and its findings, in progress, see our Web site, *UT-UW Prior Genre Study*, at <http://utuwpriorgenre.blogspot.com/>.

Works Cited

Bazerman, Charles. "Call for Program Proposals: Writing Realities, Changing Realities." 2008 Conference on College Composition and Communication Annual Convention. New Orleans. 2–5 April 2008.

Freadman, Anne. "Uptake." *The Rhetoric and Ideology of Genre*. Ed. Richard Coe, Lorelei Lingard, and Tatiana Teslenko. Cresskill, NJ: Hampton, 2002. 39–53.

Lu, Min-Zhan. "An Essay on the Work of Composition: Composing English against the Order of Fast Capitalism." *College Composition and Communication* 56 (2004): 16–50.

Trimbur, John. "Linguistic Memory and the Politics of U.S. English." *College English* 68.6 (2006): 575–88.

13. Mapping the Cultural Ecologies of Language and Literacy

Michelle Hall Kells

Implicitly or explicitly, we writers chart our way through language, culture, and multiple spheres of belonging to position ourselves in a world of relationships. We write to navigate our way through the people, ideas, places, resources, and work that constitute our local and global communities. Juan C. Guerra calls us all "transcultural citizens" (296). I like that notion—this emphasis on the idea of movement, migration, transition. It aligns with the migratory history of human existence. We are, after all, on one very long journey. How then do we map the cultural ecologies shaping language and literacy? I argue that this has become the central question challenging us as teachers in the classroom, scholars in the field of composition studies, and educational activists in colleges and universities.

Mapping the field from multiple points of view, the contributors to this volume recognize and articulate the linguistic shifts in and beyond our classrooms. They respond to the ideological constraints of our discipline and acknowledge the consequences of linguistic imperialism and racism on our institutions and students. Moreover, these scholars engage the broad range of discourses shaping the worlds in which our students live and work. They chart the terrain by interrogating "English Only" policies, problematizing the phenomena of language shift and mixing, and examining the multifarious forms and functions of linguistic codes. Together, these authors illustrate that language diversity is intrinsic to our local, national, and global identities. This volume steps ahead of, alongside, and away from the political and social pulse of the moment.

The national conversation on "diversity" initiated by the Conference on College Composition and Communication Committee on Diversity in 2008 similarly foregrounds questions related to ethnolinguistic pluralism.[1] The impetus to construct a formal statement on diversity by the national-level professional organization of college composition teachers emerges out of a sociopolitical climate increasingly intolerant of difference (culturally, linguistically, nationally, ideologically, and so on). Colleges and universities locally and nationally grapple with the rise of incivility and violence on campus, a disturbing trend in public and private institutions across the nation. In her article in the *Hispanic Outlook in Higher Education*, Marilyn Gilroy details growing reports of aggressive student behavior as well as "incidents of racist and degrading remarks shouted out loud and scrawled on boards and posters around campuses" (8). Language and diversity are the proverbial two sides of the same coin in this public exchange.

In 2008, Barack Obama, then a U.S. senator and Democratic presidential candidate, called for a national campaign to promote bilingualism, a bold and timely public recognition of the inherent and irrepressible linguistic heterogeneity of global citizenship.[2] In turn, the acerbic responses to Obama's affirmation of linguistic pluralism indexed the enduring volatility of these issues as exemplified by citizen groups across the nation—some bitterly expressed, as in a recent letter to the editor in Albuquerque, New Mexico: "As an American who clings to his religion and guns I am outraged that Sen. Barack Obama would make such a statement. . . . Sen. Obama has alienated many Americans and continues to demonstrate that he is not one of us. . . . English is the language spoken within our country which unites us."[3] When did bilingualism become a marker for being un-American?

Min-Zhan Lu and John Trimbur in this volume delineate the push-pull tendency toward hypernationalism, anti-immigrant attitudes, and English Only policies that historically erupt along political fault lines during the most fractious periods in U.S. history. The alarmist xenophobia of the post-9/11 period and subsequent enactment of the Patriot Act have plunged the national consciousness into wholesale adoption of what Paul Kei Matsuda calls in his chapter the "myth of linguistic homogeneity." The range of public reactions to language-use issues currently circulated in the media, questioned in the U.S. educational system, and debated in the civic sphere calls us as educators to consider carefully and examine closely the complex social, political, educational, economic, and historical dimensions of ethnolinguistic diversity. This volume responds to that call. These essays on cross-language relations provide a topo-map limning the contoured, rich, and often precarious terrain of linguistic pluralism. Each straddles the prescriptivist/descriptivist dilemma inherent to our field, seeking to describe language-in-use (Caribbean Creole, Ojibwe, Spanglish, Chinese, Japanese, Tamil, living-English, and so on) and at the same time to prescribe appropriate pedagogical practices for linguistically diverse students.

Ten years ago, I struggled with this same dilemma when I argued that "leveling the linguistic playing field of the college writing classroom is not possible until we confront the linguistic chauvinism and prescriptivism inherent in our roles as teachers of so-called standard American English (a prestige variety of English, among many)" ("Leveling" 131). The authors in this collection together confront the language ideologies that perpetuate social inequities and hinder access. They illustrate how linguistic hegemony operates as a tool of social control and oppression. They join a growing cohort of scholars and leaders in our field who recognize the intricate alignment of linguistic diversity, social justice, and citizenship. In her 2007 University of New Mexico Civil Rights Symposium keynote address, Jacqueline Jones Royster delineated what she calls the "three basic assertions" critical to understanding the relationship of language, literacy, and rhetorical action. First, Royster argues, "literacy is an instrument of power." Second, she maintains, "a primary use of power is to fulfill needs and desires." And finally, Royster contends,

> among the most persistent desires that human beings have exhibited across human history are the desires for: freedom, justice, and the capacity to function with agency and authority within an accommodating environment—which we often articulate as the capacity to have securely in one's life food, clothing, shelter, and meaningful work, with a sense of community and a sense of prosperity. (2)

Language and literacy are the means by which we seek to secure these inalienable human rights.

A recent series featured in *Newsweek* terms the emerging competency for engaged twenty-first-century citizens "global literacies" (Meacham). But *Newsweek* fails to define the term. Moreover, the magazine, like most of our media and national institutions, does not begin to contemplate the implications or the ethics of advancing global literacies. If we live in an exponentially diverse social world, how do we construct our relationships with one another? How do we distribute our cultural, political, and material resources equitably? We as compositionists might describe global literacy as the capacity to read (interpret) and write (respond to) the world. Rhetoric then becomes the means by which we (as teachers, scholars, and citizens) constitute and protect the presence and participation of the diverse groups within a deliberative democracy. I would extend that definition further and argue that global literacy involves both the recognition and affirmation of "difference" (racial, linguistic, class, cultural, sexual, generational, religious, regional, national, physiological, social, intellectual, perceptual, political, and so on). Global literacy in and of itself is not enough—we need a cultural ecology ethic that promotes social justice. Not all variations (linguistic, cultural, racial, sexual, and the like) have equal social value. Systems of hereditary privilege ascribe privilege to selected groups over others. These disparities inform the underlying framing questions for this book and ask: How does diversity constitute and get constituted within a nation (world) of heterogeneous communities?

Current research, as reflected in this volume, reveals that we are more successful negotiating this complex universe with a rich and varied communicative repertoire. If we are truly interested in helping our students thrive, we as educators will help them articulate their multiple spheres of belonging (constituted through the discourses they bring with them and those they acquire in the highly specialized discursive world of the university). As Kate Mangelsdorf, Elaine Richardson, and A. Suresh Canagarajah illustrate in this volume, communicative competence is informed by multiple linguistic and rhetorical resources. Students bring not only their language(s) and discourses but the cultural ecologies of their own experience to their writing. Literate processes in the twenty-first century remain contingent upon and conditioned by complex social networks (organic as well as virtual). *Guanxi*, those vital conditions of literacy sponsorship as explored by Gail E. Hawisher and Cynthia L. Selfe along with Yi-Huey Guo and Lu Liu in their chapter, reaffirm that education and citizenship are no longer confined by local, regional, or national boundaries. Where and how do our students claim citizenship? How do they enact what they know and who they are? The chapters in this collection attend to these questions.

To engage with these chapters, I offer both a response and proposal. It is an absence in the scholarship that prompts scholarship like the work represented here. Until very recently, there has been scant work focusing on ethnolinguistic diversity and college literacy education. As Matsuda and Shondel J. Nero contend in this volume, most of the composition scholarship before the twenty-first century focused on language diversity as problem rather than potential. It was that very absence that prompted me to question the constructs of "basic writing," literacy, and linguistic diversity with the releases of *Attending to the Margins: Writing, Researching, and Teaching on the Front Lines* (1999) and *Latino/a Discourses: On Language, Identity, and Literacy Education* (2004). Complex issues like linguistic pluralism require collaborative effort, as illustrated with this collection. And because social justice and inclusion are never once-done-always-done conditions, there is always an absence calling for a response.

Matsuda, Trimbur, and Richardson grapple with the implications of English Only policies, nativist ideologies, and notions of citizenship. Richardson asserts, "The ideas of naturalization and unity that underlie the English Language Unity Act of 2005 . . . seem to oppose the very diversity that is natural to humanity." Interestingly, the growth of ESL, bilingual education, and African American Vernacular English/Ebonics programs in the U.S.

educational system parallels the rise of English Only sentiments (and policies) throughout our national history. The realities of linguistic heterogeneity, conversely, invigorate the myth of linguistic homogeneity and the entrenched belief that we can legislate something we call "Standard American English." Matsuda, Trimbur, and Richardson illustrate how this tension has informed educational policies of containment that place and restrict contact of ethnolinguistically diverse students from "native" speakers of English. Trimbur traces national linguistic ambivalence to demonstrate that English Only is not simply a historical default attitude but rather a complex system of laissez-faire, opportunistic language policies malleable to the changing sociopolitical conditions of the rhetorical situation. This ambivalent stance is consistent with the expansionist impulse of postcolonial America. To absorb and colonize requires acting on values of expediency and the belief in the "inevitability of English" (Trimbur). What are the implications for teachers of composition? To be marked as "different" and a "non-native" speaker of English remains a strong stigmatizing practice within our classrooms (within and beyond Departments of English). As Matsuda concludes, "Although definitions of what constitutes a better writer may vary, implicit in most teachers' definitions of 'writing well' is the ability to produce English that is unmarked in the eyes of teachers who are custodians of privileged varieties of English." Even if we advocate pedagogical, placement, and evaluation models that accommodate ethnolinguistically diverse students within Department of English writing programs, our job is not complete. If we fail to extend our advocacy efforts across the curriculum, ethnolinguistically diverse students will continue to meet with failure, censure, and discrimination in other courses and writing contexts.

Lu, Nero, and Hawisher and Selfe illustrate the consequences of linguistic contact and the permeability of codes to further confront the myths of monolingualism. Misconceptions about the fixity of language obscure the dynamic and multilateral process of second language learning. Moreover, the stigmatization of language mixing, shifting, and code-switching denigrates the creative and innovative impulse that continually makes language new. Individual language resources, acquired through the sociolinguistic and psycholinguistic processes of becoming symbol-users, ultimately constitute the distinct and flexible idiolect that is the linguistic fingerprint of every unique human being. Linguists are quick to remind us about the distinctions between competency and performance. We all know more than we can perform. And none of us has identical phonosyntactic, lexical, or orthographic repertoires. How then do we unwittingly suppress and subordinate the linguistic agency of ethnolinguistically diverse writers and speakers? Tragically, the stigmatization of "non-native" speaker production of English can be so severe and deleterious that some second language learners take extreme measures (turning even to surgical solutions) to "improve one's career prospects in the capitalist global market" (Lu). As Lu asserts, "We need to probe the ways our sense of ease with a particular usage might inadvertently sponsor systems and relations of injustice." Language purity myths play a central role in the denigration of diverse language processes and changing linguistic systems.

Scott Richard Lyons, Mangelsdorf, and Canagarajah further examine the multilateral and generative resources of multilingual writers. As Canagarajah argues, "Competence is more than the sum of its parts, going beyond the resources provided by the individual languages." Research by Lyons, Mangelsdorf, and Canagarajah suggests that the relationship between linguistic systems is not simply additive but synergistic. Ethnolinguistically diverse writers draw upon the rhetorical and linguistic resources available to them to respond to the rhetorical situation of the writing task. We cannot expect direct or perfect one-to-one correspondences between linguistic systems: as Lyons contends, sometimes "there's no translation for it." As educators, we need to implement pedagogies that stimulate the creative rhetorical coping strategies of multilingual writers to invent and apply the literacy traditions that help them achieve their aims academically, professionally, and personally with their writing. At the same time, we must respect the limits of our students' spheres of belonging as Lyons, Mangelsdorf, and Canagarajah caution. We cannot expect students to include us as audiences for the insider discourses of their home languages. We might help them articulate the constraints that condition the communicative context, but we cannot (and should not) transgress the limits of their home communities with the naïve expectation that writing in their "mother tongue" will directly transfer or translate into academic fluency. Every language carries a culture necessitating entrée by invitation. We invite our students into academic discourse and literacy practice through the pedagogies we implement and the ideologies we circulate. Canagarajah concludes, "Compositionists have to turn their attention to developing pedagogies of shuttling between languages and communities."

Together with the contributors to this volume, I argue that we as educators need to exploit the available means within our field, our colleges, and our communities to promote linguistic justice within and beyond our classrooms. In the words of Geneva Smitherman, quoted in Trimbur's chapter, we need to "take up the unfinished business of the Committee on Students' Right to Their Own Language." It is time to advance Smitherman's call for enacting language policies that protect and promote ethnolinguistic heterogeneity. Where is the national counter-discourse to the rhetoric of English Only? Who is generating public dissent to monolingual hegemony? It is not enough that we are talking among ourselves. Our national organization and our local academic communities (two-year colleges and private and regional universities as well as research institutions) need to engage in the public debate about the language rights of our students. And as Lyons argues, the decline of endangered languages needs to be given priority, "not because they are 'authentic' in some essentialist manner but because they are threatened." Our historical languages (Nahuatl, Diné, Ojibwe, and so on) represent cultural maps, social lifelines to the ancients—linguistic guides to ways of knowing and ways of being. College and university language programs (WPA, WAC, writing centers, first-year writing programs, service learning, distance learning, technical and professional writing programs, and the like) nationwide need to be advocates of the ethnolinguistic diversity within and beyond the academy.

We as educators need to be leading sustained conversations on writing instruction and student diversity in our own institutions at all levels of college careers (first year through graduation). Over thirty-five years have passed since the 1972 CCCC Executive Committee passed the resolution declaring: "We affirm the students' right to their own language patterns and varieties of language—the dialects of their nurture or whatever dialects in which they find their own identity and style. . . . We affirm strongly that teachers must have the experiences and training that will enable them to respect diversity and uphold the right of students to their own language" ("Students' Right" 2–3). We need strategies for institutionalizing linguistic advocacy beyond the college composition classroom. We need to exploit the rhetorical resources within our domain as language and literacy experts.

Royster asserts that language, literacy, and rhetorical action are inextricably connected to "our capacity to carry out meaningful lives" (2). She further reminds us that our focus on literacy should not be so much on a set of skills and abilities "but on rhetorical action as a demonstration of will in asserting a right to agency and authority in the negotiations of our lives using language and literacy as vital and flexible tools" (5). The legacies of twentieth-century social activists in civil rights, labor, human rights, women's rights, and indigenous sovereignty reveal deep discursive identification with people, places, moments, and visions of social justice. All operated on the assumption that rhetorical situations not only shape discourse but are shaped by discourse. Language constitutes agency. Framing conversations on language "diversity" and enacting advocacy initiatives within the institution should be our primary roles in the university. This volume offers us a guide for this work—a map for conducting new research, facilitating new conversations, and implementing new pedagogies. This research helps to complicate the monolinguistic grand narrative of U.S. English Only language politics. These are our enduring challenges as educators of an endangered generation.

Notes

I wish to extend my heartfelt gratitude to Jacqueline Jones Royster for her cogent and inspiring keynote address, "Literacy and Civic Engagement," delivered at the 2007 University of New Mexico Civil Rights Symposium. Her triangulation of the concepts of "literacy" and "civic engagement" deeply informs my position on literacy education reform as explored in this commentary. I would also like to thank Juan Guerra for the vibrant dialogue and rich intellectual exchange that has defined our friendship and partnership over the past ten years. His notion of "transcultural citizenship" is key to this chapter and central to the "Writing Across Communities" project at the University of New Mexico.

1. This chapter is an expansion of my statement "Diversity, Metaphorical Constructions, and Enacting Deliberative Democracy in Teaching, Scholarship, and Service" featured on the *CCCC Conversations on Diversity* Web site on 24 July 2008, <http://cccc-blog.blogspot.com>.

2. For this news report, see Jeff Jones, "Obama: Kids in U.S. Need to Learn Spanish," *Albuquerque Journal*, 12 July 2008: A1.

3. For this letter to the editor, see "English Unites America" on the op-ed page of the *Albuquerque Journal*, 17 July 2008: A9.

Works Cited

Gilroy, Marilyn. "Colleges Grappling with Incivility." *Hispanic Outlook in Higher Education* 18.19 (June 2008): 8–9.

Guerra, Juan C. "Writing for Transcultural Citizenship: A Cultural Ecology Model." *Language Arts* 85.4 (Mar. 2008): 296–304.

Kells, Michelle Hall. "Leveling the Linguistic Playing Field in First-Year Composition." *Attending to the Margins: Writing, Researching, and Teaching on the Front Lines.* Ed. Michelle Hall Kells and Valerie Balester. Portsmouth: Boynton-Cook, 1999: 131–49.

———. "Writing Across Communities: Diversity, Deliberation, and the Discursive Possibilities of WAC." "Exploring Diversity in Community-Based Writing and Literacy Programs." Special issue, *Reflections* 6.1 (Spring 2007): 87–108.

Meacham, Jon. "The Stories We Tell Ourselves." *Newsweek* 7–14 July 2008, 26–28.

Royster, Jacqueline Jones. "Literacy and Civic Engagement." University of New Mexico Civil Rights Symposium. Albuquerque, NM. 28 Sept. 2007. 22 Oct. 2009 <http://civilrights.unm.edu/resources/symposium_archive. htm#presentations>.

"Students' Right to Their Own Language." Special issue, *College Composition and Communication* 25 (Fall 1974).

14. Language Diversity and the Responsibility of the WPA

Susan K. Miller-Cochran

As a writing teacher and writing program administrator, I often find myself struggling to respond to a perplexing dilemma: the more I understand about my students' complex linguistic backgrounds and literacy histories, the more I question the long-accepted practices and assumptions of the profession. I question the ways in which we structure programs, place students into classes, design curricula, and prepare graduate students. Shondel J. Nero points out in this collection that "teaching writing in the twenty-first-century composition classroom is, and will continue to be, about coming to terms with linguistic diversity as the norm rather than the exception." The paradox is that, as Scott Richard Lyons reveals in his chapter, most writing programs are in the business of assimilation yet at the same time say that they value diversity. Therefore, writing programs and writing program administrators (WPAs) are caught in a dilemma that Nero eloquently articulates. We want to honor (and if possible, preserve) students' home languages and cultures, but we are expected to teach them "Standard Academic English." While I sometimes find myself blaming the nature of the first-year writing requirement and its function as a "gate-keeping" course (Crowley), I don't necessarily see the existence of the paradox as negative. Rather, I see it as a step on the way toward developing a better approach to teaching writing and structuring writing programs. But acknowledging the paradox, and realizing that our classes are much more linguistically diverse spaces than we might have previously recognized, is the first step in a process that can lead to change.

The authors in this collection enrich our understanding of the language backgrounds of students in college writing classes in three ways: they identify many of the unique challenges of working with linguistically diverse populations, they reveal the inadequacies and inconsistencies of current practices, and they point the direction toward potential solutions to these problems. Nero, A. Suresh Canagarajah, Kate Mangelsdorf, and Paul Kei Matsuda complicate our understanding of who second language writers[1] are and how they compose; Gail E. Hawisher and Cynthia L. Selfe with Yi-Huey Guo and Lu

Liu enrich our understanding of the interconnectedness and complexity of digital and linguistic literacies; Lyons and Elaine Richardson raise our awareness of marginalized groups that represent rich areas of language diversity the profession has historically ignored; and Min-Zhan Lu and John Trimbur reveal the histories and implications of English dominance. While the histories they outline are compelling, the problems they identify are complex and ingrained through decades of institutional practice. The call for some kind of action is clear, but the specific direction is less so and the obstacles can seem insurmountable. What should a WPA do with this knowledge, and in which direction should this awareness point the profession?

The WPA's Dilemma

Once a WPA realizes that "the presence of language differences is the default" in U.S. college writing classes (Matsuda, this volume), then he or she is caught in the aforementioned dilemma. Examining the curricula and structure of most writing programs in institutions of higher education in the United States reveals several assumptions about students and pedagogy that—when stated outright—most rhetoric and composition specialists would agree are false. Even a cursory glance demonstrates that most writing programs are structured around (at least) five myths about second language writing that negatively impact students in our writing classes by ignoring their linguistic diversity. When the implications of these myths are extended to other linguistically diverse groups of students, the impact is enormous:

1. *Second language writers are easy to identify.* As Linda Harklau, Meryl Siegal, and Kay M. Losey, Patricia Friedrich, and others have shown, terms such as "second language writer," "ESL," and "native/non-native" are not easy to define. Students who come from linguistically diverse backgrounds might include international students, resident ESL students (sometimes called Generation 1.5), immigrant students, bilingual students, bidialectal students, and students who speak unprivileged varieties of English, among others. The common practice of placing first-year students into mainstream or second language writing classes based primarily on nationality, or simply putting all students who are "underprepared" into basic writing classes without paying attention to the underlying language differences that should impact our pedagogical approaches (Matsuda, this volume), is woefully inadequate. The profession needs to develop a more nuanced understanding of who these students are, what linguistic strengths and challenges they bring to the classroom (Friedrich), and which students could benefit from classes that address language issues historically reserved for classes designed only for second language writers.

2. *Second language writers are a small minority.* On the contrary, more English speakers in the world speak English as a second language than as a first language (Matsuda, *Internationalizing Composition*). More than half a million international students were studying at U.S. colleges and universities in 2007 (Mangelsdorf, this volume), and the 2000 census revealed that 5.5 million English language learners were enrolled in U.S. public schools (Matsuda et al.). These students, nearly a decade later, are quickly becoming our students in higher education. Furthermore, we have typically left many groups of students out of second language writing conversations because they are not identified as "ESL," even though they come from diverse linguistic backgrounds that indicate they would benefit from working with teachers specifically prepared to address language issues in a writing class. Students who speak indigenous languages, for example, have often been ignored by both the second language writing community and the larger composition profession. This entire group of students, along with other students from diverse language backgrounds, is erased by our inadequate placement policies and program structures, and this is another instance of how our assumptions about students can render them "invisible in the discourse of composition studies" (Matsuda citing Prendergast, this volume). We also render students, and their unique language challenges, invisible when we expect that their linguistic backgrounds will be irrelevant beyond their first year of college. Linguistic diversity occurs in upper-division WAC courses and programs as well, but these courses are rarely designed to address the needs of second language writers.

3. *As long as you have a second language writing specialist at your school, that person can handle any language challenges that students might face.* While having a second language writing specialist on the faculty to work with second language writers is definitely preferable to not having anyone trained to work with second language writers, a better use of that faculty member's expertise might be to familiarize other faculty with ways of identifying language diversity issues in the classroom and equipping those faculty with methods that will help them work effectively with students. Gail Shuck has described the complex demands on the second language writing specialist's time and the tendency to relegate second language writing issues to specialists, and she also provides practical strategies that can be implemented at the classroom and department level to help second language writers. If specialists are expected to "fix" all second language writing "problems," that leaves little time for them to work on such faculty development, and it doesn't help the students who fall through the cracks because their linguistic challenges weren't appropriately identified and understood in the first place. In situations where no faculty member has second language writing expertise, writing

center tutors and specialists are often called on to fill this role, whether or not they are prepared to do so. Shanti Bruce and Ben Rafoth's insightful guide for writing center tutors who work with second language writers addresses the multiple challenges that tutors must be aware of when working with a linguistically diverse student population.

4. *Second language writing students can just be placed in a separate class, and then you don't have to worry about them anymore.* Matsuda discusses how the policy of containment in writing programs creates "the false impression that all language differences could and should be addressed elsewhere" (this volume). Several scholars, including Tony Silva, Friedrich, and Shuck, have described the various learning contexts in which second language writers can succeed. Not every learning context is appropriate for every second language writer, and separate classes may work well for some students and not others. And, as mentioned earlier, identifying second language writers in the first place is a challenge in itself. Designing a placement strategy that takes into consideration a student's learning style, writing development, prior experience with academic writing in English, confidence level, and personal preference makes more sense than using a one-size-fits-all approach that might be more economical but often detrimental to the students it seeks to serve. Determining placement and curricular options needs to be context-specific, and a placement strategy needs to be realistic, given the institution's mission and resources.

5. *Second language writers need to focus on grammatical issues more than rhetorical ones.* Not much has changed in the twenty years since Ann Raimes first noted a disconnect between what we know about writing instruction and what we do in ESL writing classes. Even in programs that offer classes specifically designed for second language writers, these classes often focus primarily, or sometimes exclusively, on grammar.[2] The textbooks and curricula designed and adopted for second-language writers tend to be focused on surface-level issues instead of larger-scale rhetorical issues that are addressed in the textbooks and curricula for mainstream classes (Miller-Cochran). Very few textbooks are designed with second-language writers in mind that provide even a cursory introduction to rhetorical principles.

The profession's problematic placement practices and program structures stem from an "assumption that a clear line of demarcation can be drawn between the languages that people speak" (Mangelsdorf, this volume). From this assumption, we classify students as native English speakers or second-language/ non-native/ESL students, separate them, and prescribe a curriculum that attempts to erase linguistic differences to achieve the mythic linguistic homogeneity described by Matsuda. But the complex nature of our students' linguistic backgrounds makes this sort of division unproductive, let alone inaccurate.

A better solution to this sorting and placement dilemma is to argue that all writing teachers should be prepared to address issues of language diversity in writing classes. While such preparation is obviously beneficial for working with students historically identified as second language writers, understanding language diversity can help address the needs of other groups of students as well. For example, Richardson argues that speakers of African American Vernacular English "should be taught their own linguistic history, not at the expense of 'standard' English but as a way of positioning oneself and understanding oneself in relation to it" (this volume, citing Woodson). Indeed, evidence is mounting that argues for the relevance of classes focused on language, cross-cultural writing, and language policy for all students, such as those described by Lyons, Nero, Matsuda and Silva, and Shuck. While providing placement options for students offers a potential solution, implementing such a strategy requires that all writing teachers "study and honor students' lived languages" (Mangelsdorf, this volume). Requiring such preparation, or providing adequate professional development, would mean rethinking current patterns of graduate preparation and faculty expectations in rhetoric and composition.

Working toward Potential Solutions

In this collection, Nero offers specific guidelines for teachers that are designed to help them be more responsive to their students' linguistic backgrounds. The foundational first guideline—"Have training in language diversity"—equips teachers to reach the other objectives Nero lists (for example, "Introduce language diversity as an object of study in the writing classroom"). The CCCC Statement on Second Language Writing and Writers, adopted by the Conference on College Composition and Communication in 2001 and ratified by the Board of Directors of Teachers of English to Speakers of Other Languages that same year, provides similar guidelines to this effect:

- Writing programs should offer pre-service and in-service teacher preparation programs in teaching second language writing.
- Any writing course—including basic writing, first-year composition, advanced writing, and professional writing as well as second language writing courses—that enrolls any second language writers should be taught by a writing teacher who is able to identify and is prepared to address the linguistic and cultural needs of second language writers. (672)

The CCCC Statement on Second Language Writing and Writers also provides guidelines about the logistics of classes (placement, assessment, and class size, for example), but the two guidelines listed above are some of the most challenging for WPAs to implement. While these guidelines might seem to make logical sense, many WPAs—whether they direct first-year programs, WAC programs, professional writing programs, or writing centers—are faced with a very real dilemma: given the challenges inherent in identifying and placing students with linguistically diverse backgrounds, how can we be certain that all second language writers are working with someone trained to teach a linguistically diverse student population? The obvious solution is to require training in language issues for all teachers, yet this solution is equally difficult to implement. Preparation in working with second language writers is not generally a prerequisite for teaching writing, and it is not a required component of most graduate programs in English, where most writing teachers are initially trained (Preto-Bay and Hansen). This realization brings with it a new dilemma: How do we prepare teachers on-the-job to identify and work with second language writers if they have no prior training or experience, and how does a WPA implement appropriate teacher preparation and ongoing professional support in second-language writing if the WPA doesn't have a background in second language writing himself or herself?

The WPA's Responsibility to Students

According to the same CCCC position statement, "writing teachers and writing program administrators (should) recognize the regular presence of second-language writers in writing classes . . . understand their characteristics, and . . . develop instructional and administrative practices that are sensitive to their linguistic and cultural needs" (670). While meeting this objective doesn't require becoming an expert in second-language writing, it does means that part of the WPA's professional and pedagogical responsibility to students is to take steps toward gaining an understanding of the linguistic and cultural influences that affect students and their written language. And the WPA, then, with that knowledge, could

- incorporate attention to second language writing issues into preparation of teaching assistants;
- consider training and experience with second language writers as part of the standards for hiring faculty in writing programs;
- incorporate these issues into the curriculum itself through pedagogical strategies like the cross-cultural composition approach that Matsuda and Silva describe or through a course that focuses on writing about issues related to language policy or language awareness;
- make second language writing a part of the graduate curriculum for students specializing in rhetoric and composition. The CCCC Statement on Second Language Writing and Writers urges "graduate programs in writing-related

fields to offer courses in second language writing theory, research, and instruction in order to prepare writing teachers and scholars for working with a college student population that is increasingly diverse both linguistically and culturally" (670). I argue that such classes should not just be offered but should be a requirement for a specialization in rhetoric and composition.

Preparation for working with a linguistically diverse population would also help teachers develop what Canagarajah calls in his chapter a "multilingual orientation." By building such an orientation, teachers become more aware that second language writers have agency and can make deliberate choices about texts and languages when moving between languages/discourse communities. In addition, a multilingual orientation would prepare teachers for designing pedagogical strategies to help second language writers develop a sense of linguistic context and awareness of their own agency when moving between communities.

Implementing the four strategies listed above would mark a foundational change in the structure and substance of most writing programs. These strategies are program features best included in the design stage, however, and they will likely be more difficult to implement in those contexts where programs are already established, where faculty members have already been hired, and where graduate students have been or are already being trained. Or perhaps such large-scale changes are too ambitious for particular institutional contexts. Regardless, several strategies could serve well as first steps for adapting a writing program's approach to addressing the needs of linguistically diverse students:[3]

1. *Develop workshops for writing faculty that will help them work with language diversity.* Such workshops could be developed for faculty in writing programs at all levels, and they might address issues such as responding to second language writers and writers from other marginalized language groups, designing effective assignments that are inclusive of language diversity, and identifying and working with language differences. Shuck describes specific classroom and department-level strategies that she has presented to faculty in her program that could be adapted to other contexts (76–79).

2. *Make discussions about working with a linguistically diverse student population an integral part of TA training.* Such discussions could mirror the kinds of topics that might be offered for all writing faculty in the program. Preto-Bay and Hansen argue that training for TAs should be longer and more in-depth as a result (51).

3. *Begin hiring faculty with preparation for working in linguistically diverse environments.* Ultimately, experience working with linguistically diverse writers should be one of the priorities in hiring, especially if a program or

department works with many writers who have not been readily and previously identified as such.

4. *If such faculty are difficult to find, consider incorporating preparation to work in a linguistically diverse classroom into a new faculty orientation.*

Not all solutions will work equally well for all programs. Some programs have greater degrees of language diversity than other programs, and the demographics of the student population might vary greatly. Likewise, the faculty teaching in a program can affect the solution that might work best, and the considerations are different for programs that employ primarily full-time faculty, part-time contingent faculty, or graduate students. But language diversity is the norm in writing classrooms nationwide, and teachers need support and continuing professional development opportunities to work with students successfully. And to support these teachers, the WPA's first responsibility is to develop a personal understanding and awareness of language diversity issues.

Notes

1. As Mangelsdorf reveals in this collection, terms such as "second language," "ESL," "native," and "non-native" contain problematic assumptions that contribute to, and reify, the effects of what Matsuda calls "a policy of linguistic containment." I have chosen to use the term "second language" in my discussion of these writers, knowing that, while it is an imperfect term, it can be a more inclusive term than many others.

2. This acknowledgment opens another area of potential discussion, focusing on the content of programs preparing ESL instructors. While it is outside the scope of this paper, it is a compelling area for exploration.

3. The 2006 special issue of *Writing Program Administration: Journal of the Council of Writing Program Administrators* (volume 30, issues 1–2) focusing on second language writing and writers provides additional resources that WPAs would find helpful in addressing the challenges mentioned in this chapter.

Works Cited

Bruce, Shanti, and Ben Rafoth, eds. *ESL Writers: A Guide for Writing Center Tutors.* Portsmouth, NH: Boynton/Cook, 2004.

"CCCC Statement on Second Language Writing and Writers." *College Composition and Communication* 52.4 (2001): 669–74.

Crowley, Sharon. *Composition in the University: Historical and Polemical Essays.* Pittsburgh: U of Pittsburgh P, 1998.

Friedrich, Patricia. "Assessing the Needs of Linguistically Diverse First-Year Students: Bringing Together and Telling Apart International ESL, Resident ESL and Monolingual Basic Writers." *Writing Program Administration: Journal of the Council of Writing Program Administrators* 30.1–2 (2006): 15–35.

Harklau, Linda, Meryl Siegal, and Kay M. Losey. "Linguistically Diverse Students and College Writing: What Is Equitable and Appropriate?" *Generation 1.5 Meets College Composition: Issues in the Teaching of Writing to U.S.-Educated Learners of ESL.* Ed. Linda Harklau, Kay M. Losey, and Meryl Siegal. Mahwah, NJ: Erlbaum, 1999. 1–14.

Matsuda, Paul Kei. "Internationalizing Composition: A Reality Check." Paper presented at the annual meeting of the Conference on College Composition and Communication, New Orleans, 3 Apr. 2008.

———, Michelle Cox, Jay Jordan, and Christina Ortmeier-Hooper, eds. *Second Language Writing in the Composition Classroom: A Critical Sourcebook.* Boston: Bedford/St. Martin's, 2006.

———, and Tony Silva. "Cross-Cultural Composition: Mediated Integration of U.S. and International Students." *Composition Studies* 27.1 (1999): 15–30.

Miller-Cochran, Susan. "What We Know, What We Do, and What We Adopt: Revealing Assumptions in L2 Writing Textbooks." Paper presented at the annual meeting of the Conference on College Composition and Communication, Chicago, 26 Mar. 2006.

Preto-Bay, Ana Maria, and Kristine Hansen. "Preparing for the Tipping Point: Designing Writing Programs to Meet the Needs of the Changing Population." *Writing Program Administration: Journal of the Council of Writing Program Administrators* 30.1–2 (2006): 37–57.

Raimes, Ann. "Teaching Writing: What We Know and What We Do." Paper presented at the annual meeting of the Conference on College Composition and Communication, New Orleans, 13 Mar. 1986.

Shuck, Gail. "Combating Monolingualism: A Novice Administrator's Challenge." *Writing Program Administration: Journal of the Council of Writing Program Administrators* 30.1–2 (2006): 59–82.

Silva, Tony. "On the Ethical Treatment of ESL Writers." *TESOL Quarterly* 31 (1997): 359–63.

15. Resistance to the "English Only" Movement: Implications for Two-Year College Composition

Jody Millward

This collection is not just timely but overdue. The implications for two-year college teaching and scholarship are profound, and perhaps that is why I, a former chair of the Two-Year College English Association, have been asked to write a response. I do not claim to speak for all community college writing faculty, but I am certain that many will share my excitement in exploring how this research can inform our pedagogy. I believe this collection will initiate a conversation that will continue in our journals (*TETYC* and regional ones) and conferences, a conversation that will bring together teachers/scholars (including graduate students) across institutional boundaries.

The authors provide insight into the range of linguistic diversity of those Min-Zhan Lu defines as "living-English users." In addition, they argue that any examination of how we address language diversity in college composition courses must take into account the political, economic, and cultural forces that reinforce existing power structures. "Language containment" policies (Paul Kei Matsuda's term) have systematically devalued students (Kate Mangelsdorf, Elaine Richardson, Lu) and have resulted in the eradication of languages, cultures, and ways of knowing (John Trimbur, Richardson, and Scott Richard Lyons). Their scholarship explores the implications for international students, immigrants (including the 1.5 generation), African Americans, Native Americans, and those whose dialects these policies define as "low status." In short, they address the needs of the students populating community college classrooms. Viewed within the political, economic, and cultural context of the two-year college, their rich, multilayered analyses of the English Only movement suggest new avenues of research and a concomitant re-visioning of curriculum and classroom practices.

Two-Year College Culture

Community colleges have an open admissions policy, compared to 12.5 percent of public universities. Students in four-year classrooms share a common goal, completion of the bachelor's degree. By contrast, composition courses in the public two-year colleges bring together students seeking transfer readiness (including high school students completing university requirements), those seeking associate degrees, and those focused on workforce training, lifelong learning, and/or English language learning. According to data available before January 2008, we enrolled 11.5 million students. Fifty-five percent of all Hispanic and Native Americans and 46 percent of all Asian-Pacific Islanders and African Americans chose a community college as their gateway to education ("CC Stats"). Hey-Kyung Koh of the Institute of International Education reports that community colleges saw the largest percentage increase (57.9 percent) in international enrollment of all postsecondary institutions in the last decade, citing the "low-cost, quality education, which offers flexible and innovative programs of study not found at the traditional four-year colleges and universities." Yet, the neat categories (and identities) captured by these statistics deny the realities of the community college student and faculty teaching/learning experience.

According to "Most Spoken Languages in California in 2005," my own state leads the nation in the number of immigrants (47 percent), with 43 percent of its population speaking a language other than English in the home. To put this in perspective, Californians speak almost 100 unique languages in addition to those the MLA has grouped South/Central American Indian, Indo-European, Asian, and Pacific Island. Yet in 1986, voters initiated an English Only amendment to the constitution and in 1998 passed Proposition 227, "English for the Children Initiative," banning "bilingual education and the use of languages other than English in the use of instruction in public schools" (Mora 1).

We may argue that economic, cultural, gendered, family, racial, linguistic, and academic identities intersect in complex ways for all students. But 89 percent of community college enrollees are defined as "nontraditional," a governmental term for those whose profile includes any of the following: did not complete high school, delayed enrollment or attends part-time, is one of the first in family attending college, works thirty-five hours, is financially independent, or is a single parent. Fifty-five percent with two or more of these markers and 64 percent with four or more markers enroll in community colleges ("Special Analysis 2002" 18). Clearly, two-year students evidence complex identities shaped by the intersections of class, working status, ethnicity, and language, and two-year college teachers struggle to find ways to address these complexities in their classrooms.

These realities have shaped our curriculum and placement procedures. As JoAnn Crandall and Ken Sheppard document, community colleges offer English Language Learner (ELL) students multiple points of entry, from non-credit Adult Education to separate for-credit ESL programs to ESL strands in pre-transfer through transfer composition. They document, too,

- the lack of integration between ELL levels and programs,
- problems with placement (an over-reliance on standardized tests [13] and misplacement into "developmental education" [9]), and
- pedagogical challenges related to the diverse nature of the learners (eighteen or older, generation 1.5, international, world English–speaking, and ESL literacy students [2–3]).

They also report that the shortage of programs providing English proficiency prevents many of the nearly eight million immigrant adults eligible to apply for citizenship from doing so (8). These numbers are confounding. Composition scholars must pay more attention to ELL programs—from ESL noncredit to community college transfer to bachelor's degrees—through cross-institutional collaborations.

Shared Cultural Realities—Defining the Problem

This collection makes visible the systemic features of U.S. public education policies and practices that ensure language containment and the subsequent devaluation of students—from "exceptionalizing" students who speak Caribbean Creole English (Nero) to Spanglish-speakers' perceptions of how their language is viewed by the academy (Mangelsdorf) to the pedagogical abandonment of international students who do not "fit the dominant image of students" (Matsuda) to "the subordination and fracturing of the cultural identities of African Americans" (Richardson) to the eloquent recording of Native Americans' "decreasing fluency" and "the shame [that] cut both ways: I am bad because our language is bad, and I am bad because I can't speak it anymore" (Lyons). The image in Lu's chapter documenting tongue-surgery offers a chilling representation of how U.S. economic and political dominance promotes these practices through the geo-political contexts of globalization, thus "sponsor[ing] systems and relations of injustice."

This is possible, as Trimbur reminds us, only if we remain ignorant of our own linguistic heritage and embrace the "relentless monolingualism of American linguistic culture, the strategies by which English is meant to replace and silence other languages." Tragically, this is what we continue to do. Trimbur and Richardson note a profound silence in composition classes and across disciplines about our multilingual past and present, about how language conveys a culture's history, political views, heart, and spirit. The failure of graduate schools to include this instruction and the lack of preparation for teaching multilingual composition courses is, as Matsuda rightfully claims, a de facto endorsement of English Only (1). Systemic exclusion continues despite position statements issued by our professional organizations: the Conference on College Composition and Communication (CCCC) "Students' Right to Their Own Language" (1974, updated 2003), "Teaching Second Language Writing and Writers" (2001), "Ebonics Training and Research" (1998), "The National Language Policy" (1988, updated 1992), and "The Preparation and Professional Development of Teachers of Writing" (1982) and the TYCA "Guidelines for Academic Preparation of English Faculty at Two-Year Colleges" (2004) urging graduate programs to provide instruction in ELL pedagogy.

Some Modest Proposals

If change is to occur, "language difference" must "become a central concern for *everyone* who is involved in composition instruction" (Matsuda), not just the leadership of professional organizations. On a practical level, job descriptions for postsecondary faculty who will teach primarily composition could add instruction in ELL pedagogy as a job requirement. The market may then drive programmatic change. But ongoing professional development is what is most desperately needed, an area woefully underfunded in community colleges. As Gail E. Hawisher and Cynthia L. Selfe with Yi-Huey Guo and Lu Liu argue (see Richardson as well), technology provides ways for users to cross linguistic borders and to transform language. While many of us may be impatient with the ways in which access and pedagogical use of computers continue to "vary widely across socio-economic levels" ("Changing World" 2–3), most postsecondary institutions are wired in ways we could not have imagined a decade ago. In addition, professional development funds and other support (at least in two-year colleges) continue to privilege technology-based training or projects. WPAs and composition faculty might secure funding for training in language difference by including such instruction as a necessary facet of training in technologies (I'm remembering the early collaborations of CCCC chairs Victor Villanueva and Cynthia Selfe in their NCTE summer workshops).

Trimbur's analysis of the fracturing of language studies through academic specialization and Matsuda's call to revise preparation in the teaching of composition to include ELL pedagogy resonate with me. I teach the range of composition courses at my college, from pre-transfer to transfer. My college has four separate departments—ESL, Foreign Languages, English Skills (pre-college reading and writing), and English—and few avenues for interdepartmental collaboration to address ELL issues despite the multiplicity of languages encountered in our classrooms. While departmental structures may vary throughout the community college system, the challenges identified by Trimbur and Matsuda do not. We must take into account, too, faculty demographics: in 2003, only 33.3 percent of public community college faculty were fulltime compared to 68.1 percent of public university faculty ("2004 National Study" 30). Given the high numbers of contingent faculty (who receive little support for training or for departmental contributions), curriculum is often textbook-driven to assure program consistency. Currently, textbooks designed for pre-college-level reading/writing tend to recycle the same articles, mostly by creative writers. A. Suresh Canagarajah's discussion of the rhetorical shifts made by a Sri Lankan scholar based on audience and publishing contexts could serve as a model for the writers of a textbook that would legitimize "shuttling between languages" and provide the historical and cultural knowledge that faculty and students desperately need.

Finally, it is time to change the rhetoric, to co-opt English Only justifications of monolingualism as the avenue to academic achievement, economic prosperity, and global influence. Economics and politics are profoundly culturally bound, and language is the primary conduit of culture, as these writers demonstrate. Inclusion of "alternative" discourses promotes critical thinking (as functioning as a form of resistance, a critique of the status quo) and extends networks of influence. The principles articulated throughout this anthology provide a foundation for advocacy with public policy makers whose influence on teacher training, curriculum, and assessment in postsecondary education continues to grow.

Proposed Solutions and Implications for the Community College Classroom

The proposed solutions—full multilingualism (Trimbur), "shuttling" between languages as critical to meeting academic requirements while transforming and enriching academic discourse (Canagarajah, Richardson, Lu, Mangelsdorf, Nero, and Lyons), and *guanxi* (defined in Hawisher, Selfe, Guo, and Liu), a culturally specific notion that is, in my opinion, transcultural—should inform two-year college research and praxis. As this collection illustrates, minority discourses not only convey and strengthen family, social, political, and cultural ties but also encourage border crossings, which technology facilitates (Hawisher, Selfe, Guo, and Liu and Richardson). Using these principles to inform assignments and curriculum, faculty can encourage community college students to create multilingual, multicultural networks beyond classroom walls.

What forms might such assignments take? The work has already begun at community colleges, but the range and variety of forms it has taken require (and deserve) further research. At the 2004 CCCC, I attended Suba Subbaro's presentation on Project e-PAL, a site linking classrooms across national borders in joint academic projects. Subbaro linked her Oakland composition students with several countries through various assignments: interviews that allow each student to create a profile of the interviewee within the cultural context of the partner country, a discussion of miscommunication based on linguistic or cultural barriers prior to partnership, an assignment based on business etiquette and customs with a joint, cross-national analysis of how they differ. Community college faculty could easily adapt such assignments. Building on Subbaro, we could ask students to assess family and community economic choices. Where do they spend their money and why? What part does culture play? What differs from their partner country? Richardson's record of how Hiphoppas crossed national and linguistic borders offers the potential for multiple assignments focused on pop culture. Asking students to share perceptions of music, movies, or television shows or to trace a theme over several decades and investigate how home countries adapt trends would generate fruitful discussions about the appropriations of pop culture for multiple purposes. This would, I believe, enrich any analysis of how an artistic work or genre incorporates, excludes, or inspires cross-national exchange and would encourage students to focus on the history of cross-cultural borrowings and appropriations between the home countries.

Linking the research to local experience and communities across borders helps students develop a voice and increases learning, as my colleague Denise Bacchus demonstrates in her "Student Oral Histories Project." Her interest in the fate and role of women in the African diaspora took her to an Afro-Mexican community where she began to construct oral histories of the women in the village, and she has continued these efforts in several countries. Using her research as a model, Bacchus provides a variety of technologically enriched ways for students to discover women's contributions to the Americas (especially in resistance movements). By requiring students to link their own histories (personal, familial, or drawn from the local community) to the stories they uncover, she makes visible both those women left out of history books and the students who discover and write about them.

In my own classrooms, I have had success with assignments that make students aware of "language shuttling" and when and why this occurs. For example:

- Students document how they shuttle between languages in terms of context—family, friends, social organizations, church, business transactions, and/or school—and analyze why they do so. What is gained? What, if anything, is lost?
- Students write personal narratives on how language or cultural differences led to misunderstandings, if and/or how these were resolved, the consequences when left unresolved, lessons learned.

- Students visit classes of roughly the same size—three in English, two in other disciplines—to determine who speaks and when (noting gender, ethnicity, and age), teachers' responses, what patterns emerge, possible causes for those patterns.
- Students locate examples and purposes of language shuttling by public figures or in pop culture (music, comic routines, and/or cartoon strips—for example, *Boondocks, La Cucaracha, Candorville*—as resistant art forms) and write a multimedia analysis of the purposes/gains of doing so.
- Students from disparate communities (urban/rural, critical numbers of minority ethnic populations versus low numbers, different geographic regions, two-year/four-year institutions) analyze language and culture differences of classroom, family, community, and/or workforce.

Yet, after reading this anthology, I can see ways to reframe assignments. I have focused on language differences and asked students to identify what is lost if one community eschews the ethic(s) of another. I encourage them, as well, to examine what cultural values the traditional U.S. academic essay reflects. They have little difficulty discovering the promotion of self as expert (research), the celebration of the can-do, problem-solver ethic (the thesis-driven essay), and the celebration of efficiency (no wasted words or subthemes that may charm or interest nonacademic readers). But I am more concerned now with the critical thinking possibilities inherent in reframing the issues. While I celebrate multilingualism in all my classes as the mark of a true intellectual, I'd like to make the benefits more explicit in the readings I choose and in the ways students employ technology. In short, the goal is not to just teach ELL students the traditional format of the U.S. academic essay but to provide them (and their monolingual peers) with assignments that encourage a trans-formation of this genre, a transformation that incorporates the contributions of "living-English users" as evidence of cultural preservation, understanding, linguistic extensions and crossings.

Doing so requires providing students with the information and themes these scholars (and others) have identified. What struck me as I read these chapters is that much of the new research should draw on student knowledge of heterogeneous language practices. For example, students might survey their peers to determine how many are multilingual and how they view their multilingualism. Following Lyons's model, we might ask students to construct a dictionary of terms and phrases they frequently use that cannot be captured in standard written English to create lexicons of texting and other technological forums or lexicons of indigenous and home languages and then to analyze what these terms in aggregate convey about cultural views and mores. Assignments would encourage a critique of the consequences when cultural views of these languages are embraced or lost (giving voice to students from the United States and elsewhere who speak indigenous languages). Or we might ask students to investigate a country of choice where languages are disappearing, discover why this is so, and explore the cost to the home culture, to all cultures, when we lose these perspectives.

Admittedly, these assignments are sketched in broad strokes and require refinement. But brainstorming such ideas is a step toward what could prove to be fertile ground for research—a research not unlike the literacy narratives scholarship in this work. Four-year scholars and graduate students can partner with two-year college faculty to examine the content, culture, and pedagogy of multilingual, multimission classrooms, working together to refine assignments and to establish research goals, protocols, and boundaries. At the core would be "living-English users"—students, faculty, the public here and abroad—and would include undergraduate student analyses of multilingualism within the context of culture. I envision such research as essentially collaborative and resistant in nature, a research that will move multilingual students, too often marginalized and rendered invisible, to the center of the academy.

Works Cited

"CCCC Position Statements." *NCTE: Conference on College Composition: CCCC*, 15 Aug. 2008. 29 Oct. 2009 <http://www.ncte.org/cccc/resources/positions>.

"CC Stats." *American Association of Community Colleges*, Jan. 2008. 6 Nov. 2009 <http://www2.aacc.nche.edu/research/index.htm>.

Crandall, JoAnn (Jodi), and Ken Sheppard. *Adult ESL and the Community College*. CAAL Community College Series: Working Paper 7. *Council for Advancement of Adult Literacy*. 13 Dec. 2004. 1–65. 14 July 2008 <http://www.caalusa.org/eslreport.pdf>.

"Guidelines for the Academic Preparation of Two-Year College English Faculty." *NCTE: Two-Year College English Association*, 2004. 18 July 2008 <http://www.ncte.org/tyca/positions>.

Koh, Hey-Kyung. "The Impact of Community Colleges on International Education." *Institute of International Education: Open Doors Report on International Educational Exchange*, 2004–08. 14 July 2008 <http://opendoors.iienetwork.org/?p=42055>.

Mora, Jill Kerper. "Debunking English-Only Ideology: Bi-lingual Instructors Are Not the Enemy." *Cross-Cultural Language & Academic Development (CLAD)*, 24 Nov. 2006. 7 July 2008 <http://coe.sdsu.edu/people/jmora/Prop227/EngOnly.htm>.

"Most Spoken Languages in California in 2005." *MLA: Language Map Data Center*, 2005. 10 Aug. 2008 <http://www.mla.org/cgi-shl/docstudio/docs.pl?map_data_results>.

"Project e-PAL." *e-PAL: Extending Professional Active Life*, 2008. 12 July 2008 <http://www.epal.ev.com/Home>.

"Special Analysis 2002: Nontraditional Undergraduates." *National Center for Education Statistics*, 5 Sept. 2002. 9 June 2005 <http://nces.ed.gov/programs/coe/2002/analyses/nontraditional/index.asp>.

Subbaro, Suba. "Using E-pal Project to Enhance Writing Classes." Presentation. 2004 Conference on College Composition and Communication. San Antonio, TX. 25 Mar. 2004.

"21st-Century Literacies." *NCTE*, 2007. 9 Aug. 2009 <www.ncte.org/library/NCTEFiles/.../21stCenturyResearchBrief.pdf>.

"2004 National Study of Postsecondary Faculty: Report on Faculty and Instructional Staff in Fall 2003." *National Center for Education Statistics*, May 2005. 4 June 2005 <http://nces.ed.gov/pubsearch/pubsinfo.asp?pubid=2005172>.

16. In Praise of Incomprehension

Catherine Prendergast

The most significant achievement of the chapters in part 1 of this volume is that they bring attention back to language; such sustained attention has not been the focus of the field's energies since the years immediately following the Students' Right to Their Own Language resolution. Cross-language work demonstrates that rhetorical concerns of purpose, argument, and ethos are animated through language choices. Yet how cross-language relations can be animated in our too often monolingual classrooms is another question entirely. As Geneva Smitherman and more recently Scott Wible have observed, efforts to design writing pedagogies informed by the language research of the Students' Right to Their Own Language resolution and background statement were thwarted when political shifts in the 1980s redefined progressive pedagogy as irresponsible pedagogy. This precedent suggests that efforts to implement the insights from this volume in the classroom are likely to meet similar political pressure.

And then there remains the question of whether such efforts should be undertaken at all. Perhaps I'm reading in, but I imagine Scott Richard Lyons felt taxed by the implicit task of relating his long-standing cross-language work to the enterprise of teaching composition. He writes: "Readers of this collection will doubtless want to know what role might be played by today's teachers of writing in the struggle to preserve Native tongues and linguistic diversity. Unfortunately, my answer is: probably very little." I agree with Lyons that composition is an inherently imperial enterprise and therefore not a natural environment for cross-language work. As Lyons points out, readers of this volume shouldn't expect its chapters to provide lesson plans, particularly on the weighty topic of preserving languages whose existence is directly threatened by continued imperialistic action. Composition can't help but partake of those "gross actions and inactions" that, as Min-Zhan Lu puts it in her chapter, "directly and indirectly pressured users of English to see symbolic and surgical fixes," including pedagogical fixes for imagined brokenness. But I do think there is a difference between the administrative apparatus that is composition (problematic, as most can agree) and the acts of writing and teaching writing, which are transcendent enough to take flower even in the unfertile ground of the required first-year course.

That said, I hasten to also acknowledge that only a small portion of language acquisition and use, particularly of any form of English globally, takes place in the classroom at all. In environments of political and economic oppression, language learning goes underground. As Elaine Richardson reminds us in her chapter of the American context: "Historically speaking, Black folks didn't get their rhetorical training through the classroom." The same could be said for many across the globe in developing countries who have little choice but to acquire English for themselves and their families in whatever ways they can both afford and embrace. Where the classroom becomes an expression of political control, as it did, for example, in Czechoslovakia during the communist regime, the most vibrant forms of language learning happen elsewhere. Slovaks I have interviewed who learned English during communism uniformly attested to retaining little from English classes at school, even where English classes were available to them. On the other hand, these same people participated in a subculture of unofficial English lessons: they read smuggled-in paperbacks, learned the lyrics to Beatles songs, made their own cassette tapes of English expressions, and devised language games that would force exercise of their English.

While I would in no way argue that the political climate in post-communist Slovakia rivals the level of oppression experienced pre-1989, there remain global inequities that have resulted in continued expansion of the boundaries of the classroom. Although English classes are now required at many Slovak schools and workplaces, and a supplemental education market is booming, to the many who seek to learn English—fast—these resources are not enough. A wealthy few can afford to send their children abroad to intensive courses in English-speaking countries. The less wealthy pay for after-school courses and tutoring to augment school offerings and look for opportunities within their daily lives and circumstances to improve their English or that of their family members. I met one repairman who listened to tapes while driving in his car on service calls to far corners of Slovakia. I watched a scholar and father of two wash dishes at night wearing headphones so he could listen to English-language podcasts while his wife put the children to bed. I talked to a couple who listened to BBC radio broadcasts while preparing breakfast, writing the phrases they culled from the program in black marker all over their white kitchen cupboards. Not everyone has welcomed this permeation of English into so many aspects of daily life. While the fluent podcaster enjoyed time spent refining an expression in English here or there, another woman I spoke with took a dimmer view of the imperative to perfect English: "It's like a kind of new slavery, which is of course different from the previous one," she observed (Prendergast 64).

Aside and apart from these largely middle-aged efforts to convert the domestic sphere into a site of either vexed or enjoyed learning, global Hiphop and international gaming also thrive in post-communist Slovakia, both dominated by world and Black Englishes. A case in point: on my most recent visit to Slovakia, a friend persuaded her seventeen-year-old son to accompany us on a trip to the mountains in the hopes that her son, who otherwise faced limited opportunities for conversation in English, would practice speaking with us. Hanging out with his mother's friends was far down this teenager's weekend agenda, however, and he went unwillingly, smiling little and speaking English even less. Much of his time was spent on the Internet or listening to rap and Hiphop. Indeed, Hiphop culture, and not middle-aged white Americans, proved to be the source of his interest in English; he wore almost exclusively South Pole–brand clothing his sister had acquired during a trip to America, following his very specific orders for shirts and pants. Nor did he confuse his mother's friends with his sources of global English, just because both came from the United States. When I sat down to use the computer to check e-mail, the computer's speakers still softly bleating a rap song with particularly obscene (and, I would have to add, misogynistic) lyrics, he raced across the room to turn the music off. Because I couldn't resist teasing him for it, I said in Slovak the equivalent of "Nice song." It was probably the first time I expended energy in Slovakia trying to convince someone I understood English; formerly stilted relations improved markedly from that point on.

The teen's quick crossing of the room exposes how many axes can overlap in cross-language relations: for starters, axes of aspiration, mode, gender, generation, "coolness" (for real lack of a better word), and, of course, language. Lu issues no small challenge, then, when she asks us, "How might U.S. composition articulate a global perspective that attends to rather than blurs the actual, specific, physical-social-historical contexts of individual students' life and work?" I believe if Lu's challenge is to be met within the composition class, it will not be through engagement with any one axis of the cross in cross-language relations but rather through consideration of intersections, by which I mean those moments of accidental and purposeful comprehension—and, more crucially, incomprehension—that result in some upending of the established linguistic order. We might call such upending "cross-languaging," with deliberate reference to the more familiar term "cross-dressing." Both acts are inherently political (as well as artistic), inviting us to consider how our rigid categories were formed in the first place.

I find one incidence of "cross-languaging" with great potential for class-room discussion in the 2007 Irish film *Once*, directed by John Carney. Set in Dublin, the film tells the story of the relationship between "the guy," an English-speaking Irish busker, and "the girl," a Czech immigrant who is functionally bilingual, even if her English isn't perfect. The pivotal moment of the film is one in which the two, who have theretofore negotiated the thickets of their ambiguous relationship primarily through music, engage in an act of cross-languaging: using a Czech phrase she has taught him at his request, the guy asks the girl if she loves the husband she left behind in the Czech Republic. Her response—answering both the central question of the film as well as that of their relationship—is given in Czech with no accompanying subtitle or verbal translation. The Irish busker doesn't understand what she said and neither do most of the movie's viewers, but those viewers equally understand that what they've missed is the key to unraveling the meaning of the film and the fate of its central characters.

In a composition class, I would first ask students to consider the signifi-cance of this scene of cross-languaging in the world of the film itself. Why does the Irish busker feel he needs to ask this question in Czech? Otherwise in the film, the busker is the one to whom others linguistically accommodate: when, earlier in the film, he is in the girl's living room, surrounded by her Polish neighbors who, since they don't have a TV, come in nightly to get their English lessons from the soap *Fair City*, he is treated to some hilarious phrases of the English they've picked up from the program, including, "Are you not pregnant?" Interestingly, at the end of this domestic scene that affords the Irishman his greatest moment of intimacy with the world of the immigrant, one of the Polish neighbors looks directly at the camera—in other words, at the audience, rather than at the TV where he's supposed to be looking. The viewer is reminded that the line between the film and reality is razor-thin. The Polish neighbor is not just any English-language learner, the glance tells us. He is your neighbor, the real English-language learner.

The girl's answer in untranslated Czech to the busker's question is similar to the Polish neighbor's quick glance at the audience in that both moments violate the audience's expectations of the genre. I would ask students to write about the effect of the cross-language moment on them personally. How did they deal with the moment of incomprehension or uncertainty? Did they try to figure out what the girl said from context? Did they find themselves trying to sound out what she said or write it down? Did they feel irritation or excitement? Did they want to jump on the Internet and look it up? Did they feel good because they understood it exactly? Extrapolating from their experiences, I would ask them to imagine the effect of that moment of in-comprehension on (most) viewers. How would it play in various towns in the United States, including cities like Chicago where many of my students are from, with its substantial Slavic language–speaking population? What would its effect be on the audience in newly cosmopolitan Dublin, where the many Eastern European viewers might audibly laugh or gasp, leaving the film's Irish viewers sitting in bafflement and possibly discomfort in a reversal of everyday linguistic hierarchies and the general drift of Irish/Eastern European relations (the Irish recently rejected a crucial European Union treaty in referendum, largely due to dissatisfaction over growing immigration from the former Soviet Bloc countries)?[1] Potentially, as viewers whisper their questions to their neighbors in the dark, the theater becomes a classroom. And when no native speaker is in easy range, either physically or sociologically, and the question is sent over the Internet—as multiple confused English-speaking viewers actually did to the *Yahoo! Answers* Web site, receiving answers from Czech and Polish responders—the classroom gets a little larger again, and teacher and student change sides. Or perhaps on some Web sites, the question just hangs there in cyberspace, unanswered, while those in the know silently smile to themselves, as did the girl in *Once*.

"I made a lot of funny mistakes when I was trying to learn Ojibwe, and sometimes speakers would play tricks on me," Scott Lyons tells us. This is the part of Lyons's chapter that I find most striking, because it reminds us that what drives language work is the promise of mysteries uncovered and con-nections forged. The "dirty farts" trick that the elder plays on Lyons brings him as much into the community as the words he learns correctly. Though the current political climate may strive to convince us otherwise, incomprehen-sion is not simply lack, the absence of comprehension. Incomprehension is generative—of longing, of effort, of meaning. Once the girl in *Once* delivers her answer in Czech, the busker wants to know what she said—so do we—and relationships are forged anew.

Note

1. The director and actor's commentary on the DVD of *Once* is revealing of the fraught state of Irish/Eastern European relations and how they penetrated the world of the film. Markéta Irglová, who plays "the girl," commented that while in character as a wandering rose-seller in a street scene, she received a lot of dis-approving looks from the native Irish passersby. Glen Hansard, who plays "the guy," explains: "The idea that you were walking up and down the street selling roses . . . was really offensive to them, because they're the flower-sellers. They were calling you a 'Bosie,' as in 'We don't want any Bosnians here.'" Here would be a

good place to note that Czechs and Slovaks do not consider themselves Eastern Europeans at all. The consider themselves Central Europeans.

Works Cited

Once. Dir. John Carney. Bórd Scannán na hÉireann/The Irish Film Board, 2007.

Prendergast, Catherine. *Buying into English: Language and Investment in the New Capitalist World*. Pittsburgh: U of Pittsburgh P, 2008.

Smitherman, Geneva. "CCCC's Role in the Struggle for Language Rights." "A Usable Past: CCC at 50, Part 1." Special issue, *College Composition and Communication* 50 (1999): 349–76.

Wible, Scott. "Pedagogies of the 'Students' Right' Era: The Language Curriculum Research Group's Project for Linguistic Diversity." *College Composition and Communication* 57 (2006): 442–78.

17. Sustainable Writing

Marilyn M. Cooper

A ll my thoughts now about writing are inspired by taking literally what I used to think was a metaphor—the ecology of writing. Ecology was how I first encountered what is now commonly known as complexity theory, and for me the environmental forms of complexity are still the most accessible. The understanding I've come to is that writing is structured and given life by the same dynamics that structure all living systems and that the most significant aspect of systems that thrive or survive is their complexity, that is, complexity in a particular sense that I will define presently.

The advantage of thinking about cross-language writing in terms of complex systems, I believe, is that it enables a compelling answer to the question of why diversity in language matters. The authors of the chapters in this collection have all suggested answers to this question: Scott Richard Lyons and Elaine Richardson argue that it is because language is a carrier of culture, that systems of language represent ways of being in the world; John Trimbur argues that more widespread multilingualism enables reciprocal exchanges; Paul Kei Matsuda, Kate Mangelsdorf, and Gail E. Hawisher and Cynthia L. Selfe with Yi-Huey Guo and Lu Liu state that multilingualism is a twenty-first-century reality that cannot be ignored by writing teachers; Shondel J. Nero and A. Suresh Canagarajah argue that diverse languages offer diverse resources to writers; and Min-Zhan Lu argues that engagement with diversity in language is a way to resist the logic of fast capitalism. These are all good answers. But I want to suggest an answer that underlies these: that diversity in language is necessary to survival—not just the survival of cultures and identities but perhaps the survival of the human species.

Complexity theory offers an explanation of why change is inevitable in real world systems and how it comes about. It posits that organization arises out of dense interactions in systems that are sufficiently complex, systems that consist of a very large number of frequently interacting agents. Through these interactions, the agents change in response to one another as well as to the ambient conditions, which are, in turn, modified by the changes in the agents; they become "structurally coupled," in Humberto R. Maturana and

Francisco J. Varela's terms (75). Because the organization that arises depends on the particular, contingent sequence of interactions, it is not predictable. It is also, therefore, dynamic—in other words, changeable—and not amenable to control. Complex systems are also open to inflows and outflows of agents, products, and energy, and thus "by trading their stuff they collectively produce a [larger system], one that inexorably becomes more complex" (Kauffman 129). One of the main theorists of complexity, physicist Ilya Prigogine, explains the implications of seeing social systems as complex in this sense:

> We know now that societies are immensely complex systems involving a potentially enormous number of bifurcations exemplified by the variety of cultures that have evolved in the relatively short span of human history. We know that such systems are highly sensitive to fluctuations. This leads both to hope and a threat: hope, since even small fluctuations may grow and change the overall structure. As a result, individual activity is not doomed to insignificance. On the other hand, this is also a threat, since in our universe the security of stable, permanent rules seems gone forever. (Prigogine and Stengers 312–13)

In the field of writing studies, we are coming to understand more fully that stable, permanent rules offer security only to some and that, as Lu concludes, "all of us interested in the future of a world sustainable for not only the few of us benefiting from the logic of fast capitalism but also the majority grossly impoverished by it need to get involved in living-English work."

Like cultures, languages are immensely complex systems, but adherents to the doctrine of standard language try to treat them as if they were the closed systems of classical physics, systems that are predictable and can be controlled. Reading Trimbur's, Lu's, and Matsuda's critiques of the monolingualism assumed by U.S. writing classes and Trimbur's and Lu's explanations of how that assumption arose from the economic situations of the merchant-planter coalition that was the Founding Fathers and from the current structure of fast capitalism, I was continually reminded of Michael Pollan's and Barbara Kingsolver's critiques of the U.S. food production system. Like language, food production is a complex system that U.S. agribusiness treats as if it were predictable or at least controllable, and like standard language ideology, agribusiness is wary of diversity. Extolling monocultures and fast, cheap food and dismissing heirloom species and small local farms as privileges for the elite, agribusiness exhibits some ambiguity about species diversity in the food supply: it's a nice luxury but not the way the world is fed. Traditional small farming is tolerated as long as it stays on the margins and does not cut too far into the profits of agribusiness. Similarly, standard language ideology extols monolingualism and efficiency in communication and welcomes diversity only as an exotic luxury (sending one's children to private schools in Switzerland to learn French) or grudgingly as a temporary necessity (tolerating first-generation immigrant laborers' incomplete mastery of American English). Trimbur refers to Mary Louise Pratt's argument that Americans are ambivalent about multilingualism and notes that exceptions to Standard English have been tolerated only on the grounds of expediency, as with the plantation creoles that facilitated the transatlantic triangle trade but were later suppressed because they "embodied the potentiality for an international anti-colonialism of the dispossessed." My argument in this response is that just as it is increasingly clear that U.S. agribusiness is not feeding the world but leading to starvation for many and obesity for the few, so too we need to realize that monolingualism does not improve but rather debilitates language and deprives humans of the resources that enable them to make meanings flexibly in response to ever-changing conditions.

Lu and Hawisher and Selfe explain some of the principles that support this argument. In her notion of living-English, Lu emphasizes the organic nature of language and the importance of recognizing change; she posits that language is "kept alive by many and many different ways of using it" and that ideal users are "attentive to the capacities, rights, and necessities of change in all living things: people, their lives, society, culture, the world, and the language itself." And Hawisher and Selfe, referring explicitly to complexity theory, explain that "the ecology of literacy is seldom monocultural and never static," driven by "a dynamic mosaic of patches, mini self-organizing systems characterized variously by different languages and histories and locations, different literacy practices and digital environments, different belief systems and hegemonic relationships, different 'organisms, artifacts, landscapes, dialects, communities, cultures, and social individuals'" (quoting Lemke).

On some level, everyone must realize that languages continually change over time (Chaucer's English or even George Orwell's is not the same as twenty-first-century American English), and everyone should know that languages cannot be controlled (decades of "correction" by writing teachers have still not eliminated split infinitives from reputable published texts). But the belief that languages, like nature, need to be subjugated to make them more amenable to human purposes persists, for clear economic reasons. Lu comments, "Subjugation is the end objective of any instruction underwritten by the fantasy of a world using one language, English, and using English strictly according to a fixed set of usages."

The attempt to subjugate language (and its users) through the establishment of monolingual Standard English, like agribusiness's establishment of the system of monocultural, chemically fertilized, and pesticide-protected food diminished in nutritional quality, not only diminishes the use value of language but also benefits only the few and only in the short term. Both are extractive systems designed explicitly to move profit toward the owners, and, like all extractive systems, both are destined to collapse. Kingsolver describes how after World War II the need to repurpose surplus ammonium sulfate used to manufacture explosives led to the development of chemical fertilizers, which produced surpluses of midwestern corn and soybeans, surpluses extended by rewritten commodity subsidy rules that no longer safeguarded farmers but instead guaranteed an oversupply of cheap corn and soybeans that were converted to high fructose corn syrup and hydrogenated oil and fed to cattle in concentrated animal feeding operations. The result was intensively marketed, cheap, fast foods that caused a 33 percent rise in the consumption of added fats, a 1,000 percent rise in the consumption of high fructose corn syrup, and the production of twice as many calories as the population of the United States needs, which, in turn, increased rates of obesity, diabetes, and heart disease and, finally, produced immense profits for fertilizer manufacturers and food distributors and marketers. Decisions at each step of this development (except, perhaps, the consumers' "choice" to consume) were a response to the demand for profit. Kingsolver concludes, "We all subsidize the cheap food with our tax dollars, the strategists make fortunes, and the overweight consumers get blamed for the violation. The perfect crime" (15). As she notes earlier, "That is the well-oiled machine we call Late Capitalism" (14). In the case of language, Lu describes the same extraction of profit at the expense of those supposedly served by the system: the construction and imposition of Standard English is driven by "the interests of 'developed' countries such as the United States to globalize their hyper-competitive, technology-driven market economies, what critics have termed 'flexible, information economies' or 'fast capitalism'" (citing Castells; Harvey).

These systems may be profitable in the short term, but they are not sustainable: they attempt to control a system through simplifying it, but simplification depletes the resources that fuel the system and requires tireless, and ultimately futile, efforts to maintain. Chemical fertilizers produce high yields in the short term, but they deplete the fertility of the soil by killing off the biological activity in the humus, a complex system of bacteria, phages, fungi, earthworms, and other organisms that decompose organic matter into nutrients, provide nutrients to roots in a form they can use, and prevent water from seeping away (Pollan 146–49). Pollan also notes how the reduction of a complex living system to a machine-like system of inputs and outputs requires ongoing maintenance: "When the synthetic nitrogen fed to plants makes them more attractive to insects and vulnerable to disease, as we have discovered, the farmer turns to chemical pesticides to fix his broken machine" (148). And now farmers are also losing the chemical battle against pests, which quickly evolve resistance to each new pesticide.

Mangelsdorf observes the same depletion of resources caused by simplification in the application of standard language ideology to international and generation 1.5 students who come to college "with a variety of complex, creative, and constantly changing literacies" (this volume). Spanglish-speaking students at the University of Texas–El Paso creatively combine the vocabulary and grammar of local varieties of English and Spanish into "a complex language that allows its speakers to strategically interact with their worlds." When asked about their attitudes toward Spanglish, some students recognize its advantages: "Spanglish is cool because it demonstrates how inventive and creative the human mind is, especially when the mind plays with words." But most students, persuaded by standard language ideology that dictates that each language (Spanish as well as English) has one correct variety and that languages must remain pure to be useful, speak and write Standard English in their classes and at their workplace (or feel they should, even if they don't actually succeed in doing so), even when Spanglish is clearly more appropriate and useful.[1] Constant reminders of the ideals of standardization and purity in language ("my mom would hit us if I would mix [Spanish] with English," "natives [were] constantly criticizing either my Spanish or English"), like applications of pesticide, are needed to kill off the linguistic resources that nurture varieties of language that have arisen through the structural coupling of diverse groups of people and their particular economic, social, and physical surroundings. Just as chemically fertilized soil lacks the resources to produce crops that are adapted to local conditions, the standard language Mangelsdorf's students are pressured to accept "cannot address their needs to use English to articulate—work out meaningful connections across—experiences and circumstances of life consistently discredited by standardized English usages" (Lu, this volume). And like pests, the resources from diverse languages may be warded off, but they are resilient and slip back in when needed. Speaking of her workplace, one of Mangelsdorf's students explains, "It is very common for us to have complete conversations in Spanish, but when it comes to explaining technical concepts, we have to shift to English since we learned those concepts in English."

It is this loss of linguistic resources and the ability to use them flexibly in response to a changing world that leads me to say that diversity in language is as essential to the survival of the human species as sustainably produced crops and flocks of animals. Writing, in the broad sense I define it, is the unique way humans live in the world; it is how we make the connections among people, technologies, and the natural world that enable us to survive. Restricting writing to a monolingual standard code prevents us from making new connections, as it cuts us off from the resources available in other cultural patches as well as prevents us from transforming (or redesigning, as the New London Group calls it [Cope and Kalantzis]) the resources in our own patch.

Lyons and Richardson explain in their chapters the kinds of distinctions and meanings white American English could adapt from other language patches: a new way of thinking about the distinction between animate and inanimate, for example, or a way of thinking about what abolition meant. By "trading stuff" like this, the larger human society becomes more complex and thus more sustainable. Cross-language writing also raises our consciousness of how language conventions continually change in response to the needs of their users. Canagarajah's analysis of how Professor Sivatamby adapted a research report for readers of different languages and situations illustrates how writers can create new rhetorical strategies that allow them to partially accommodate readers while also honoring their own way of making meaning. Sivatamby used hedges to project "a very objective and restrained researcher-like ethos" expected in Western academic communities but also to display the humility ethos expected by the Tamil community, and this "paradoxical" way of using a convention inspires reflection on possible nuances of each community's ethos as well as enabling Sivatamby's report to communicate to diverse audiences.

Canagarajah suggests that this way of working with cross-language resources is most often intuitive and that it doesn't necessarily come from "a vacuum in the brain" but instead may draw on mixed-code traditions. I'd add that in multilingual—actually, in all—writers, such rhetorical strategies can also arise through brain dynamics, for the brain is a complex system in itself, continually creating new patterns from combinations and permutations of old ones: as brain scientist Walter J. Freeman says, "Our brains are the foundry of new meanings, which come into our awareness when they are already self-organized" (154–55).

Lu argues in her chapter for more conscious work to uncover how tinkering with standardized usages allows users "to limn [their] actual, imagined and possible lives" (quoting Morrison). She suggests paying attention to "non-idiomatic English lexicons and grammar" in order "to consider the ways in which various usages in the English-only, standardized version might also directly and indirectly undercut conditions and relations critical to the day-to-day being of individual students" and to pay attention to differing translations of words in order to understand why certain translations were chosen and what lived experiences were elided by that choice.

While it is true that the long-term effects of conscious efforts to change complex systems cannot be accurately predicted, as Prigogine argues, changes in an individual's actions may be reinforced by other factors and thus change the overall structure. Some understanding, continually updated, of how the system works—such as the understanding achieved by the practices Lu advocates—can enhance this possibility. Joel Salatin, a "grass farmer" that Pollan observed at work, calls his Polyface Farm a postindustrial enterprise because it requires much nuanced local information and juggling "the various elements of his farm in space as well as time, relying on his powers of observation and organization to arrange the appointed daily meeting of animal and grass in such a way as to insure maximum benefit for both" (191). One of his strategies is an "eggmobile," a covered wagon housing a chicken coop with attached feeding pens that every day is moved to a new patch of pasture recently vacated by cattle. The chickens feed on the grubs growing in the cowpats (the protein makes their eggs rich and tasty) and in the process fertilize the grass by kicking apart the cowpats and dropping their own high-nitrogen wastes; at the same time, the chickens sanitize the pastures so that the cattle don't have to be treated for parasites or worms. Pollan concludes, "This is what Joel means when he says that the animals do the real work around here. I'm just the orchestra conductor, making sure everybody's in the right place at the right time'" (212). This is the way to ensure the sustainability of a complex system, whether it's a farm or a writing class, and this is why diversity, through ensuring that multiple resources are available to interacting agents, is an important factor in the survival of all species on our planet.

Note

1. Mangelsdorf suggests that one of the reasons students do not accept her invitation to use Spanglish in their writing is that they perceive it as an oral language, so that "stabilizing it in writing may seem unnatural." Canagarajah, too, suggests that the "graphocentric" mode of writing valued in Western societies influences students' acceptance of monolingualist assumptions in composition classes, and he urges writing teachers to "reconsider the place of orality in writing." Though it is true that written language is more conservative than oral language and that "slips of the tongue" (nonconscious uses of forms from nonstandard varieties) are slightly more amenable to control in writing, written languages are just as complex—and changeable—as oral languages. Standard edited English and academic discourse are policed by professional editors, but editors (with the help of electronic discussion lists and continually updated guides like the *Chicago Manual of Style*) work to ascertain what usages are currently accepted by published writers and are careful to not impose their own preferences or varieties of language on the texts they work on. Or they should.

Works Cited

Cope, Bill, and Mary Kalantzis, eds. *Multiliteracies: Literacy Learning and the Design of Social Futures*. New York: Routledge, 2000.

Freeman, Walter J. *How Brains Make Up Their Minds*. New York: Columbia UP, 2000.

Kauffman, Stuart. *At Home in the Universe: The Search for the Laws of Self-Organization and Complexity*. New York: Oxford UP, 1995.

Kingsolver, Barbara. *Animal, Vegetable, Miracle: A Year of Food Life*. New York: Harper, 2007.

Maturana, Humberto R., and Francisco J. Varela. *The Tree of Knowledge: The Biological Roots of Human Understanding*. Rev. ed. Boston: Shambhala Press, 1998.

Pollan, Michael. *The Omnivore's Dilemma: A Natural History of Four Meals*. New York: Penguin, 2006.

Prigogine, Ilya, and Isabelle Stengers. *Order Out of Chaos: Man's New Dialogue with Nature*. New York: Bantam, 1984.

18. Reflections

Victor Villanueva

I'm troubled that this conversation still goes on, that the matter hasn't been settled, that there still remain attempts at what Arnold Kemp calls "genopsycholinguisticide," genocide through language. And so I find myself reacting to what I've just read by thinking of what's already been said, finding that the chapters that so wonderfully tell of living language and multilingualism and language legislation and pedagogy all recap, in some sense, even as I learn of the English of Sri Lanka and travel a Sino-American cyberhighway. I think, for instance, of how Kelvin Monroe described genopsycholinguisticide a few years back and how what he wrote enters into a dialectic with Scott Richard Lyons and Elaine Richardson, explaining what they're explaining intimately:

> This genocide through linguistics—genopsycholinguisticide—is really dead-on-the-money. It speaks to me in so many ways. When I reflect on the idea of language, the way and how it means for me, I remember thinking only of it in terms of spoken discourse—as real as the body and intratextual in many ways, even beyond the verbal. Take, for example, my attending graduate school for the first time. I walk through the doors of a new fancy building, and because of my previous historical location, this building signifies a type of upper-crusty-ness about it. I know—or at least it means to me—that the program that is housed here has resources to accomplish what it desires. In that instant, language is intrinsic, in that the architecture was designed to say (to speak) to the onlooker—me, at that time—modern, up-to-date, even futuristic, and ultimately, white. This is not to say that schools with primarily a color demographic cannot have nice buildings or even futuristic buildings. My point is that where I am located the language being spoken, conveyed, projected is not a language that welcomes people of color—despite endless multicultural campaigns. As Stuart Hall notes, language "speaks us" . . . , a language that is constructed, situated by dominant structures around subordinate bodies, that invades and occupies, colonizes, and inhabits the terrain of those subordinate bodies.

In other words, to say that one is a college student or that one attends such and such university is to assert a language that is, first, situated in the premise that there are inferior beings as well as superior beings. Second, the institutions of higher learning have historically been instruments in the wider campaign to further that myth of superior-inferior and make distinct the lines of knowledge as they relate to who has authority to speak and be heard and who does not. Last, is the need to widen the economic gap between economic classes so as to naturalize hegemonic production and reproduction vis-à-vis exploitation of the subordinated groups.

We are spoken for because this historically bound legacy attached to institutions of higher learning precedes, even preempts, any utterances we attempt. I like to think of this as preemptive rhetorical situatedness (to borrow from Molefi Asante). Linguistic occupation has seized our utterances before they flow and while they flow—a violent act. Our voices have been seized and silenced. Genopsycholinguisticide plays out by mass-murdering the language that relates to how we behave in the world that suppresses us, to how we use language to make sense of the world. So our language—being a part of how we become—suffers death for the sake of and at the hands of the empire: the white power structure in this country. (106–7)

I'm troubled that institutes of higher education would still need to be convinced of the power of multiple language access as we demand that students learn "a foreign language," when so many of us carried a domestic language that would be foreign only to monolingual English speakers, many of whom— including those who have enjoyed great power—speak in dialects not at all standard or standardized (thinking here of Kennedy or Carter or G. W. Bush). Troubled at the truth in Paul Kei Matsuda's assertion that composition studies is "English Only" by default, that we seem unable to play with language.

Maybe I'm troubled by having to read this set of arguments retold, even as I'm enlightened by a new historicity in John Trimbur, a newer set of understandings about language and languages, but I am glad to have read A. Suresh Canagarajah's assertion that to be bilingual is not to be monolingual in two languages, because that says something abut competencies, about what we might aim for, what Shondel J. Nero presents. And for me, Canagarajah and Nero and Matsuda complement Kate Mangelsdorf's questions about Spanglish, about how this is itself a kind of bilingualism, even as fragmented, even as receptive more than productive. And in recognizing that, we can reduce the shame. Today, I find myself—in part thanks to Canagarajah—speaking the Spanish I know, able to say I can't think of a word (like the other day trying to find the word for "hat," and only able to come up with "chapeau" or "beret," even "petasi," but not "sombrero," I reckon because of some association between that word, sombrero, and Mexican Westerns of my childhood—language and prejudice and competence; so much to work through).

A decade ago I told this story:

> That morning I had spoken with Ceci, my friend the Cuban English Professor. Her husband had said something to me over the phone that I had to unravel quickly, immediate translation from my first language to my only language, slipping the Spanish into the English to understand. . . .
>
> During that phone conversation, I tried to come up with a familiar Spanish saying. It was there: at the tip of the mind. But I could never. I said it in English. Ceci said it. Quickly. Then again more slowly. I heard it. I understood it. I recognized it. I still feel unsure that I could produce it. My Spanish is limited to single sentences, never extended stretches of discourse. I can't. At least I don't believe I can. And I listen to salsa and mambo and bomba and plena—the music of my childhood. But I can't dance to it in front of anyone. And phrases from the CDs slip by me, untranslated. I am assimilated. I am not.
>
> There was a time when a person came to the US to begin a life separated from the homeland, having to give it all up, all that came prior. It's what separated us from the peoples of the Eurasian continent. They crossed borders and languages, but were always near the homeland, so that they acquired a language if they needed to stay in some country and culture other than home, without giving up home, because there would be reasons to return sometimes. So Europeans remain multilingual. So Asians remain multilingual. Mr. Fawlty on the TV comedy speaks a bit of French, pokes some fun at German, and speaks a broken Spanish to Manuel, the Spanish waiter, who in turn speaks a broken English. And though there is always the presumption of the superiority of English in an English TV show, though the studio audience laughs at the parochial Mr. Fawlty, an archaism, the general assumption among that audience that languages will cross.
>
> Today, the world is a few hours away. And some might have to scrimp and save for a year before affording a flight home to Germany or to Russia or to Cuba, but the fare is rarely really out of reach. And a week's vacation can be spent in the homeland. No one—no one, whatever the race—needs to give up the home tongue anymore, now that the world is

small. And most of the world knows its English, and most of the world knows another language, at least one more.

So I was driving home from some chore or other on the afternoon of the morning I had spoken to Ceci. And in the midst of a left turn I thought: "I'm 50 now, maybe a third of my life left. I wonder if I'll die without ever being fluent in the language that first met my ears." English is the only language I know, really. Yet Spanish is the language of my ear, of my soul. And I try to pass it on to my children. But I'm inadequate.

For any other value—anything—a parent would not deny his or her children what he or she had been denied. We wish our children to know and enjoy those things we lacked. It's what motivates most of us. We're even in the business of legacy, of passing on, we teachers. I'm saddened by my loss. I'm saddened by my sister's lack, who has even less of the legacy than I. It wasn't necessary. Ceci stands as an indicator. One gives up nothing by being adept at two languages or more. One gains. So many have had to give up so much to be part of the US. It was the price, when going back meant prison or famine, at best an expensive and long trip on a steamship. That price is no longer necessary. Why deny the children a richness because it had been denied to the parents? The story that begins "my grandfather had to" is wrongheaded. We don't limit on the basis of our ancestors' limits. We break through the limitations of the past. Our children—the children—will learn English. There is no stopping it. Why should the learning be painful? The new residents of this land will learn English. There is no stopping it. Why should their rights be denied during the process of acquiring this new language? Why legislate a kind of assimilation that no longer obtains, is no longer necessary, and was never not painful? (339–40)

But maybe I should be gratified more than troubled. Things could be worse. We could still not be recognizing how language lives in the ways that Min-Zhan Lu makes clear, how the live language moves in cyberspace as Gail E. Hawisher and Cynthia L. Selfe with Yi-Huey Guo and Lu Liu make clear. We might even overlook the legislative limitations that have always been with us, as Trimbur reflects. The point is clear. Kenneth Burke tells us that "rhetoric is concerned with the state of Babel after the Fall" (23). And we are, we who profess language, language learning, and language instruction—no matter our disciplinary affiliation (composition or linguistics or literacy studies)—we are all of us rhetoricians, not concerned with creating an imperial lingua Adamica, a solitary language spoken and understood by all. That is nonsensical. We are concerned with finding the richness in language multiplicity, recognizing that languages and dialects bleed into one another and that we can have a greater community in learning from one another, finding our ways through Babel.

Works Cited

Burke, Kenneth. *A Rhetoric of Motives*. Berkeley: U of California P, 1969.

Monroe, Kelvin. "Writin da Funk Dealer: Songs of Reflections and Reflex/shuns." *College English* 67 (2004): 102–20.

Villanueva, Victor. "On English Only." *Language Ideologies: Critical Perspectives on the Official English Movement*. Ed. Roseann Dueñas González and Ildikó Melis. Urbana, IL: NCTE, 2000. 333–41.

Contributors
Index

Contributors

Anis Bawarshi is associate professor of English and director of the Expository Writing Program at the University of Washington. His publications include *Genre and the Invention of the Writer: Reconsidering the Place of Invention in Composition, Scenes of Writing: Strategies for Composing with Genres* (with Amy J. Devitt and Mary Jo Reiff), *A Closer Look: A Writer's Reader* (with Sidney I. Dobrin), and articles and book chapters on genre, uptake, invention, and knowledge transfer in composition.

A. Suresh Canagarajah is the Kirby Professor in Language Learning and director of the Migration Studies Project at Pennsylvania State University. He has taught before at the University of Jaffna, Sri Lanka, and the City University of New York. His books include *Critical Academic Writing and Multilingual Students, A Geopolitics of Academic Writing,* and *Resisting Linguistic Imperialism in English Teaching.* He currently serves as editor of *TESOL Quarterly.*

Marilyn M. Cooper is professor of humanities at Michigan Technological University, where she teaches grammar, editing, rhetoric, and composition. She is a past editor of *College Composition and Communication* and is currently working on a book project that argues that writing emerges from and structures our interactions with biological, technological, and social systems.

Gail E. Hawisher is University Distinguished Teacher/Scholar and professor of English at the University of Illinois. Her work probes the many connections between literate activity and new information technologies, as reflected in her ongoing research and recent book with Cynthia L. Selfe, *Literate Lives in the Information Age: Narratives of Literacy.* She continues to coedit *Computers and Composition: An International Journal* with Cynthia Selfe. Her latest project is a coauthored multimodal book for Computers and Composition Digital Press (CCDP) titled *Transnational Literate Lives.*

Bruce Horner is Endowed Chair in Rhetoric and Composition at the University of Louisville. His books include *Terms of Work for Composition: A Materialist Critique,* winner of the 2001 Winterowd Award, and, with Min-Zhan Lu, *Representing the "Other": Basic Writers and the Teaching of Basic Writing* and *Writing Conventions.* "English Only and U.S. College Composition," coauthored with John Trimbur, was the recipient of the Richard Braddock Award for outstanding article in 2002.

Michelle Hall Kells is associate professor of rhetoric and writing in the English department at the University of New Mexico. She is coeditor of *Attending to the Margins: Writing, Researching, and Teaching on the Front Lines* (with Valerie Balester) and *Latino/a Discourses: On Language, Identity, and Literacy Education* (with Valerie Balester and Victor Villanueva) and author of *Hector P. Garcia: Everyday Rhetoric and Mexican American Civil Rights*. Her current book project is *Vicente Ximenes and LBJ's "Great Society": The Rhetoric of Mexican American Civil Rights Reform*.

Shirley Wilson Logan is professor and director of writing programs in the Department of English at the University of Maryland, where she teaches writing, the history of rhetoric, African American rhetoric, and composition theory. Logan's most recent publication, *Liberating Language: Sites of Rhetorical Education in Nineteenth-Century Black America*, examines some of the locations where African Americans developed their rhetorical abilities across the nineteenth century.

Min-Zhan Lu is professor of English and University Scholar at the University of Louisville. Her books include *Shanghai Quartet: The Crossings of Four Women of China*, *Comp Tales* (coedited with Richard Haswell), and, with Bruce Horner, *Representing the "Other": Basic Writers and the Teaching of Basic Writing* and *Writing Conventions*. She is winner of the Richard Braddock Award (2005) and the Mina Shaughnessy Award (1992).

Scott Richard Lyons (Leech Lake Ojibwe/Mdewakanton Dakota) teaches Native American and global indigenous literatures in the English department at Syracuse University. He is the author of *X-Marks: Native Signatures of Assent*.

Kate Mangelsdorf is professor of rhetoric and writing studies and directs the University Writing Programs at the University of Texas–El Paso. Her research interests include critical literacies and second-language writing. In addition to publishing journal articles and book chapters, she has coauthored several textbooks. She currently serves on the executive committee of the Conference on College Composition and Communication.

LuMing Mao is professor of English at Miami University. His publications include *Reading Chinese Fortune Cookie: The Making of Chinese American Rhetoric* and *Representations: Doing Asian American Rhetoric* (coedited with Morris Young). His recent essay "Studying the Chinese Rhetorical Tradition in the Present: Representing the Native's Point of View" won the 2007 Richard Ohmann Award for the most outstanding essay published in *College English*.

Paul Kei Matsuda is associate professor of English at Arizona State University, where he works with doctoral students in rhetoric, composition, and linguistics as well as in applied linguistics. Founding co-chair of the Symposium on Second Language Writing and the editor of the Parlor Press Series on Second Language Writing, Matsuda has edited over ten books and journal special issues. He has also published widely in journals and edited collections in both rhetoric/composition and applied linguistics/TESOL. His essay "The Myth of Linguistic Homogeneity in U.S. College Composition" won the 2006 Richard Ohmann Award.

Susan K. Miller-Cochran is associate professor of English at North Carolina State University and director of the First-Year Writing Program. Her research focuses on the intersections of technology, second-language writing, and writing program administration. She is an editor of *Rhetorically Rethinking Usability* and *Strategies for Teaching First-Year Composition* and coauthor of *The Wadsworth Guide to Research*.

Jody Millward, former chair of the Two-Year College English Association, is a professor of English at Santa Barbara City College, California, where she cofounded the Multicultural English Transfer Program and the College Achievement Program, both designed to increase the success rates of underserved and underrepresented students.

Shondel J. Nero is associate professor of TESOL at New York University. Her research focuses on the education of speakers of ESL and of Standard English as a second dialect, especially Caribbean Creole English speakers. She has authored two books and numerous articles on speakers of Caribbean Creole English and other world Englishes.

Catherine Prendergast is professor of English, University Scholar, and director of First Year Rhetoric at the University of Illinois. Her most recent book, *Buying into English: Language and Investment in the New Capitalist World*, examines the role of English in introducing language learners to capitalism.

Elaine Richardson is professor of literacy studies in the College of Education and Human Ecology at Ohio State University, where she specializes in Afrodiasporic literacies. Richardson won the 2006 National Reading Conference's Edward Fry Award for outstanding research in literacy studies for *African American Literacies*. She is author or editor of five books. Richardson's most recent book, tentatively titled *PHD 2 Ph.D.*, is both street literature and educational memoir chronicling her descent into street life and rise into the academy.

Cynthia L. Selfe is Humanities Distinguished Professor at Ohio State University. Her most recent scholarly accomplishment includes the Digital Archives on Literacy Narratives (DALN) and, with Gail E. Hawisher and colleagues, the new Computers and Composition Digital Press (CCDP), an imprint of Utah State University Press. She continues to coedit *Computers and Composition: An International Journal* with Gail Hawisher.

John Trimbur is professor of writing, literature, and publishing at Emerson College. He has published widely on writing theory and has won a number of awards, including the Richard Braddock Award for outstanding article in 2002 for "English Only and U.S. College Composition," co-written with Bruce Horner.

Victor Villanueva is Regents Professor at Washington State University. He is a former chair of the Conference on College Composition and Communication and has been honored with the organization's 2009 Exemplar Award. All of his efforts have centered on the connections between language and racism.

Index

abolition, in Douglass's writing, 101–2

access promise, living-English users, 45–46. *See also* economic factors

Achebe, Chinua, 45–48, 50, 186

Adams, John, 21, 42

admission procedures, as linguistic containment policy, 85–86, 88

African American Language: in center-periphery model, 97–99, 107–9, 146; contributions to English, 7, 99–100; cultural identity factors, 100–103, 147; education strategies, 102–5, 108–9, 193–94, 216; freestylin practice, 105–6; hiphop practices, 106–7; shuttling awareness, 173

African American Vernacular English. *See* African American Language

"African Writer and the English Language, The" (Achebe), 45

Afrocentric Multicultural Writing Project, 108

agongos, in Ojibwemowin language, 132

agricultural production comparison, 10, 237, 238–40, 242

Alabama, truck driver story, 189–90

Allen, Harold B., 92

alternative discourse, defining, 144–45

Anderson, Benedict, 23

Anglo-Saxonism, surrogation process, 32–37

anishinaabeg, in Ojibwemowin language, 131–32

Anzaldúa, Gloria, 115

Ardila, Alfredo, 115, 116

Arizona, language legislation, 117

Arrow of God (Achebe), 50–51, 186

Asian rap, 194

asin, in Ojibwemowin language, 137

Attending to the Margins, 207

Auginaush, Joe, 129

avai aTakkam, Tamil language, 165–66

Baca, Damián, 115

Bacchus, Denise, 226

Baldwin, James, 45, 46, 47

Barajas, Elias Dominguez, 121

Bawarshi, Anis, 9, 123

Bayley, Robert, 121

Bazerman, Charles, 196

Bean, Janet, 142

Benjamin, Walter, 32

Bilingual Education Act, 121–22

bimaadizi, in Ojibwemowin language, 135–36

Bizzell, Patricia, 144, 145, 146

Borderlands/La Frontera (Anzaldúa), 115

Bourdieu, Pierre, 58

Brandt, Deborah, 74–75

British English, Webster's claim, 35–36

Broken Speak, 194

Bruce, Shanti, 215

Burke, Kenneth, 247

Butler, Judith, 190–91

bwaan, in Ojibwemowin language, 132

California, language legislation, 117, 222

cálo, as Spanglish attitude, 115

Canagarajah, A. Suresh, 5, 7, 8, 146, 147, 151, 183–84, 198, 207, 209, 212, 225, 236, 241, 242n.1, 245–46

Caribbean Creole English, 7–8, 147–52. *See also* creole languages

Carney, John, 233

Carpenter, Karen, 147

Carrington, Lawrence, 147–48

CARS model (Create a Research Space), 162–64. *See also* multilingual writing, negotiation model

Castillo, Manuel, 189

CCCC Statement, 216–17

center-periphery model, 97–99, 107–9, 146

Chávez, César, 123